THE FALLOUT

THE
FALLOUT

How a guilty liberal lost his innocence

Andrew Anthony

JONATHAN CAPE
LONDON

THE
FALLOUT

How a guilty liberal lost his innocence

Andrew Anthony

JONATHAN CAPE
LONDON

Published by Jonathan Cape 2007

2 4 6 8 10 9 7 5 3 1

First published in Great Britain in 2007 by
Jonathan Cape
Random House, 20 Vauxhall Bridge Road,
London SW1V 2SA

Address for companies within The Random House Group Limited
can be found at:
www.randomhouse.co.uk/offices.htm

The Random House Group Limited Reg. No. 954009
www.rbooks.co.uk

A CIP catalogue record for this book is available from
the British Library

ISBN 9780224080774

Mixed Sources
Product group from well-managed
forests and other controlled sources
www.fsc.org Cert no. TT-COC-2139
© 1996 Forest Stewardship Council

Papers used by Random House are natural,
recyclable products made from wood grown in sustainable forests.
The manufacturing processes conform to the environmental
regulations of the country of origin

Typeset by Palimpsest Book Production Limited,
Grangemouth, Stirlingshire

Printed in the UK by CPI Mackays, Chatham ME5 8TD

In memory of my mother

Emotions

Emotions

1

Shock

I was in a dark bunker beneath the heart of London when it happened, sealed off from reality, protected from the intrusions and distractions of life outside. A film called *Greenfingers* had just come, mercifully, to an end, but the small and overdue pleasure of watching the credits roll was not one I wished to savour. The audience of critics was starting to leave and I was anxious to be the first among them. All I wanted to do was get out into the fresh air, to return to the resuscitating smell of the real world, or what passed for it in the late-summer streets of Soho. I was fed up with sitting in cramped basements watching poor films. And *Greenfingers* was another poor film. A textbook example of British cinema at its most insipid and formulaic, it would have instantly disappeared from memory even if it had been released in a normal week. Clive Owen did his brooding best and Helen Mirren her comic worst, but neither could divert the story – about a lovable group of prisoners that enters a flower competition – from the overfamiliar course plotted by *The Full Monty* and its endless imitators. I would describe it in print the following Sunday as 'a hackneyed romance that feels about as organic as DDT'. But come Sunday no one would care about the film, much less the review.

On that Tuesday, I had endured two days of back-to-back screenings and *Greenfingers*, for its many faults, was by no means the most feeble. The only comfort I could draw was the knowledge that I would never again have to sit through

The Martins or *The Fast and the Furious*. The low quality of feature films, that's what roused my anger on a nondescript afternoon in September, the disservice done to popular art. And it was a righteous anger, an anger born of a firm belief in some core values: aesthetic beauty, narrative richness, wit, subtlety, intelligence. I knew how bad these films were and I was not going to pretend otherwise. There was no point in searching for subtexts or hidden meanings that didn't exist. Even the most slippery semiotician, the most elastic relativist, would have had his work cut out intellectualising his way to a defence of this piffle. Sometimes things were just plain wrong.

How, I wondered as I searched for my coat and bag, could film critics stomach this meagre diet week in, week out? I was already regretting agreeing to cover for Philip French, the estimable *Observer* film critic, who was on holiday. After four decades of reviewing the weekly releases, the guy deserved the break but, on this evidence, I thought he couldn't return soon enough. As I shuffled along the aisle to the exit, the final credits were replaced by a flickering image of a burning skyscraper. Yet another Hollywood cliché, I thought. The picture was presented as if it was newsreel but, due to an apparent problem in the projection room, there was no sound. It was a little odd to see another feature played immediately after the previous one had finished. Was this a preview of a forthcoming attraction? Was it one of those guerrilla advertising campaigns?

Then in an instant I recognised the building, and its untouched twin, and in that same instant I saw a fast-moving shadow enter the frame and fly straight into the structure that wasn't burning. It was a shocking sight, but my mind absorbed the shock because it was still operating on the assumption, not unreasonable in a cinema, that the footage was a shocking *cinematic* sight. Still, credit where it was due, the film achieved a compelling authenticity. They had got that flat video texture just right. And on some nagging level of consciousness, for those strange few seconds in that darkened room, it was a

4

struggle to suspend the suspicion that it was real. I lost that struggle a moment later when the image stabilised and it suddenly gained the accompaniment of sound. I saw the 'Sky News' logo in the corner of the screen. The reporter was saying that aircraft had flown into both towers of the World Trade Center. The audience audibly inhaled and exhaled, first a gasp then a hush, and I slumped back down. The details were limited and confusing but I thought I picked up either that one of the planes had been heading for Washington or that there was another plane, still in the air, that was DC-bound. I took a couple of seconds to process the information and then I was off, up out of my seat, out of the room and up the stairs, trying to locate my phone as I rushed out into the street.

My wife was in New York and she was flying to Washington DC that day. I couldn't get through to her number. I tried again and again without success. Panic started to rise up from my stomach into my shallow-breathing chest. Was this how it happened? Was this how a nightmare invades your life, masquerading as a movie, as a cheap action flick? What were you doing, people like to ask, when you first heard the news of this or that momentous event? It's a largely redundant question nowadays in the age of twenty-four-hour rolling television news because almost invariably the answer is watching the news on television. But I was watching a film in a cinema, as I had been for most of that day and the previous one as well, when the second jet flew into the architectural fjords of lower Manhattan. And I was having trouble readjusting to the world of non-fiction. After what I imagine was just a few minutes, but felt infinitely longer at the time, I got through to my wife's London office. They had heard from her. She was OK. Life would continue. The panic was over. I could rejoin most of the rest of the world as an appalled voyeur, but a voyeur nonetheless. I could stand in murmuring awe in a bar with the other critics, silently reviewing the incredible atrocity happening live on TV. I could note the innocent clarity of that blue sky and the shimmering glory of those twin totems of capitalism, which stood proud even as the thick smoke gushed, like arterial blood, from their obscene entry wounds. I could try to imagine, and then try not to imagine, the last hellish moments of the passengers on those planes, and the hopeless plight of the workers trapped on the floors above the fire. I could address the unforeseen and earth-shaking collapse of the buildings by studied recourse to metaphor and history, all the while stifling the childish, vicarious and despi-cable thrill of witnessing the creation of devastation. I could reflect on the planetary nature of this broadcast, how it would captivate and unify, if mostly in horror, the whole world in a way nothing else, including the fall of the Berlin Wall, had done since the moon landings. This was the antithesis of that day in 1969, not a celebration of America's power and humanity's ambition but a statement of America's vulnera-bility and humanity's division. I could do and think all this and more from the civilised safety of Bar Italia on Frith Street, but it was OK, my wife was alive. This was a global event. But this was not our story.

I was just a few months into my fortieth year in September 2001. The previous year I had become a father for the first time and published my first book. I had a good job as a feature writer and a life that was not without comfort; a middle-class, middle-aged urban professional with plans and expectations, but more than that a growing sense of rootedness, social investment, dare I say a kind of ominous contentment. It is in such conditions, of course, and at such times that a man, particularly a man, can start to question himself and his purpose in life. If the midlife crisis is a figment of the psychi-atric and literary imagination, it's a figment that has migrated to the male imagination at large. The option of fleeing one's responsibilities seems, paradoxically, to grow more appealing as the responsibilities themselves become more rewarding. And in the same counter-intuitive fashion, there is nothing like the arrival of new life to focus the mind on the proximity of death. You become more grounded and simultaneously the ground becomes less steady. My daughter was just starting to walk and suddenly the world was full of dangers, and not of the interesting variety. A vegetable knife protruding from the dishwasher became a mortal threat, an unguarded staircase a potential descent into hell. How would such heightened sensitivities contend with the gruesome incineration of three thousand people and the destruction of two of the most recognisable structures on earth, buildings in whose dizzying elevators I had ridden to what was once the highest man-made point in the world? How steady would the ground seem after that?

A midlife crisis did indeed ensue after 9/11. In truth it had been brewing for some time. It wasn't my midlife crisis, however, but that of Western culture at large. No matter what other aims may have motivated this singular act of terrorism, it was beyond question that it was planned as a symbolic, as well as a lethal, attack on 'the West', whether the target was militarism (the Pentagon), capitalism (the WTC), or cosmopolitanism (the heterogeneity of the victims). The problem was many in the West were not sure that it was worthy of defence. For some time in the post-Soviet era, as America established its position as the sole superpower, a West-based movement had been growing that rejected the spread of free-market capitalism and the Western values that underpinned the global market. Known as anti-globalisation, it drew attention to the poverty and deprivation that was such a common feature of life in the Third World. But it also posed some stark existential questions about the Western way of life. 'What was the point?' the anti-globalisers seemed to be asking, all we do is buy stuff, turn everywhere into a market, and force McDonald's and Starbucks down other people's throats. Our culture is nothing but consumption. As the anti-globalist writer Naomi Klein argued a few weeks after 11 September: 'Part of the disorientation many Americans now face has to do with the inflated and oversimplified place consumerism plays in the American narrative. To buy is to be. To buy is to love. To buy is to vote.'

No wonder Americans were disorientated. It was a disorientating time. Even in Europe, it was hard to regain one's bearings. In the immediate aftermath of the attacks, I did what everyone did, I watched the news obsessively, impatient for each new piece of amateur video, each new visual perspective on the impact that served only to increase my appetite for further, better, more definitive angles. I read newspapers, magazines, comment, analysis, anything I could get my hands on, hungry for more detail, more description, more drama. There is a pornography of atrocity, an idea which J.G. Ballard explored many years ago, and few of us are immune to its morbid lure. The more you see, the more you want to see. To be sure my interest was propelled by outrage, but the preoccupation with the awful minutiae was also, perversely, a form of denial. The more one focuses on the effects, the more blurred becomes the cause. It's a natural reaction, a human reaction, a way of coming to terms with a new situation before dealing with what it means.

For those first few hours and days I was caught up in the unfolding story. My wife was grounded in New York, unable to leave Manhattan island, which was temporarily cut off from the rest of the world. She is a journalist too, and the reason she was in New York was to shadow the Duchess of York, Sarah Ferguson, for a magazine story. The rumbustious former royal was engaged in charity work on a mini American tour. It so happened that her New York office was in the WTC, tucked away in a corner of Cantor Fitzgerald, the international brokerage firm. Cantor Fitzgerald was spread between the 101st and the 105th floors in the north tower, some way above the crash site. Over seven hundred of its employees perished. None that was in the building survived. According to Ferguson, she and her entourage, including my wife, were due to pay a visit to her office that Tuesday morning.

It was not our story, but it could have been.

There were macabre might-have-beens everywhere you looked, that's what made the whole horror fit so perfectly into the dimensions of our nightmares. If this father hadn't left home early that day, and that fiancée hadn't got the express train, if that daughter had caught the plane she originally intended to take, then they would all be alive. It's a vortex of torture, this kind of thinking, and the temptation to disappear into its fathomless depths must, for the relatives of the deceased, have seemed like a trial beyond endurance.

As I drank in the devastation, numbed and intoxicated by the scale of what had taken place, I struggled, like everyone else, to make sense of it all. And in my case, as with many people from the liberal-left side of the political spectrum, that job was made more difficult by the fact that the United States was the victim. From where I came from, the United States was always the culprit. There was Vietnam, Chile, and the dreadful support for repressive and often debauched regimes right across Latin America, Africa and Asia. I was a veteran of CND anti-cruise missile marches in the 1980s. I had gone to Nicaragua to defend the Sandinista cause against American imperialism. I had stood smiling in Managua's Revolution Square as the assembled crowd chanted death to the Yanquis. America was the bad guy, right? America was always the bad guy.

Clearly some basic moral calculations needed to be performed. Starting with which vision of the world represented more closely my own liberal outlook. The cosmopolitan city of New York, a multiracial city of opportunity, a town where anyone on earth could arrive and thrive, exuberant, cultured, diverse, a place I had visited and loved for its liberty and energy and excitement? Or the people who attacked it, those arid minds who wanted to remove women from sight, kill homosexuals, banish music, destroy art, the demolishers of the Bamiyan Buddhas who aimed to terrorise everyone they could into submission to the will of their vengeful God. It was, as they say, a no-brainer, or should have been. But was there not also an obligation to ask if this heinous crime was more complex than it first appeared? That was the progressive instinct: don't be fooled by the mass media, which we all knew was a propaganda industry, look behind the scenes, examine the bigger picture, think about the context, study history. And so if you wanted to consider yourself a member of the thinking classes, it was not enough to recoil in horror, you also had to take into account America's own score sheet in matters of cold blood.

'It's terrible,' was the often heard formulation, 'but . . .' Did I think there was a but? And if there was a but, could it be any kind of justification for what had taken place? And if it wasn't a justification, what was the point of the but? Was it there to show one's even-handedness and sense of fair play? Or purely for decoration? I knew right from the first second where my emotional sympathies were located but what was my intellectual position?

What helped guide me to the answer was the alternative analysis, the 'It's terrible, but' in which the 'It's terrible' was the decorative part of the equation. A number of commentaries that articulated this response quickly began to appear in different newspapers. Perhaps the most indignant came, with impressive alacrity, on 13 September in the newspaper that I had read since I was a teenager, the newspaper for which I had been writing for over ten years, the voice of liberal Britain, the *Guardian*.

'Nearly two days after the horrific suicide attacks on civilian workers in New York and Washington,' wrote Seamus Milne, 'it has become painfully clear that most Americans simply don't get it . . . Shock, rage and grief there has been aplenty. But any glimmer of recognition of why people might have been driven to carry out such atrocities, sacrificing their own lives in the process – or why the United States is hated with such bitterness, not only in Arab and Muslim countries, but across the developing world – seems almost entirely absent.'

One doesn't need to work for a newspaper – though it probably helps – to realise that Milne was underselling his own speed of analytical thought. To get his piece published on the 13th meant that he would have needed to have completed it by around 6 p.m. or 7 p.m. on the 12th. Allowing for its considered tone, which must have been the product of several hours of sober reflection, it would be fair to assume that he would have begun writing it, at the latest, at around 2 p.m. In other words, at about 9 a.m. New York time. That left the Americans a whole twenty-four hours to absorb the shock, deal with the grief and then move on to some cold, hard self-criticism. And they flunked it.

Milne's savaging of American self-absorption was the most conspicuous example of an attitude that could be heard in plenty of sophisticated conversations, or should I say conversations between sophisticated people, and read in a number of left or liberal publications. But it was not the earliest. That prize has to go to George Galloway, still then a Labour MP, who published his own litany of American crimes and misdemeanours in the *Guardian* on 12 September (i.e. written on September 11), and noted, not entirely without approval, that many people around the world 'will consider the US to have had to swallow some of their own medicine'. It could not have been easy to have mastered that kind of dispassionate observation as scenes of the most visceral despair were being screened live on television, but Gorgeous George rose, or sank, to the occasion.

However, perhaps the most telling instance of this blame-the-victim outlook was to be found in the 4 October issue of the *London Review of Books*. If the *Guardian* is the voice of liberal Britain then the *LRB* is where the liberal intelligentsia takes its time to reflect on politics and culture. Twenty-nine intellectuals responded to the *LRB*'s commission to write about 9/11 and its fallout. Contrary to some reports, a number of differing views were filed, but it's not inaccurate to say that overall the sentiments tended towards anti-Americanism. In some of the pieces that tendency was not disguised by anything so polite as a show of sympathy. The Cambridge historian and classicist Mary Beard gained a measure of notoriety with her summary of public reaction. 'But when the shock had faded, more hard-headed reaction set in. This wasn't just the feeling that, however tactfully you dress it up, the United States had it coming. That is, of course, what many people openly or privately think. World bullies, even if their heart is in the right place, will in the end pay the price.' September 11, she wrote, was the West's price for its 'refusal to listen to what the "terrorists" have to say'. Those doubting speech marks around the word 'terrorist' would become the badge of enlightened scepticism in the weeks, months and years to come. Beard also disparaged Peter Mandelson for suggesting that the secret services should be recruiting in Bradford rather than St James's. And she derided the notion that there existed a plentiful supply of suicide bombers.

What all these reactions had in common, I realised, was not complexity but simplicity. For all of them this was an issue of the powerless striking back at the powerful, the oppressed against the oppressor, the rebels against the imperialists. It was Han Solo and Luke Skywalker taking on the Death Star. There was no serious attempt to examine what kind of power the powerless wanted to assume, or over whom they wanted to exercise it, and no one thought to ask by what authority these suicidal killers had been designated the voice of the oppressed. It was enough that Palestinians had danced in the West Bank. After all, everyone knew that America, the most aped nation on earth, was the most hated nation on earth.

It was Beard who was the focus of counter-criticism in the ensuing debate but there were several other contributions that caught my eye. There was the *Village Voice* film critic, J. Hoberman, who wrote: 'It seems incredible to me that the period between the fall of the Berlin Wall and the collapse of the World Trade towers will be perceived as some sort of golden age – albeit one characterized by the production

of disaster movies ranging from the Gulf War to *Pearl Harbor*.'
It seemed incredible to me that, after all that had happened,
the object of anger was still the movies. Even as a recent
survivor of *The Fast and the Furious*, I could not now muster
the smallest antipathy towards overblown blockbusters. That
could wait for another time. Yet Hoberman was not alone in
targeting Tinseltown. Amit Chaudhuri finished his denunciation of American power with a plea to the American public,
then immediately added the pessimistic caveat: 'but the
American public's main source of information about its
country's foreign policy is Hollywood with its images of terror
and frightening rhetoric of "good" and "evil".'

I remember being struck by the recurring expression of what
seemed to me like minor concerns. I was amazed how these
celebrated thinkers appeared to take in their stride a mass
homicide that no one foresaw. The scale of the suffering, the
innocence of the victims, and the aims of the perpetrators
barely seemed to register in many of the comments. Was this
a sign of shock or complacency? Or was it something else, a
kind of atrophying of moral faculties, brought on by prolonged
use of fixed ideas, that prevented the sufferer from recognising
a new paradigm when it arrived, no matter how spectacular
its announcement? Marx referred to something similar when
he noted how even revolutionaries turn reflexively to the past
'in order to present the new scene of world history in this
time-honoured disguise and this borrowed language'.

The cultural theorist, Frederic Jameson, another contributor to the *LRB* special, has often been described as a Marxist.
But his entry offered no challenge to the prevailing ortho-
doxies of the left. I had once attended a seminar on film
theory Jameson gave at the National Film Theatre, back in
that period when the subject seemed to be the last refuge for
Marxists, structuralists, Freudians and every other intellectual seeking asylum from the failings and disappointments of
the real world. After sitting through a couple of hours of
impenetrable jargonised discourse I was, I recall, embarrassed

to acknowledge that I hadn't understood a word of what had been said – if Jameson's language was borrowed, it was on terms of zero interest. But that embarrassment, in a nimble piece of historical rewriting of which Jameson would doubt-less approve, was retrospectively erased when I read what he had to say about 11 September.

'I have been reluctant to comment on the recent "events",' Jameson opened in characteristically lofty fashion, 'because the event in question, as history, is incomplete and one can even say that it has not yet fully happened.' Well, I remember thinking, it's certainly happened for the many thousands who were dead. The 'event' was unlikely to get any more complete for them. 'Obviously,' he continued, 'there are immediate comments one can make, in particular on the nauseating media reception, whose cheap pathos seemed unconsciously dictated by a White House intent on smothering the situation in senti-ment in order to demonstrate the undemonstrable: namely, that "Americans are united as never before since Pearl Harbor."'

Jameson prides himself on his critique of postmodernism but could there be a more nauseating illustration of the warped priorities of postmodern thinking? All things considered, it wasn't the mass murder that was cause for distress but instead its media coverage. After the customary impeachment of American foreign policy, Jameson concluded with a breath-taking example of what, to use his own language, might be termed 'dialectical reversal'.

'As for the future, no one (presumably including our own Government) has any idea what the promised and threatened "war on terrorism" might look like. But until we know that, we can have no satisfactory picture of the "events" we imagine to have taken place on a single day in September. Despite this uncertainty, however, it is permitted to feel that the future holds nothing good for either side.'

In two metaphysical swoops, Jameson had upended the twin towers of sequential truth: cause and effect. We cannot describe what has taken place, he seemed to say, until we see what the response is to it. Yes, you may think – or 'imagine' – your daughter was flown into a skyscraper but that's just an interpretation of 'events' that cannot be verified – or presumably dismissed – until we have seen the reaction it may provoke at some unknown point in the future. We can't acknowledge a crime, as it were, until its punishment has been delivered. Hold on a moment, I recall thinking as I reread the passage to make sure I hadn't missed something, what is this self-hatred doing to our powers of reason? Into what moral quicksand had intellectual obfuscation led us? And how sinister was that 'permitted'?

Still, in the satellite age of relentless news, a tiny circulation ink sheet like the *LRB* was surely of limited influence. True enough, but it's also fair to say that its influence was limited to influential people: academics, writers, commentators. The issue of consumer reach, however, was not really the point for me. I was more concerned with moral scope, in particular how the magazine, or rather these contributors, exerted influence on me. Curiously for a movement that so often invoked the masses and the underprivileged, the left has always set great store in the ability of intellectuals to extract the buried significance and truth from the rubble of history. To have a left outlook, if it means anything at all, is to be on guard against easy explanations and popular (manufactured) opinions. Intellectuals, in this respect, form a kind of priesthood, interpreting not just the sacred texts of Marx, Freud et al., but also reality itself. And so much of what leftist intellectuals have had to say, in an effort to explain the success of capitalism, has been devoted to the problem of rejecting the myths and untruths of the controlling elite. All that stuff about hegemony and false consciousness and the culture industry was aimed at inspiring doubt in the appearance of the world and respect for those whose analytical approach was such that they could penetrate the misleading surface of things. If I'm honest, I think I had always been a little intimidated by such 'first-class' minds. There was a sense in which, when it came down to the nitty-gritty, when things got difficult or bloody, it was a relief to defer to the better read, the more keenly informed. And here were a number of *LRB*-approved intellects, some of them of world renown, cutting through the nonsense and telling it, in small bite-sized pieces, just exactly how it was. They had made an effort to set the parameters of debate for the thinking left, to prescribe, if you like, what was permitted.

For those of a progressive sensibility, it was permitted to 'move on' from the vast graveyard of Ground Zero, which was seen as a tiresome media circus, and vent outrage at the real adversary: President George W. Bush and his 'War on Terror' against prime target Afghanistan. There were, and remain, plenty of things that could be said about Bush's statements at that time, his careless and emotive use of the word 'crusade', his macho posturing, and his worrying lack of gravitas. But whatever the criticisms of the American president they did not alter the fact that Afghanistan was harbouring the chief suspect in the attacks, Osama bin Laden, whom the Taliban refused to hand over; or that the country was a home to an extensive network of terrorist training camps. And nor – most disturbingly for those of us who thought universal human rights should be universal – did a dislike of Bush change the reality of the Taliban as a sadistic regime that had imposed a medieval dystopia on its long-suffering citizens. In this respect, at least, Jameson was correct: there were two sides. One side focused entirely on Bush's shortcomings and America's unsavoury history, the other on the psychopathology of the Taliban and the murderous ambition of bin Laden.

Most people I knew were against the invasion. War was wrong because war was avoidable. I had some sympathy with that viewpoint. War, even the most brief and precise war, is always bloody and there has never been a war in which innocent people haven't died. To resist the urge for revenge was surely the mark of a civilised authority. The problem with the pacifist approach is that it didn't address what was to be done about bin Laden, or the possibility of repeat attacks. No one was quite sure what the 11 September killers wanted, not least because no one had claimed responsibility, but in the minds of the appeasers that was no reason not to give it to them. On top of which, it was widely believed that any war in Afghanistan, the nation that defeated the disciplined might of the Soviet army, would turn into a protracted bloodbath. Some even argued that the bloodbath was America's true aim. Noam Chomsky, the dissident American academic whom the *New Statesman* described as 'our greatest unraveller of accredited lies' told an audience at MIT on 18 October that a 'silent genocide' was underway. He estimated that America was deliberately 'trying to murder 3 or 4 million people' in Afghanistan. A figure roughly one-thousandth of that size is the generally accepted figure for the death toll in the Afghanistan campaign. But let's allow a margin of error, and say it is perhaps one hundredth. Again, does it matter what Chomsky says? Isn't he just an unheard voice up against a vast military machine? In a global opinion poll organised by *Prospect* magazine in 2005, Chomsky was named the world's leading public intellectual. He may have no power, as such, but it cannot be said that he is without influence.

After 11 September, and right up until the fall of Kabul in November, I was still labouring under the impression that one could hold both opinions: that Bush was mad and bin Laden was bad (or was it the other way round?). And, naturally, one could. I wrote a piece for the *Observer* in November criticising the blind entrenchment of the opposing positions. It seemed to me that once a line had been adopted no one was prepared to allow changing events to change their minds. Thus the anti-war lobby warned of a fierce campaign, but when the Taliban, lacking popular support, quickly collapsed, the anti-war *New Statesman* instantly ran a front cover with the headline: 'WHY BIN LADEN IS STILL WINNING'. Both sides, the pro-war and anti-war, saw only what they wanted to see. 'The urge to prove that they have been right all along is so much greater than the need to adapt to new circumstances,' I wrote at the time. 'So it's the circumstances that are adapted to fit the pre-existing line. All sides will say that it is a question of morality. But the suspicion remains that deep down it is a matter of pride.'

Yet, when all was said and done, it was not possible to maintain a foot in both camps. The more I learned about bin Laden and the global jihad, the more I realised that it was not impotence that was their salient characteristic, but rather the totalitarian ambition of their ideology. The Nazis in Germany, the Bolsheviks in Russia and the Maoists in China started out as powerless irritants who sought support among the marginalised and alienated. In each case, many of those who should have known better decided to look the other way or even lionise their appeal. The result was that the madmen seized power and, between them, were responsible for well over 100 million deaths in the twentieth century. If mass, indiscriminate murder is one of the hallmarks of totalitarianism, then 11 September proved that, given the opportunity, al-Qaeda and its sympathisers had what it took to become a new totalitarian force: a complete indifference to human life. It may have been fun and exhilarating, in an angry student way, to call Bush a fascist. But what words did that leave to describe democracy-hating fanatics with a pronounced aim of global domination and a willingness to kill civilians in their thousands?

In the end I reached the conclusion that 11 September had already brutally confirmed: there were other forces, far more malign than America, that lay in wait in the world. But having faced up to the basic issue of comparative international threats, could I stop the political reassessment there? If I had been wrong about the relative danger of America, could I be wrong about all the other things I previously held to be true? I tried hard to suppress this thought, to ring-fence the global situation, grant it exceptional status and keep it in a separate part of my mind. All those other questions that would begin to taunt me, I resolved to ignore. I had too much vested in my image of myself as a 'liberal'. After all, I was not only a *Guardian* reader, I was, from time to time, a *Guardian writer*. Some fundamentals could not change. I had bought into the idea, for instance, that all social ills stemmed from inequality and racism. I knew that crime was solely a function of poverty. That to be British was cause for shame, never pride. And to be white was to bear an unshakeable burden of guilt. I held the view, or at least was unprepared to challenge it, that while all cultures may not be deserving of equal praise, it was wrong to single out any for censure, except, of course, Western culture, which should be admonished at every opportunity. Oh yes, I had many times quoted Mahatma Gandhi's famous line when asked what he thought of Western civilisation – 'It would be a good idea.' I was confident too that Israel was the source of most of the troubles in the Middle East. These were non-negotiables for any right-thinking decent person. I couldn't question these received wisdoms without questioning my own identity. And I had grown too comfortable with seeing myself as one of the good guys, the well-meaning people, to want to do anything that upset that image. I viewed myself as understanding, and to maintain that self-perception it was imperative that I didn't try to understand myself. In a sense 11 September was the ultimate mugging, a murderous assertion of a new reality, or rather a reality that already existed but which we preferred not to see. Over the years I had absorbed a notion of liberalism that was passive, defeatist, guilt-ridden. Feelings of guilt governed my world view: post-colonial guilt, white guilt, middle-class guilt, British guilt. But if I was guilty, 9/11 shattered my innocence. More than anything it challenged us all to wake up and open our eyes to what was real. It took me far too long to meet that challenge. For while I realised almost straight away that 9/11 would change the world, it would be several years before I accepted that it had also changed me. I had been wrong. This was my story, after all.

2

Shame

Like most people of a liberal sensibility I have been a long-time inhabitant of the state of conscientious denial. Though 9/11 forced me to confront my views, it would be wrong to say they had never previously caused me doubt. But rather than examine those doubts I chose to suppress them. Over the course of three decades I learned to evade, ignore, dismiss, excuse or explain away those aspects of reality that did not fit with how I believed, or wanted to believe, the world to be. As the world so seldom tallied with my prescribed version of events I was called upon to spend a lot of time pretending otherwise. This pretence took many forms – from wishful thinking to wilful refusal to think – but its most common manifestation was silence. Not the stealthy conspiratorial silence of the activist, but the passive silence of prevailing attitude, implicit, assumed, unsaid. For the establishment of an orthodoxy tacit acceptance serves almost as well as fervent agreement. And I found myself tacitly accepting a progressive orthodoxy that was increasingly set against progress.

I am a product of the liberal-left consensus that has dominated informed opinion in Britain since 1945. The term 'liberal-left' is of course imprecise and amorphous, one of those terms that can mean anything or nothing, depending on circumstance. But I use it here as a description of a way of understanding, a mentality, rather than an exact set of principles. For many of those who like to think of themselves as open-minded, a liberal-left outlook has become almost second nature. More reflexive than reflective, it's an attitude that has successfully smothered debate among liberal-minded people. What's more, because this attitude is nebulous, because it's not tied to a major party or a particular doctrine, it remains resilient and adaptable. It's precisely because it has wriggle room over the specifics that the liberal-left mindset has survived the ravages of communism, the collapse of communism, and the triumph of market economics without having to do any serious mental revision.

In spite of all these provisos, I would describe my views even today as liberal-left, if we can take that hyphenate as a commitment to both liberty and equality. However, the liberal-left in the West currently appears less interested in striving towards those dual Enlightenment ideals than in fostering the twin human emotions by which they are distorted: guilt and grievance. The left half of the equation draws on grievance while the liberal half is sustained by guilt, and as such they enjoy a symbiotic relationship: the more grievance the left can generate, the more guilt the liberal will feel, and the more guilt the liberal feels, the more grievance the left are able to generate. Those of a liberal-left outlook therefore risk being locked into an escalating emotional spiral that leads to some conspicuously irrational positions.

In my own case I can't really lay claim to the excuse of *feeling* guilty. I never sat around beating myself up over the uneven distribution of the planet's wealth and health – though I have met people who do and, it must be said, they're no fun at all. No, my guilt was far more notional and abstracted, a kind of adopted social obligation rather than a genuine personal emotion. The effect of this kind of guilt is not to purge the heart but to censor the mind. To register liberal guilt is also a sign of sophistication and sensitivity, a badge of civilised decency. Within the arts and social sciences, in particular, guilt remains the major currency of debate. So central is it to the Western liberal sensibility that a guiltless Western liberal is an oxymoron, like a penniless philanthropist or a chaste whore.

But from where does this guilt originate and to what end is its purpose? These are questions that the good liberal doesn't ask. They seem like conservative questions, doubting, cynical, ungenerous. Even to pose them implicitly suggests that the status quo is acceptable, that the privileged bear no responsibility for the world's manifold inequalities.

Nonetheless, they are necessary questions and in my case, at least, they call forth some instructive answers. When I examine my own experience it strikes me that I didn't develop a sense of guilt as a result of material success. On the contrary, it would be more accurate to say that I gained a measure of material success as a result of developing a sense of guilt. If that makes me sound a little mercenary then it also points to the near monopoly that guilt has held on liberal ideas in education, academia and the intellectual professions. So firm was its grip when I was at school and university that I very soon inculcated the widely disseminated notion that someone like me – white, British, male – had an unfair advantage in life. What was perhaps most significant about adopting this belief is that, in common with the majority of white British males, I had enjoyed scarcely any of the privileges for which I was supposed to feel guilty.

In fact, when I arrived at my north London comprehensive school in 1973 for what proved to be my liberal induction, I had known only the kind of poverty that used to be the subject of award-winning TV plays. The British can be oddly competitive and sentimental about being poor. It's a trait that was well satirised in *Monty Python's* 'Four Yorkshiremen' sketch. Devotees will recall that the eponymous characters, all successful businessmen, share a bottle of Chateau de Chasselas at an upmarket vacation resort as they attempt to best one another with tales of their childhood deprivation. It starts with one Yorkshireman reminiscing about how he used to live in an old house with holes in the roof and progresses with each trumping the others' misfortune until at some point one of them boasts of having lived 'in a shoebox in t' middle o' road'. 'Cardboard?' says another. 'You were lucky.' The sketch ends, after a series of ever more fantastic exaggerations, with all of them agreeing that 'you try and tell the young people today that . . . and they won't believe yer'.

In reality the disbelief is not just limited to young people. Despite our ongoing fixation with heritage and twentieth-century history, few us now think of poverty as a defining feature of our recent past. We're familiar with stories of hardship, of course, we know that it could be 'grim up North', and we're aware that ours was a class-bound society in which something as superficial as the choice of the word 'toilet' or 'lavatory' could define your position in life. But overall, and in particular on the international stage, the collective British story has become one of the exploiters, not the exploited. It's notorious that Britain controlled a quarter of the planet at the height of its empire. We dominated the downtrodden masses of the world and as they got poorer we got richer. That's the story, anyway, that most progressive people more or less accept. The fact remains, however, that during this golden age of empire, from around 1850 to 1950, the British themselves, with a minority of exceptions, were uncomfortably poor. Not starving, perhaps, but frequently hungry and usually malnourished. Economic historians are still divided over whether the empire provided a net financial gain or loss to Britain, but whatever the answer it seemed to do little for the well-being of most Britons. It was not until the empire was relinquished after the Second World War that there was a meaningful redistribution of wealth, and even then its effect was slow and limited. For many years following the war, surplus of any kind was notable by its absence in the lives of most Britons. Somehow, though, amid all the queasy sentiment and hand-wringing, this past has become a nostalgic anecdote, a false memory, another country that bears no relevance or relation to the place we inhabit today. As a consequence I find it almost impossible to recall my childhood without feeling as if I've pulled up a chair alongside those Yorkshiremen and poured myself a long glass of the Chateau de Chasselas. My own instinct, honed by irony and schooled in ridicule, is to view the I-had-it-tough memoir as an exercise in self-appreciation, as if the real point is to establish one's moral bona fides or street credibility. Yet that considerable reservation aside, I think it's worth briefly describing the conditions of my upbringing, if only because they would appear to be so unfavourable to the development of guilt.

I was born and spent my first nine years in Rhyl Street in the Kentish Town area of north London. The street was demolished in the early seventies as part of a slum clearance programme and replaced by a large council estate that looked from the outside like a purpose-built correctional facility. Rhyl Street, like those around it, was made up of dilapidated Victorian three-storey terraces that opened, with the briefest of pathways, directly on to the street. We shared our house with an old crone who lived upstairs with her budgerigar. There were no subdivisions or separate entrances. Inside the house there was neither a bath nor a lavatory (nor, come to that, a toilet). The only loo – and it was shared with the crone – was a damp crumbling shack in the backyard. There were seven of us in my family and we would all wash in a sink in the kitchen, the hot water dribbling from a tiny Ascot water-heater that looked and sounded as if it was about to explode each time it was used. The place was rodent-infested and, naturally, there was no heating, save for a coal fire in the sitting room. I shared a bedroom with my two sisters, who shared a single bed. I've been told by older siblings, over another metaphorical glass of the burgundy, that I had it easy. For when I was very young, beyond my memory but not theirs, six of us lived in two damp rooms.

To look at photographs of my childhood in the sixties is to see a world ingrained with the austerity of the post-war years. This was not 'Swinging London' of colour-supplement fame. Indeed, were it not for their compositional flaws, the snaps from my family album of that period might be mistaken for Bill Brandt's work from the thirties and forties. I grew up around 'bomb debris' sites and the prefabricated houses that were 'temporarily' erected after the war. Children wore functional clothes in functional colours and we had no say in the matter. Our lives were centred on the outside world, in the street, women were mothers in the home, and men worked and went to the pub. There were very few digressions or distractions from this arrangement. A restaurant, for example, or even a café that was not dedicated to feeding workmen was something that was simply not part of the life I knew as a child. Not even as a conceptual possibility. No one I knew had ever travelled abroad, unless abroad was from where they had come or they had served in the army. Holidays were a fortnight on a spartan caravan site or if you could afford it – and I can still recall the excitement when we first went to Butlins – a forlorn British holiday camp that, with its perimeter fences, rows of barracks-like accommodation and strict regime of timekeeping, appeared to be a leftover from national service. Cars were a rarity and all of them were second-, third- or fourth-hand. I remember that on the other side of our backyard there lived a short man, his enormous wife and their five children who wore the permanently alert expressions of woodland animals. They were the proud owners of a motorbike with a sidecar and it was in this tiny vehicle, the father struggling to remain earthbound, that they ventured out on family trips and camping holidays. All seven of them.

Not that I thought of myself or my neighbours as poor. Poor kids, as far as I understood it, were those whose parents couldn't afford school dinners and really poor kids were those whose parents couldn't afford underwear. A number of children in my class in primary school were allowed to sit out PE, or perform in their trousers, because they did not possess the luxury of pants. I was also aware of how lucky I was that corporal punishment was not a feature of home life. I walked in trepidation of my father, a big man with a sharp mind and a volcanic temper, but I can only remember him hitting me on a single occasion. For most kids I knew, being hit with a slipper or a belt was a weekly, if not daily, occurrence.

In *Postwar*, his compendious history of modern Europe, Tony Judt describes this period in Britain's and Europe's history as the 'Age of Affluence'. And it was. For poverty, to an extent at least, is relative and by comparison with what had gone before we were upwardly mobile. My mother was born locally and her family had lived in the area for generations. Her father, my grandfather, died when she was seven. Her mother, a classic big-hearted cockney matriarch, had spent much of her childhood in the workhouse, sent there by her violent and alcoholic mother. My father's father was from Ireland, the son of a barefisted fighter from Cork. I never knew my paternal grandfather either. He was a First World War veteran who lost his health in the Depression and eventually died in 1947 while my father was stationed in Japan. My father's mother was a fastidious but rather cold woman, and she had reason for withholding her emotions. An orphan, she too was no stranger to the workhouse. Though possessed of a nimble mind and great beauty, she was reduced, in her prime, to scrubbing doorsteps of the wealthy on Christmas Day to earn money for her family. It all sounds so Dickensian, this kind of story, but it was a common enough narrative in my youth. So common that no one, least of all my grandmothers, would have thought it worthy of special mention. Neither of my parents completed their formal education. A few years after her father died, my mother was evacuated to the countryside for most of the war. She was moved back and forth to a number of locations across England, disrupting what little schooling she received. This was just as well because the area around her street, The Grove, was bombed so heavily that it was literally removed from the map: no sign of The Grove remains in Kentish Town. She eventually left school at fourteen to start work as a seamstress. My father fared slightly better, completing his studies at fifteen. As I say, there was nothing remotely unusual about any of these biographical details in the part of London I lived in the 1960s. The fact is that from the perspective of most Londoners, and for the overwhelming majority of my neighbours, these were normal life stories. As they would have been for millions of other families across the country. We were not members of some feared and alienated underclass. We were simply an inconspicuous part of the mass of working people living in Britain at that time.

Due to its proximity to the major train stations in the south of the borough (King's Cross, St Pancras, Euston) and the presence of a Catholic church and school, our neighbourhood had a large Irish population. Most were second or third generation, the children of navvies and labourers who worked on the railways. Most of the local pubs were more or less Irish pubs, the most obvious exception being one at the end of Rhyl Street called the Ponsford Arms. On Sunday afternoons in the summer the customers would spill out into the road to play a game of cricket. In those days car traffic was so infrequent that it hardly ever interrupted play. The games were loud and boisterous and the men, dressed in their best clothes, wore their shirtsleeves rolled up with their braces exposed. It was like a scene from an earlier era, which in a way it was. Like most decades, the 1960s arrived late, and they failed to arrive until the 1970s in our corner of north London. The Malden Road area of Kentish Town remained fixed in an age that had nothing to do with hippies or social rebellion or pharmacological experimentation or protest. The only thing about the cricket players that marked them out from other men who would have behaved and dressed in a similar fashion any time in the previous three decades was their black skin. The Ponsford was one of the few pubs in the borough back then that welcomed black people. There were a few black families from West Africa and the West Indies in the surrounding streets but not enough to qualify as a 'community'. The patrons of the Ponsford came from outside the neighbourhood.

I didn't know there was such a thing as a de facto colour

bar in those days but I did realise that the Ponsford, so to speak, was a coloured bar. And the neighbourhood was sufficiently traditional in its character and attitudes that the sight of twenty or thirty black men shouting and running around on a Sunday afternoon, I now realise, must have caused something of a stir. I don't recall being aware of any real tension or flashpoints but it would be surprising if feelings of suspicion and resentment were not aroused. After all, the very fact that black men – and they were all men accompanied by a handful of white women – felt compelled to congregate in one pub very likely points to the prejudice they encountered elsewhere in the area. For while the publican of the Ponsford may have been admirably inclusive, it's not as if our street was particularly forward-thinking about such matters. My mother, who was one of the most selfless people I've ever known, would certainly, by modern standards, have been found guilty of racism. She didn't think black people were bad or immoral, she simply felt that they were out of place in England. If there was ever a fight at the Ponsford, which there was from time to time, it served only to reaffirm her conviction that this is what happened when foreigners found themselves a long way from home. And to her, black people back then were foreigners. By contrast, my father, a trade unionist who had flirted with communism and was better disposed to other cultures, made a point of lecturing us on the evils of judging people by their race, a task he would usually combine with a quick primer on British colonial misdeeds. I distinctly recall him insisting very firmly that we should never, under any circumstances, use the word 'nigger'. Which was presumably why his own preference was 'spade'.

Kentish Town in the 1960s, then, was an insular and unenlightened place that was ill-prepared for the dramatic social changes by which the locality and the nation at large were soon to be transformed. Overwhelmingly white and working class, it boasted a thriving criminal culture in its pubs and markets and scrap-metal yards but at the same time its streets were reasonably safe, certainly for those who lived there. Though hard-core Labour in its voting habits, it was essentially conservative in its attitudes. Gentrification, multiculturalism, drug use and abuse, working mothers, single-parent families, among much else that was to change the area, were hardly known at that time.

The term 'gentrification' was coined in 1964 by the British sociologist Ruth Glass. She used it to describe the process that was underway in Islington, the neighbouring borough to Camden in which Kentish Town is located. But it was a number of years before an advance party of gentrifiers reached our part of town. I was ten before I came across anyone who could be described as 'middle class'. A boy arrived at my primary school in my final year. He stood out so much that everyone in the school took an interest in him, particularly after he broke down in tears one day in assembly. We had never seen such a public display of weakness before. He was called Gann and outside of science-fiction books no one had a name like that. He spoke in a funny way, stuttering and expressive, with a marked absence of the expletives that formed the basis of our vocabulary. His accent to our ears was impossibly and offensively posh. I later learned that his father was an actor – an unknown profession around our way – who was out of work. So Kentish Town was not, like Islington, on the way up; Gann's father was on the way down. And his son was beaten up every day of his school life.

I felt sorry for Gann, though doubtless I bullied him too on occasion. He seemed to represent a sensibility that was an insult, even a threat, to our more robust codes of behaviour. I suppose it was class hatred in its embryonic form. In any case it was not the kind of neighbourhood that welcomed outsiders or difference, if such a neighbourhood has ever in fact existed. Like all children, I took what I saw around me to be the normal state of affairs that would remain indefinitely unchanged. Of course, aged seven, eight, nine, I was largely ignorant of the events that were unfolding across the world. I knew nothing of the significance of the 1968 riots or the civil rights movement or Bloody Sunday or the Vietnam War, though I heard them mentioned. They formed an intermittent and largely inaudible transmission whose signal, like that of the pirate radio stations of the period, drifted in and out of range. I didn't know what racism and sexism were, and I had never heard of the word 'gay'. It was in this state of innocence or ignorance that I arrived at Haverstock comprehensive school in September 1973.

Located on the border of the affluent foothills of Hampstead and the council flatlands of Kentish Town, Haverstock was a school with a properly comprehensive intake. It was mixed sex with over thirty different nationalities represented among the pupils. There was also a significant minority of children from the intellectual and artistic communities of Primrose Hill and Belsize Park, as well as a smattering of kids whose parents were professionals – lawyers, doctors, public administrators – with either an idealistic or economic interest in avoiding the private or grammar school systems. And in addition, owing to a specialised department, there were a large number of deaf children. It was a time of great optimism, when the classroom was seen as the place in which to end the class system. Teaching back then was governed less by a determination to correct spelling than a commitment to put right social injustice. I was a bright kid, the kind that a few years before would have been 'rescued' from the oblivion of a secondary modern school – a sort of dumping ground for the menial classes – and hothoused at a grammar school, the state-supported facsimiles of the traditional private school.

Haverstock was no hothouse. It was ideologically opposed to all forms of competition. There was only one area of endeavour that remained beyond the school's egalitarian control: fighting. When it came to violence there was no shortage of competitive spirit. And a strict hierarchy existed, organised along class and race lines, with the white middle-class kids at the bottom, little more than walk-on victims, and the black working-class kids at the top – a perfect inversion of academic expectations. The simmering and often explosive atmosphere permeated all the lessons, but to say that they were a distraction would imply that there was some core element of learning from which we were distracted. Almost without exception, that was not the case. Classes were a matter of damage containment and not infrequently total anarchy. Kids smashed up desks, fought with one another and attacked staff. The year I arrived at the school a teacher was crippled in an assault by a pupil wielding a chisel. Gangs of black and white kids did battle with Chinese pupils inspired by the Bruce Lee films of the time and the police were regularly called to patrol the school exit at the end of the day. Bullying was rife and largely neglected. Years later I was disturbed but not too dismayed to learn that the serial killers and rapists David Mulcahy and John Duffy formed their psychopathic bond after being bullied at Haverstock (unfortunately they were far from being the only murderers-to-be who graduated while I was there). There were only two teachers who were able to impose some level of calm on the Hobbesian proceedings. Both, as it turned out, were male homosexuals, both traditionalists in their methods, and both were viewed by the rest of staff as reactionary eccentrics. In return they observed the hapless efforts of their colleagues and the disorder wrought by the new orthodoxy with barely concealed contempt.

Most of the staff could best be described as well-meaning – if not particularly industrious – liberals who were manifestly ill-suited to the profession of teaching. But a number were outspoken Marxists and my maths teacher was an avowed Maoist. She looked like a gothic or Pre-Raphaelite hippy with long black hair, long black clothes, a long powder-white face and a long pointed nose through which she seemed to talk. She was the first person I heard use the phrase 'petty bourgeois' and she was also the first person I'd ever encountered who seemed permanently angry about the state of the world. Much to the approval of her male pupils, she had no time for the petty bourgeois convention of wearing a bra. She carried round a copy of the *Little Red Book* and she spoke of the forthcoming revolution as if it were as inevitable as the new football season.

One day, a few weeks into my first term at Haverstock, she asked if there were any socialists or communists in the class. An uninhibited girl from the Hampstead tendency put her hand up and said that her parents were communists and so was she. The teacher gave her a big smile, which was a rare expression to see in place of the militant scowl that seemed set like a sphincter in the middle of her thin face. I thought we were socialists but I wasn't sure, so I didn't put my hand up. I knew we were Labour. Everyone was Labour. But were Labour socialists? I asked my brother about this when I got home. He was five years older than me and something of a practical joker. I told him that my teacher supported Chairman Mao and I asked if we were socialists. He confirmed that I was right. 'Yeah, we're socialists,' he said. 'National socialists, tell her. She'll like that.' And so I went in the next day and announced that I was a national socialist, ready to be rewarded with the approving smile that none of my top marks in maths had managed to secure.

'A Nazi!' she exclaimed in her nasal whine. 'I fucking hate Nazis.'

Then she turned to the class and announced that I supported the National Front and I believed that all black people should be sent back to Africa. She wanted to know what the black kids thought of that. Needless to say, several let me know in the playground afterwards. Suddenly I was NF, one of the goons from the television, a slander that took me several awkward days to correct. It was only an appeal to the maths teacher in which I told her about my brother's joke that moved her to call off the black guard and salvage my reputation. Warning me that it was no joke to bandy around a phrase like that, the self-proclaimed Maoist said I should never use political terms I didn't understand.

I suppose you could say that in the sequence of false accusation, punishment and ideological rehabilitation I had received a U-certificate preview of the re-education process that at that time was still terrorising China in Mao's Cultural Revolution. And in a sense the re-education worked. Perversely, given that she had instigated my beating, I was still more keen to gain my maths teacher's respect. So I would ask her opinion about politics and she would explain that the British Empire was a global crime syndicate without equal. She told me that all white people were culpable in the historic crimes committed against the non-white peoples of the world. And she said that after the revolution everyone would be equal. Though she reserved a special loathing for the National Front, whose pernicious influence she saw everywhere, it was the Labour Party that most often earned her abomination. What particularly angered her was the Labour Party's position on immigration control. She believed that there should be no controls at all, that any controls were intrinsically racist. I found all of these ideas hard to position in the reality that I knew, but I began to wonder if that was because I didn't understand reality.

Though few of the Haverstock staff were quite as forthright in their opinions, many of them, including my science teacher, my tutor, my English teacher, my history and my art teachers, made it apparent that they were broadly sympathetic to my maths teacher's way of thinking. They were hard left, revolutionary left, at a time when barricades were still discussed without irony. There were, however, obvious limits to their revolutionary fervour. Even at my tender age I noticed that while they invoked the working class in heroic terms, in vanguard language, so to speak, it was the middle-class children that they would treat as equals. From time to time, this apparent favouritism would ignite in me a vestigial class resentment that I could never quite build into outright hatred. Partly, I think, because I secretly admired the manner in which the middle-class children also saw the teachers as their equals, and partly because it was the middle-class girls after whom

I lusted. I think I also sensed a philosophical problem in being a class warrior. I came from generations of a Labour-voting family. I lived in subsidised housing in a borough that had been Labour, and hard-left Labour, for many years. There was from 1974 to 1979, roughly my secondary school years, a Labour government. And I attended a school that was the very ideal of Labour thinking. In short, I was a total product of socialist policy living through what was, in terms of industrial relations and ideological debate, arguably the most revolutionary decade of the twentieth century. What more could I want other than more? And wasn't the appetite for more what capitalism, rather than socialism, was all about?

The only logical way out of that little paradox was more socialism. That at least was what I wanted to believe. As I entered my teenage years I became increasingly aware of inequality. This was not necessarily due to the smattering of Marxism that I'd picked up from the Haverstock, in want of any formal education, but because I had begun to befriend children from different backgrounds to my own, wealthier, better informed, more travelled, and enviably more liberal. I visited their stuccoed houses in Primrose Hill and was struck by the space and comfort, and the sheer liberating style, in which they lived. By now we were crammed into a stark little council flat, no less cold and damp than the house from which we'd been involuntarily removed, though it did have an indoor lavatory and – luxury – a tiny bath. I shared a room with my brother, the joker, and it was so narrow that there was no space to walk between our single beds. I noted the difference between my living conditions and those of my recently acquired friends with the raw sensitivity only a teenager can feel. My galvanising emotion was not bitterness, however, but shame.

Where my new friends lived surrounded by art and design, I knew only of cheap ornaments and decoration. They inhabited a radical aesthetic, all polished floorboards, white walls, abstract paintings and Turkish rugs. My visual grammar was kitsch convention: the moral certainty of the three-piece suite, the fitted carpet and the net curtain. The discrepancy that most bothered me, though, was that between the abundance of books in my friends' houses and the absence of any in mine. Actually, it's not true to say there was a complete absence. There were a set of encyclopedias and a couple of paperbacks, one of them *The Godfather*, and they were hidden on the floor behind an armchair in our sitting room, as if they were contraband. My father read, but he got his books from the library, and they played no part in the presentation or atmosphere of the flat. To place a book on display was to advertise a knowledge to which very few people I knew aspired and even fewer possessed. It was therefore pretentious and pretension, from where I came from, was a cardinal sin. I remember having a fight with one of the children on my estate when I was about eleven or twelve. He accused me of using 'long words'. As a strict adherent to a minimalist vocabulary that centred on the words 'fuck' and 'cunt', he was deeply offended by my verbal extravagance (I can't remember the offence but no doubt I had said something unforgivably effete like 'prostitute' instead of 'slag'). Eloquence and erudition were not prized qualities where I lived. And unless books were Harold Robbins paperbacks thumbed for the dirty bits, they were a 'load of bollocks', a dangerous threat to the collective identity.

Of course, it is of a collective identity that adolescents, even the most rebellious ones (especially the most rebellious), are in search. Individualism at that age is the preserve of freaks and loners. And I was not enamoured by the collective identity that I had been assigned. Some people make a big song and dance, a real knees-up Mother Brown, about their working-class roots. But from where I stood, on a bleak council estate surrounded by people who revelled in their limitations, there was not much that I felt able to romanticise back then, and the passage of years has made the job no easier. By the time I was in my late teens, the choice of which group or tribe I wanted to belong to was easy. Joining that group, though, seemed impossible. As far as money and opportunity went the world of my new friends was like a film, something you could watch but never enter. No one in my extended family had ever been to university, we didn't know any graduates, and it was never discussed as an option. Nor did any teacher ever mention the possibility that I might take a degree. My eldest brother, who had been a milkman like my father, had joined the army and was serving in Northern Ireland, a situation that left my father, an admirer of military discipline but also a staunch republican, with conflicting emotions. I dealt with the relentless aggression and the paltry teaching of school by non-attendance. And when I was fifteen the school's careers adviser advised me to become a panel beater in a local car-repair workshop. I was not about to join a different economic class.

So the fork in the road that I encountered around the age of fifteen or sixteen was primarily a matter of social outlook rather than social mobility. The decision was whether to 'stay true' to my background, inward-looking, bibliophobic, TV-saturated, casually racist, intellectually unambitious, pub-focused and passively resentful or embrace ways of interacting with the world that were more in keeping with those of my new affluent friends: permissive, open-minded, bookish, exper-imental, pot-smoking, questioning, anti-racist. Of course, there were all manner of tensions and inconsistencies entwined in these superficially straightforward choices, but essentially this was how it appeared on the surface. As it happened, at just about the same time, a musical and fashion revolution had taken place that was – and still is – widely misrepresented as a political street movement of sorts: punk. Living near Camden Town, with its battery of fetid clubs and music venues, I could see that whatever it was punk was not the mythical 'working-class' backlash against music's big business. From where I stood, it was mostly a bunch of middle-class kids playing at being bad boys. At school it was the arty types who immediately took to wearing ripped clothes and talking about anarchy. No one on my estate would have dreamt of putting on bondage trousers.

You might just as well have worn a T-shirt emblazoned with the words 'Kick Me'. Though drawn to the energy and uncertainty of it all, I was never a punk. But even from the sidelines it was obvious that the people I'd grown up with were the least ready to enter into that spirit. I was tired of the apathy that seemed to echo from every concrete stairwell of the flats in which I lived. The backdrop of punk, with its do anything you want to do attitude, served to complement the more personal process of change that I was then undergoing. To the extent that I was a conscious architect of this transformation, which was not very far, it felt less like shedding an identity than rejecting a presumption.

The one element of all this bourgeois freedom that was not emancipating was the attendant and apparently obligatory sense of guilt. No one felt they had to apologise on my council estate because they were white and British. On the contrary, these were their main sources of pride. But my new friends, veterans of Rock Against Racism, connoisseurs of reggae, sympathisers with Rastafarianism, often seemed embarrassed by the colour of their skin. To be black was cool, radical, dangerous. To be white was cold, dull, safe. Suddenly my white Hampstead pals were pressing into my hands copies of Malcolm X's autobiography and Eldridge Cleaver's *Soul on Ice*. These were revolutionary texts, tales of violent black uprising against remorseless white oppression. They were also American books that dealt with particular American histories in a precise American context, and furthermore overtly macho books that relegated women to the kitchen and bedroom. The point, however, was the universal liberation struggle of black against white. That was the story and to see its relevance one needed only to look at the obscenity of the apartheid regime of South Africa.

That Malcolm X and Cleaver themselves advocated a kind of racial separation none of my anti-racist friends saw fit to condemn. What mattered by my friends' way of thinking, and they were far from alone, was that black men stood at the very top of the hierarchy of victimhood. And such a vantage point afforded them access to truths that were beyond the grasp of those afflicted by the privilege of a white skin.

It was perhaps no coincidence that I came to adopt, or at least accept, this revolutionary view of black males at the same time – the end of school – that I started to lose contact with black male friends. In the space of a couple of years nearly all of my friends were white and middle class, and nearly all of them saw something oppressed and heroic – in other words, something Other – in the skin of black men. Having successfully thrown off the shackles of my own imposed identity, I quickly got used to imposing an even more restrictive identity on people with whom I had increasingly little social connection. At school, black kids could be smart, funny, quiet, disruptive, bullies, friends. But now, as my attitudes became more liberal, I saw all blacks as victims. I wanted to be free to be the person I wanted to be. And that person, it turned out, was someone who was content to imprison other groups of people within limiting expectations. Thus in my mind, the liberal mind, a person's blackness became inextricably tied to their anger and separateness. Which is to say, the more content and the more assimilated in day-to-day life a black person was then the less *black* he was, the less true to his roots. It followed that any black person who fell into my new social orbit was by definition not very black.

In the generation before mine the same attitudes applied to class. In the fifties and sixties the working-class hero was someone – invariably a man – who wore his roughness and anger as a mark of authenticity (a scenario that has faded over the years without, alas, ever quite vanishing). The films and plays of that era are peopled with loud, often abusive, working-class men, unwilling to stomach bourgeois values. That these dramas were mostly produced by guilt-ridden middle-class men – the Lindsay Andersons and Tony Richardsons of this world – points to an abiding irony of bourgeois intellectual life. The rejection of bourgeois values is a recurring theme in art and cultural debate and yet the very forum of its expression – in theatre, for example, and literary novels – serves to maintain bourgeois values. It's impossible to spend any time around intellectuals who rail at 'bourgeois convention' without noticing how studiously they follow such conventions themselves. Guilt-ridden and self-hating they may be but very few radical members of the intelligentsia have any real intention of leaving the ranks of the bourgeoisie. Incapable of committing class suicide, they dream of a homicidal class that will do the job for them. But in the end, one comes to realise, the compromise they reach with themselves is to discourage less privileged groups from joining what they insist is a doomed enterprise.

The absurdity of that kind of thinking should, of course, be self-evident, yet it continues to form the basis of the liberal understanding of ethnic and religious identity. Many of the problems that we now face at home and abroad stem directly from this guilt-warped vision of the world. Bourgeois values, which rest on individual liberty, intellectual freedom and personal responsibility, have been the foundation of enormous power and wealth in the Western world. To renounce those values is also effectively to renounce power and wealth. Of course there is nothing wrong with renouncing power and wealth – it may even be good for the soul – but it's sense-less to do so and at the same time nurture a grievance about a lack of power and wealth. This, however, is the contradic-tory position which underprivileged groups are repeatedly encouraged to adopt by Western anti-Western intellectuals.

At seventeen I was already immersed in this mental and moral confusion. Expelled from school with barely any qual-ifications, I seemed to have no access to the world into which many of my friends were disappearing, the splendidly contained wonderland of university and opportunity and professional careers. By contrast I worked on building sites and in a multi-tude of menial jobs. It was a struggle to hold on to my recently acquired idealism when the people from whom I'd acquired it had all gone off to secure the solid bourgeois existence that I'd been reliably informed was a worthless fraud. Of course deep down I would have preferred to dismiss the shallowness of material aspiration from the position of being middle class but that was not a viable option. In Britain in the late seventies and early eighties there were far fewer paths than now that led to material success, but by way of compensation it was a much more accommodating environment in which to fail. What was the point of upward mobility when the nation at large was sinking into the comfort of its own decline? It felt momentarily good to turn my back on power and wealth, though I don't doubt it would have felt better if power and wealth had not already turned their back on me. But as I was busy making a virtue out of necessity, it was necessary to find the appropriate venue for that virtue to flower. Building sites were barren landscapes in more ways than the literal. I was ridiculed for reading books and the conversation of my workmates, mostly young Irishmen, was awash with racism and homophobia. It was life on the council estate all over again, and the more I tried to oppose those attitudes, the more ridiculed and isolated I became. But if my workmates were hard work, they were nothing compared to the labour. 'Work,' wrote Khalil Gibran in *The Prophet*, 'is love made visible.' There speaks a man who had obviously never balanced on a joist five floors up, with a sheer drop below, attacking a brick wall with a hand-held pneumatic drill. I needed a more sympathetic setting, somewhere I could reconcile the contradictions of my class consciousness without having to lift damp sacks of debris. And I found that at Harrods, the most famous shop in Britain. There I could revel in the mindless nature of my labour while at the same time nurturing a keen resentment of the conspicuous affluence I saw all around me. It was the perfect job, as luck would have it, in which to hide from the transforming decade that was about to unfold.

3

Anger

My first job at Harrods was located two levels beneath the marble ground floor of the renowned department store. Deep in the sub-basement, where natural light was a dim memory, I constructed cardboard boxes. One after the other, for eight hours a day. I worked opposite a camp Pakistani lad with a floppy bush of black hair that hung down over his eyes like the head of a new broom. His hobby, indeed obsession, was plane-spotting. At any opportunity he liked to get out his logbook and contemplate the aeroplane serial numbers he had accumulated, as if they could explain the mystery of life, or at least, perhaps, why he was boxed in by boxes, hidden from aircraft, down in the Stygian gloom. Occasionally I'd try to engage him in a conversation about our lot but he wasn't interested. He used to call me a socialist, though it was obvious he had little idea what the word meant.

I also called myself a socialist, but the difference was I knew what it meant. At least I knew what it meant in theory. In practice I was far from certain. Did it include the hopeless mismanagement, chronic waste and endemic laziness that characterised the socialist local authority in which I had grown up? Was it about the strike-plagued nationalised industries that seemed to symbolise British decline? Or the closed shop that underpinned the power of labour organisation? Did it have anything to do with communism and the Soviet Union? For socialism's enemies the answers were as plain as a bread queue, but for socialists it had always been more complicated than that. Socialism represented a possibility, a better way, an ideal that was necessarily compromised by the prevalence, in fact the very existence, of capitalism.

What socialism amounted to at the beginning of the eighties in Europe, and particularly in Britain, was a tangled knot of disparate ideas. There was traditional labourism, with its male-dominated unions and paternalist outlook. There were the hard-core revolutionaries and the Soviet sympathisers, the Trotskyists and the Stalinists. There was also the post-1968 New Left, which was more socially permissive, emphasising individual liberty in matters like sex and sexuality, and the well-meaning social reformers, who took an almost Christian line on crime and social deprivation. There was the devolved, anti-statist position that saw civic institutions as inherently ominous and controlling and at the same time there was a widespread understanding that the state should continue to be interventionist, organising as much employment, housing and social welfare as possible. There was the new town-hall left, which looked towards ethnic minorities and dispossessed groups as their constituency. And taking shape in the background was an academic, postmodern left, culturally and morally relativist, anti-Western, and in thrall to the intellectual cult of deconstruction.

In the broad consensus of post-war Britain, socialism and liberalism and even 'One Nation' conservatism had become entwined together in political life. But when Margaret Thatcher removed conservatism from that ménage and transformed it into a radical ideology, socialism and liberalism found themselves locked in a survival embrace. To be a liberal in the Thatcher years was almost by definition to be a socialist. Not in party political terms – after all, the Social Democrat Party was formed in reaction to socialism – but in the anti-Thatcherite public discourse. Naturally any self-respecting socialist would have claimed that they hated wishy-washy backsliding liberals. But such pronouncements were often more to do with Britain's incurable addiction to class posturing. Liberal was virtually a synonym for 'middle class', whereas socialist had earthier connotations. Another distinction was that liberal was often used in the passive sense, referring to a sensibility, whereas socialist implied something more active, grittier, more resistant, a commitment, an ideal. In practice the line between the two was not always obvious.

For example, it was quite possible to come across, as I once did, a dope-smoking gay squatter who extolled the benefits of East Germany, a nation that was hardly renowned for its tolerance towards dope-smoking, gayness or squatting. The implicit understanding was that 'socialist' countries should be judged by less exacting standards. That's exactly what I did. During the militant years of the early eighties I had a girlfriend whose mother was an ardent Tory from a landed, faintly aristocratic background. An embittered and energetically unhappy woman, she loathed socialism and the working classes and, as she made abundantly clear, she loathed me. One day, without much warning, she decided to take my girlfriend and her sister on holiday to Albania to show them the horrors of communism. When they returned after a bizarre fortnight spent with a Stalinist tour group, they were full of appalled tales of the country's backwardness and poverty. All I knew about Albania was its extreme ideological purity and isolation, that it had broken from Moscow because the Soviet Union was too liberal, and that it backed away from China, in protest at Mao's meeting with Nixon. Yet so aggravated was I by my girlfriend's mother's right-wing attitudes that when the sisters described what they had witnessed, I found myself attempting to mount a defence of the cartoon dictator Enver Hoxha. 'But you don't understand,' they told me, 'the people live in terrible poverty, while the top party officials drive around in limousines. How can that be about equality?' It's a process, I sagely explained, you can't change a traditional society overnight. A few weeks after my girlfriend's return, Hoxha continued the process by killing half the leadership, including his deputy.

Aside from the camp plane-spotter, there were one or two other Asians in our section at Harrods, a couple of West Indians and the rest of the twenty or thirty staff, with one exception, were Africans. I was the only white-skinned employee. It was hard to conclude that the origin of the workers and the location of their employment – underground out of sight of the shop floor – were unrelated. The work was not only mindless but seemingly faceless, deemed fit only for those whom it was best to shield from public view: Africans, Asians and, as it had turned out, me. Within a few months I began to feel as though I was going quietly mad in the subterranean gloom (many of my workmates had arrived at the same state rather more loudly) and, after a mini campaign, managed to get transferred to the furniture department. Here, in unmistakable contrast, the porters were made up of over-educated graduate dropouts, all of whom were impressively skilled at avoiding what little work there was to do. The furniture porters' warehouse, a kind of hidden retreat from the shop floor, was an especially pleasant environment in which to be – or pretend to be – a dissident. It was like some benign parody of one of the Soviet bloc factories staffed by problematic writers and artists. In place of my former workmate's recital of aeroplane serial numbers, there were long discussions on Marx, Herbert Marcuse and, in the case of one sandal-wearing born-again Roman Catholic with a monkish beard, the works of Alexander Solzhenitsyn. For this, I recall, the would-be priest was roundly mocked for being a 'reactionary'. I heard what amounted to seminars on the theory of surplus value and the nature of the unconscious, and we played three-hour-long games of football in Hyde Park. It was like university, only without the essays and exams. Books would be exchanged and furiously discussed. I remember one porter doggedly making his way through *Ulysses* during breaks in work – or, to be more accurate, occasionally delivering a reproduction Louis XIV table during breaks in Joyce. I read Dostoevsky, Heller, Orwell, Nabokov and Sartre. It was an invaluable education, the first time I'd encountered what it would not be too decorous to call intellectual debate. It was also the first time that anyone suggested that I should go to a real university. Up until that point I had thought of university as an exclusive environment, in that awful deferential phrase 'not for the likes of us', rather than a national institution to which my parents, and now I, contributed taxes. But to my new workmates, who were socialists by conviction but hippies by temperament, the three years of being an undergraduate were a basic human right – the right to idle. They did not see a degree as the entry to a career but as a state-subsidised means of postponing the world of work. They argued that everyone should go to university and I began to wonder why I should be the exception.

One lazy afternoon in the late spring of 1981 a slightly unformed young woman walked by a group of us who were languishing on the third floor of the shop. She wore a blonde pageboy haircut and a dirndl skirt, the female uniform of what had been recently labelled the 'Sloane Ranger'. 'It makes me sick,' said Adam, our foreman and a walking homage to Joe Strummer of the Clash, 'how every girl looks like Lady Di.' It was said for our amusement but also just within earshot of the young woman, who seemed to quicken her step in response. That's when we noticed the team of security men following in her wake. 'Hold on,' said someone else, 'that *is* Lady Di.'

As if propelled by the force of history, my friend Simon and I set off after the VIP customer, shouting 'Don't do it, Di! Don't do it!' Simon, who would later go on to become one of the country's leading neurologists, threw himself on his knees before the startled girl and repeated his plaintive warning against marrying Prince Charles. I chipped in with agitprop wit: 'He's an unemployed thirty-year-old – it will never work.' She gave us that coy smile that would soon become the selling point of a million magazine covers but, just as characteristically, said nothing. As it happened, mine was prophetic advice, though almost as soon as it was issued she was surrounded by her security team and whisked away to her fate: the royal wedding a few weeks later, global fame, bulimia, adultery, divorce and premature death. But before all that, in fact that very afternoon, Simon was sacked and an unsuccessful investigation was launched by Harrods management to discover my identity so that I might also be fired. For my role alongside Simon and Adam, I became known in shop lore as the Third Man. There were three of us in that engagement.

The part of Kensington in which Harrods stands has long been a heartland of snobbery, but in 1981, a gloating sense of Tory triumphalism and the hype surrounding the approaching royal wedding, made it all the more insufferable. To grab the opportunity to make a small protest, albeit involving a guileless teenager, seemed like a tiny blow for reason, though mostly, of course, it just seemed like a good laugh. Here was a pantomime dramatisation of that old story, the workers against the bosses, refashioned as the princess and the porter. The very fact that Simon was summarily dismissed for such an innocuous joke exemplified for me and my friends the petty vindictiveness of establishment values.

Unfortunately for Harrods, Simon's father worked as a printer in Fleet Street and his son informed the shop's management that unless he was reinstated with immediate effect then the story would appear in the following day's newspapers – with 3 million unemployed, that meant a lot of negative publicity for both the store and the royal family. Harrods called an extraordinary meeting of high-ups and Simon was duly welcomed back to the staff. He also received an unctuous apology from the head of personnel. It was a humiliating defeat for the bosses. Us and them: that was what industrial relations always came down to. Like most unskilled labour, we were on very low wages, and as long as there was no prospect of earning much more, the main focus of our ambition was to get one over on the employers. In this struggle everyone knew their assigned roles, like players in a game, and few deviated from the rules.

The Lady Di incident, though a minor indiscretion, was all part of the game, like sledging in cricket. What I didn't realise at the time is that it was a game drawing to a close. Two sides of Britain's antiquated class system had accidentally met, neither anticipating that they were soon to be under threat of extinction. Within a few years organised labour would lose a decisive series of clashes with the Conservative government, and not long after the monarchy would be hanging by the thread of its debased celebrity. Harrods used to hold a power-fully symbolic position in British culture. It took enormous pride in its reputation as the top people's shop, actively trading on its royal connections. At the same time it was seen by many, perhaps most, egalitarian-minded people as an objec-tionable monument to privilege. In one of Channel 4's earliest broadcasts in 1982, a youth-oriented programme with the punkish title *Whatever You Want*, the presenter Keith Allen stood outside the store and claimed that it was for Harrods that the Falklands War had been waged and hundreds of lives lost. Allen, a professional provocateur, was paid to say the unsayable. But he wasn't saying anything that a large section of his youngish audience did not already think. In some unfocused, unthought-through way I agreed with him. Was Harrods receiving cheap lambswool from the Falklands, or had it tapped into the oil that was rumoured to be some-where in the South Pacific? What did a department store really have to do with sending a task force to fight a fascist occupying army? I didn't know, of course, and nor did I much care. Harrods was a temple of materialist excess and was therefore by definition to blame, that was the main thing. What, though, was the appropriate punishment for this nebu-lous crime? The following year the IRA planted a bomb in Harrods during the Christmas sales. It killed six people and injured a further ninety. Before that and before the Channel 4 show, the armoured vehicle in which my eldest brother, a guardsman, was travelling in Belfast was also blown up. It was in March 1982, three days after the Argentinian occupation of South Georgia that precipitated the Falklands War. Two of the soldiers with him died and another was badly maimed, but my brother survived with minor injuries. I never mentioned this incident to my liberal friends. I was too ashamed that I had a brother in the army.

Until the 1980s it could be said of Britain that class was more important than money. Capitalism was held in place not just by nationalised industry and organised labour but also the old school tie. Under these social and political restrictions everyone, from whatever end of the scale, tended to know their place. For better or worse, Thatcher changed all that. If there was such an entity as the establishment, then it came under greater attack from market deregulation than it ever had from state control. Two years after it was bombed, Harrods, the establishment's establishment, was bought by an Egyptian former Coca-Cola street salesman named Mohamed Al Fayed. Rejected by polite society, Fayed's revenge came when his son, Dodi, began dating the divorced Princess Diana. It was with Dodi that Diana died in a Paris car crash, an event that is widely believed in the Arab and Muslim worlds to have been a murder orchestrated by British Intelligence – the idea being that the secret services had to act to prevent the mother of the future King of England from marrying a Muslim or, worse, giving birth to his child. The chief financier and disseminator of this conspiracy theory is Al Fayed. In 2001 the prime target of Al Fayed's accusations, Prince Philip, rescinded the store's Duke of Edinburgh warrant as outfitters. Who could have guessed in 1981 that the young innocent I saw disappearing into the clutches of the British state would emerge in death a rallying point for republicans, anti-imperialists and even Islamic grievance?

Is there a spectrum of protest that can include a teenage prank at one end and blowing limbs off Christmas shoppers at the other? Are the two acts separated simply by gradations of seriousness, of commitment to a 'cause', or is there an unbreachable moral wall between them? Back then the issue was clouded by a sulphurous atmosphere of rebellion. A few weeks before Diana Spencer walked through the furniture department, the streets of Brixton went up in flames. It was the first time Molotov cocktails had been thrown on mainland Britain. Riots spread across the nation to Toxteth in Liverpool, Moss Side in Manchester, Handsworth in Birmingham, Leeds, Leicester, Southampton, Halifax, Bristol, Edinburgh and even the genteel Cotswold town of Gloucester. There was a tangible threat of violence in the air. For a brief but anxious period it seemed as if civil order hung in the balance as a divide opened like an old wound in British society.

As the majority of the Brixton and Toxteth rioters were black it followed that these 'uprisings', to use the favoured designation of the left, were naturally situated on the good side, the progressive side, of the division, just as the police, the main target for the rioters' anger, were located on the bad, the reactionary side. At Harrods, we spoke with glee at the prospect of the riots spreading to Knightsbridge, so that wealthy areas could be put to the torch too. Naturally, we knew little about the causes of the riots. The police and racism were to blame, that was enough to know.

The Brixton riots were without doubt propelled by social inequalities and a history of heavy-handed and often racist policing, but the incident that actually ignited the trouble was a stabbing. Police came to the aid of a black youth who had been stabbed by another black youth. The false rumour went round that the first youth had died and armies of brick-throwers took to the streets. I can't recall if I knew about the 'black-on-black' stabbing, though I'm sure that even if I did, it was not a detail upon which I would have dwelt for long. I suppose I would have told myself that such incidents were inevitable in the ghetto, having already managed to forget that I'd grown up in a slum that few parts of Brixton could rival for social deprivation. The process of importing American notions – romantic and fearful – of an outlaw black under-class was well under way in Britain, particularly among the excitable sections of the white population. The Clash, Adam's heroes and the poets of vicarious revolution, had not only penned lyrics about 'Sten guns in Knightsbridge', but had also already written a song called 'The Guns of Brixton'. 'When they kick at your front door / How you gonna come? / With your hands on your head / Or on the trigger of your gun / When the law break in / How you gonna go? / Shot down on the pavement / Or waiting on death row.'

Death row? Capital punishment had been outlawed for two decades! Oh well, it was only a pop song. Except 'The Guns of Brixton' was in one sense uncannily apposite. Guns, the real kind with real bullets that caused real deaths, would become an all-too-common feature of Brixton life. A genera-tion of black kids was soon to grow up having to deal with the belief that a carrying a knife or a gun meant respect on the streets. In the eighties, before gangsta culture arrived in Britain, many white liberals saw black crime and violence as somehow sexy, an expression of 'resistance' in the face of intolerable oppression (a notion that has not altogether disap-peared). The Clash were not to blame for capitalising on that image. They just vocalised a fashionable counterculture atti-tude. I recall the tense exhilaration of watching Franco Rosso's *Babylon* around 1981, a film about a group of black youths who are backed into crime by racism. And the jolting scene that sticks like a knife in the memory is one in which a white kid is headbutted by a member of the black gang for acting 'black'. Black was black, was the message, a state of mind that comes with the suffering that comes with the skin. But that didn't stop sympathetic whites from wanting to grab a piece of that blackness by association. The 'front line', terri-tory where black youths attempted to make a stand against the law, represented the cutting edge of radicalism to many people I knew at the time. To hang out on All Saints Road in Notting Hill or Railton Road in Brixton was to achieve an intoxicating credibility, especially if you managed to buy some drugs at the same time. The whole scene was a theatre of phoniness, with young black guys talking in fake Jamaican accents and young whites adopting fake versions of the fake Jamaican accents. The racism that black men suffered at the hands of right-on whites may not have been as crude as that meted out by the police, but it fed on the same stereotype: black men were untamed, hedonistic outlaws. And too many young black men were ready enough to play the role. A number of black kids I knew from school had acquired three, four or, in one case, five 'baby-mothers' by the time they were in their early twenties. They were absent fathers up to five times over. And this too was seen as cool. Not by everyone, to be sure, but to express reservations about this particular cultural development was to nominate yourself either as a racist if you were white or a self-loathing friend to racists if you were black.

I was twenty years old when I left Harrods and returned to education. City and East London College was a far cry from Kensington. It was situated in a part of Hackney that would later become trendy in a scruffy, arty sort of way, but at that time was just scruffy in a neglected sort of way. The classes I took in English and politics were full of last-chancers, young adults from various ethnic backgrounds who had failed or been failed by the school system. Nevertheless many of the teachers at the college shared the same priorities as the Harrods furniture porters: ideological rants first, work last. I had two politics lecturers, both committed left-wingers, with tellingly divergent approaches to their students. One, a Bennite Labour supporter, thought his main responsibility was to help us to attain the best grades of which we were capable. The other felt that her prior duty was to instil a proper disrespect for all aspects of the capitalist machine, and not least the sausage-producing exam system. She smilingly informed us in her first lecture that she was a member of the Communist Party. Thereafter she would invite party officials in to give impromptu lectures on political philosophy. It was soon apparent to even the least attentive student that she had no interest in our academic plight, other than as receptacles for discontent. Little by little, they stopped coming to her class. I could see that she was a poor teacher but I lacked the clarity of thought to pinpoint the real problem, far less make a complaint about it. Instead I sought to confront her on safer ground. One day after class I saw her marching along in her bright green Kickers boots, labourer's overcoat and multi-coloured floor-length scarf, as if she were on her way to audition for the part of a loony lefty lecturer in a TV drama. I asked her as we walked together to the tube station what she thought, as a communist, of the idea of the dictatorship of the proletariat. It was a simple question but she refused to answer. She ummed and aahed, then said in her unvarying tone of jolly enthusiasm: 'If you want to discuss Marxist theory, you should come along to a meeting.'

My politics lecturer's speciality was political theory, but she wasn't qualified to answer a question on the political theory that was the basis of her beliefs, the beliefs to which she never stopped referring. Rather, she tried to sell me the guru-in-chief, the local head ideologue. He was better, she explained, at explaining. And having sat through her lectures, I could see her point. What she really meant was that she couldn't trust herself to follow the party line. The dialectic could not be reduced to simple formulations, though her critique of capitalism was made up of nothing else. It reminded me of an experience I'd had in San Francisco a couple of years before while I was travelling, near penniless, around America. I was lured to the Moonie headquarters in Haight-Ashbury by a couple of young recruits with promises of free food. They didn't tell me they were Moonies, of course, and every time I asked a question, they would fob me off, suggesting that I should wait to have everything explained by the man in charge. I went to the hotel-sized house, where I was asked to remove my shoes, which were promptly taken hostage. Eventually the top dog arrived, a frozen-smile fraud with the disposable charm of a double-glazing salesman. The fresh Moonie recruits listened to him as if immanent revelation dripped from his tongue. How could they not see through him? They were drunk on the idea of belief, but he was so patently interested in control. This same transaction between followers and leaders is re-enacted in all cults, political or religious. And each cult is convinced it's the exception to the rule.

Politics inevitably draws charlatans and opportunists, but revolutionary politics seems to guarantee their swift promotion. How else, for example, could a serial sexual abuser and con man lead a party for decades? That was the achievement of Gerry Healy, head of the Workers Revolutionary Party. A paranoid and pathologically sinister character, Healy was able to exercise dictatorial control over his party only because its members – notably the actors Vanessa and Corin Redgrave – were abject idolisers of the man. As frustrated and confused as I sometimes was as a young adult, it was at least clear to me that the far-left parties were essentially secular Moonies, with the same cast of egomaniacs and misfits.

Nevertheless, I was fascinated by the revolutionary left. I used to spend hours in Collets bookshop in Charing Cross Road reading the stacks of newsletters and publications that these grouplets (SWP, RCP, WRP, CPGB) somehow managed to produce. It was a secret world of schisms and vendettas, with each microparty competing, in the communist historian Raphael Samuel's phrase, 'for the honour of leading a non-existent revolutionary working class'. Each maintained that it and it alone understood the correct line, and all refashioned recent events to conceal the misguided direction of the previous correct line. Every word was written in high declarative style, as if the authors had imagined Lenin reading their words at the Finland Station. As with all zealots, they believed the day of reckoning was nigh. Instead of the apocalypse, revolution was on its way in, hastened by the unstinting demand for a general strike. Every week that it didn't take place meant only that it was one week nearer. And all the time, the hysterically impatient calls to action – Fight Now! March Now! Ban Now! – that exhausted parody. These rallying cries worked on me in the same way, I suspect, that they worked on many other people who did not take them seriously. That is, in some incomprehensible fashion, they still worked. Or at least had a psychological effect.

Even if it accounts for a tiny fraction of voters, the far left has managed to exercise a disproportionate influence on the British and European political scene. It has done so, in part, through traditional means: marches, meetings, newsletters, protests, entryism, industrial organisation and the like. And on the whole these agitations have had limited impact on political life at large. But where it has made a mark is with the existential challenge: what do *you* intend to do. In other words, it was easy, indeed sensible, to dismiss the far left as fantasists and sinister cranks, but it was much harder, in all conscience, to ignore the idea of dramatic social change that these small parties represented. For if you thought society was unfair, what were you prepared to do to change it? It's a question that has struck at the heart of liberal guilt, a political emotion that gradually, like an initiate to a spiritual journey, I was beginning to understand and profess.

In one way or another I spent much of the 1980s asking myself what I was prepared to do. Mostly the question was couched in philosophical terms, the better no doubt to postpone actually doing anything. I was hardly the radical son. There were some scattershot juvenilia: I graffitied a few Shell garages as an anti-apartheid protest. I was carted off by a police van at a Stop the City march. I canvassed for John McDonnell, a left-wing Labour candidate for Hampstead, in the calamitous 1983 election. I also did voluntary work for a Third World charity, took part in vigils at South Africa House, CND marches, fund-raising for miners during the strike and various other activities that could be loosely defined as 'doing something'. In addition there were a few dispiriting forays into trade union work. It was here that I first came across the boilerplate script that is used in most political meetings. The shopworkers' and delivery workers' union at Harrods was what used to be called a 'moderate' union. It had few hard-left members and none among its leadership and yet the spirit of the hard left hung over proceedings like an invisible commissar. Very soon I realised that the object of the meeting, and the object of many to come, was for each participant to appear more radical than whoever had spoken last. A kind of moral exhibitionism and inflationary zeal informed almost every utterance, as if the aim was to get to a declaration of a general strike in as few contributions as possible: 'You think we should have a 10 per cent pay rise? Well, I think it should be 15 per cent. I win.' Just how entrenched this syndrome was I realised many years later when I found exactly the same principle in operation at newspaper union meetings. On one occasion I sat at a table with a group of highly paid and not especially productive journalists as each one took it in turns to up the demand of his neighbour. The newspaper, which was losing millions, had offered a pay rise in keeping with inflation but the journalists wanted more, much more. Up and up went the bid – 5 per cent, 7.5 per cent, 10 per cent, work-to-rule, until finally one man called for an all-out strike. For this speaker the withdrawal of labour was in a sense an academic threat as he had barely written a word in months. He was one of the highest paid in the room, with many years of service (or at least employment) and a large pension awaiting him. And at the time, he was going through an internal disciplinary procedure for repeatedly downloading child pornography. Not one person present at the meeting, myself included, said a word in opposition to his proposal. Instead some openly agreed, others nodded their heads and the rest of us remained silent. Outside the meeting, such a scene would have been recognised as ridiculous, but within this looking-glass world it was completely normal.

None of my dilettante activities in the 1980s began to

address the challenge set by the hard left. They were a non-committal kind of commitment, a form of badge-wearing, like the 'Coal not Dole' sticker I wore throughout the miners' strike of 1984. They were lame efforts, to be sure, but that wasn't the principal reason they failed the test. For there was no action, no matter how committed or extreme, that could meet the challenge. This was the point of the far left, this was its psychological role, to foster a sense of an individual's impotence. The whole project was dedicated to exposing the 'sell-out', the 'bourgeois lackey', the 'Menshevik mentality'. How could it do anything else? Every communist or 'workers'' state in history had been a disaster, combining inefficiency, corruption and repression to universally miserable effect. There was nothing tangible to aim for, no proletarian paradise on earth. To be sure, those far-left parties, invariably Trotskyist, that were critical of the Soviet bloc could still maintain that, if things were done their way, then heaven was just a revolution away. But no one aside from a few crazed ideologues and the cravenly naive believed that. And yet these groups continued to exert a moral pull on the liberal heartland of the left. Labour-controlled local authorities succumbed to revolutionary fervour during the Thatcher era, with groups like the Militant Tendency, a clandestine Trotskyist sect, effectively hijacking the city of Liverpool. As this process was repeated in town halls throughout the country, leading to pantomime mismanagement and in many cases bankruptcy, it was striking how few in the Labour Party dared to speak out. Those that did left to form the Social Democrat Party – the ultimate sell-out – but in the party rump, and on the left in general, there was an institutionalised reluctance to acknowledge what was taking place. When called upon to confront the chaos and ineptitude of the 'Loony Left', the *Guardian*-reading left did what we always do: we blamed the *Daily Mail*. I lived in Camden and Islington, two boroughs that were rife with ideological initiatives and riddled with incompetence and waste; yet whenever their misdeeds were brought to my attention, I recited to myself and anyone who would listen the well-worn defence that it was all right-wing press propaganda. Ken Livingstone, then leader of the Greater London Council, was in no doubt of what needed to be done. 'The third vital task is to deal with the press,' he told Tariq Ali in a booklet published in 1984, a year in which the left saw Big Brother everywhere. Though he stopped short of advocating state control of the press, on the grounds that it was not an electable position to take, he wanted to prevent advertisers from choosing where they advertised. 'There would have to be a law,' he demanded, 'that no one launching a new Sierra or running a Guinness campaign could bypass a paper they didn't particularly like.'

That was the kind of fighting talk we liked to hear. To do anything else, to have acknowledged the councils' faults or errors and discussed them openly, would have been to betray a fictional revolution in which I didn't believe. It would have required an engagement with reality. And it was the hard left's triumph that they succeeded in blocking that process among progressive people. They had made reality a no-go area.

Socialism, in many left-wing local authorities, had become concerned with promoting policies that were selected for their 'resistance' value, how much they would thwart the government and irritate the conservative media. In this barricaded atmosphere, the worst crime was siding with the opposition. Thus when a right-wing newspaper, the London *Evening Standard*, exposed the paedophiliac abuse that was widespread in Islington's children's care during the eighties, it was dismissed by Margaret Hodge, the council's leader and later the Labour minister for children, as 'gutter journalism'. She remembered which side she was on. If the right-wing press said it was taking place, by definition it was not taking place.

The censorial spectre of the hard left also haunted the 1984–85 national miners' strike. However, in that case the fear of being labelled a capitalist running dog was far outweighed by heartfelt sympathy for the miners' cause. The strike was the last great hurrah of industrial protest in twentieth-century Britain, and the final roll of the dice for traditional class politics. The almost atavistic tribalism surrounding the dispute transcended all my own personal reservations about membership of the working class. It was the defining 'whose side are you on' moment of the decade. On the left was Arthur Scargill, the National Union of Minerworkers' fuzzy-haired president, a diehard socialist and Soviet sympathiser. On the right, Margaret Thatcher, the Cold Warrior Conservative prime minister with the armoured blonde bouffant. Each had their own troops, the flying pickets against the combined forces of the British police. The past in hand-to-hand combat with the future. It was real conflict, with real consequences, not simply a symbolic action, though it was also a battle of symbols. The miners represented a sort of proletarian ideal. They suffered so that society might benefit. There was something noble and inspiring about the miners as a collective workforce, their 'tight-knit' communities, their traditions, their bravery, their solidarity. They chivvied away in the bowels of the earth to extract the dark material that brought us heat and light. 'Coal not Dole' said the sticker on my jacket and its truth was simple: coal good, unemployment bad. But was coal mining good? Given the choice, who really wanted to dig up lung-damaging lumps of black rock in back-breaking conditions far beneath ground? Obviously Margaret Thatcher did not take on the miners because she was concerned about their health. But then neither was it upper-most in the minds of those, like myself, who professed solidarity with them. Occasionally the thought did occur, while I was raising or donating money, that I was supporting a struggle to ensure future generations of young men could work in a suffocating, claustrophobic, emphysemic hell. The kind of hell, what's more, that I was in no danger of having to endure.

Various 'minority' groups played a part in supporting the miners, which resulted in such delightful incongruities as cross-dressing gay benefits for the strike. The awkward fact remained, however, that the miners were almost without exception white working class and that was a constituency that was fast going out of political fashion. In the capital, under the leadership of Livingstone, the Greater London Council had set about promoting a 'rainbow alliance' of minorities and the marginalised. These two strands of left-wing thought, the industrial and the multicultural, made gestures of unity, but they were distinct and often inimical political visions – one the voice of white, male heterosexuals, the other, avowedly not. It goes without saying that the collapse of the miners' strike in 1985 had nothing to do with race or sexuality. It did not fail because of a lack of black, Asian, lesbian or disabled miners. Nonetheless it marked the demise of one idea of the left – class – and, in its place, the rise of another: identity.

Talking to *Woman's Own* magazine in 1987, Margaret Thatcher said: 'And, you know, there is no such thing as society. There are individual men and women, and there are families.' One of the lesser remarked-upon ironies of the Thatcher years is that the prime minister's most vehement opponents effectively agreed with her. The left had lost faith in a holistic society and had set about forming alliances with a series of self-interest groups. Between them, the free-market right and the town-hall left combined to create a perfect wave of social fragmentation. On one side, the Conservative government passed a law to enable council tenants to buy (and then sell) their rented accommodation, and on the other, local authorities had abandoned traditional community means of arranging housing waiting lists, and made need the primary determinant. When I was a child the council housing 'waiting list' was spoken of with frustration but also a kind of reverence. It was the lengthy process by which tenants were admitted to council housing and also transferred within the system. But prioritising need meant that large numbers of homeless and 'problem' families went to the top of the list.

The dispiriting and disillusioning effect that had on the Labour heartland, and its belief in the role of the welfare state, is a story that is powerfully told in *The New East End* by Geoff Dench, Kate Gavron and Michael Young, the follow up to Young's landmark study of urban kinship. The outcome in many cases was sink estates, the housing projects that no one wanted to buy into under Thatcher's new law, and everyone wanted to leave.

Nonetheless I believed that targeting need was a better means of dealing with social injustice than rewarding contribution and patience. In holding this conviction, though, I had a problem. With all but one of her children (my younger sister) having left home, my mother was living in a damp, unheated five-bedroom council flat. She was fiercely house-proud and desperate to move out of an estate that was fast sinking. As families moved in that had no sense of attachment to the area, and some of whom did not speak English, she redoubled her efforts to maintain her local environment. She was forever washing down the stairwell and mopping the communal balcony, but she was fighting a losing battle against the graffiti artists and drug users who congregated outside her flat. Each month she would go to the council and ask for a transfer and each month she would be refused, despite the fact that my parents were now paying for three unused bedrooms. The message she was repeatedly told was that she was not a priority. One day in a meeting she voiced her frustration to her local councillor, Tessa Jowell, who would later go on to become a Cabinet minister. She would also later have her mortgage paid off by a £400,000 gift to her husband from an Italian criminal. But that, for these purposes, is another story. Why was it, my mother asked, that she, who worked hard to make the estate a clean and pleasant place to live, who always paid her rent on time, who was only supposed to have been temporarily housed on the estate, having had her previous house demolished by the council, why was it that fifteen years on after continual requests she was a low priority for action, while a family that had just arrived in the country would receive immediate attention and, to my mother's mind, superior housing? At which point she received a brusque lecture on racism from the ambitious Ms Jowell.

My problem was how could I explain to a woman who had left school to work at fourteen, who had watched her neighbourhood become increasingly violent and unsafe, in which people like herself, who worked to keep up appearances, were mocked and their stalwart efforts undermined, and who was treated with barely concealed contempt by the authorities responsible for her living conditions, how could I explain to her that Jowell was right?

I listened sympathetically, with concern and understanding, trying to cast a positive light on what looked for her like a bleak situation. Many years later I would listen to a Pakistani owner of a minicab service complain about newly arrived Afghanistanis receiving more housing benefit than he claimed in Luton, where he had lived for twenty years. No one would have thought to call him racist. In 2007 a government colleague of Ms Jowell's and MP for Barking, the London suburb to which many white East Enders had moved, suggested that perhaps people like my mother had a point, perhaps a notion of investment, based on longevity and community, was vital for social harmony. 'We should look at policies where the legitimate sense of entitlement felt by the indigenous family overrides the legitimate need demonstrated by the new migrants,' wrote the MP, who was the industry minister, Margaret Hodge, the same woman who once preferred to denounce the media rather than accept the genuine anxieties of her constituents. Now that she did address a neglected issue, she was accused of doing the BNP's racist work, and that was by her friends and colleagues. Even raising the subject, she was told, was an act of culpable naivety that amounted to racism.

Back in the eighties there was an idea that traditional Labour voters like my mother could be hectored into adopting attitudes that ran counter to their interests. Yet there was never the same belief that newly arrived Britons could be hectored into adopting attitudes that ran counter to their culture. I was at university when my mother received her dressing-down, and though I could sense her frustrations, and I could imagine how she would have been patronised, my enlightened concern was that she didn't do or say anything that could be construed as racist. About the deterioration of her living conditions I had nothing helpful to say. I must have appeared, I'm sure, like so many other ineffectual liberals, busily pretending that everything was OK. I was now outside, like an anthropologist, looking in.

4

Denial

In the 1980s, in what the angrier citizens among us used to call 'Thatcher's Britain', it sometimes seemed as if history had obeyed Marx and repeated itself, this time in the farcical guise of the 1930s. There was huge unemployment, massive strikes, pitched battles between the workers and the police, and the most talked-about drama on television was *Brideshead Revisited*. A fashion developed for earnest young left-wing men to wear flat caps, as though they were heading off to the shipyards rather than the junior common room or public-sector employment in an office. And in this strange retroworld of bygone class struggle there was even, for true aficionados of the earlier period, a version of the Spanish Civil War.

It was fought in far-off Nicaragua, where a group of revolutionaries had been inspired, naturally, by a figure from the 1930s. The Sandinista National Liberation Front (FSLN), better known as the Sandinistas, named themselves after Augusto Sandino, a cowboy-hat-wearing nationalist who fought against US occupation. Sandino, who was in reality an anti-communist, became an iconic martyr when he was double-crossed and murdered in 1934 by Anastasio Somoza, the dictator whose debauched family ran the country for over forty years.

In Latin America, the style of capitalism supported by the US tended to go hand in hand with dictatorships and death squads. But even by regional standards, Somoza's son, also called Anastasio, was an exceptional piece of work. And not only as a tyrant and torturer. After an earthquake devastated the capital Managua in 1972, he diverted tens of millions of dollars of international aid into his personal bank account. There was something ghoulishly Transylvanian about the manner in which he bled the populace, literally in the case of Plasmaferesis, a company run by his cronies that extracted cheap blood from Nicaraguans and sold it abroad at a large profit.

Then in 1979 a revolution led by the Sandinistas overthrew Somoza and suddenly a country that was known previously only as the birthplace of Bianca Jagger was the height of radical chic. As if to confirm this new status, the following year The Clash, ever vigilant to revolutionary trends, named their fourth album *Sandinista!*. And when Ronald Reagan's administration enforced a trade embargo, mined the Nicaraguan ports and funded the remnants of Somoza's hated National Guard that made up the counter-revolutionary 'Contras', the Sandinistas became a rallying cause for anti-imperialism the world over. In Britain the ranks of the Nicaraguan Solidarity Campaign were swollen by thousands of sympathisers, including artists and writers like Julie Christie and Salman Rushdie. As the political essayist Paul Berman put it: 'The Sandinistas thought of their revolution as part of a vast wave of revolutions across the whole of the Third World – as an irreversible fact of history – and this belief of theirs was echoed, without Marxist theorizing, by any number of outside observers.'

Having suffered a series of humiliating defeats at the hands of Margaret Thatcher's government, the left in Britain saw Nicaragua as a symbol of hope, or revenge, or a chance to teach Thatcher's bellicose friend Reagan a lesson. It was the Third World David standing up to the superpower Goliath. Concerts and benefits were held to raise funds. Hundreds of British volunteers made their way to Central America to offer their support. And I was one of them.

In one respect the often cited analogy of the Spanish Civil War was all too pertinent. Over 30,000 Nicaraguans died in the Contra war, a figure that, relative to population size, approximates to the death toll in Spain. But of course the international brigades that went out to Nicaragua were nothing like their counterparts fifty years earlier. We didn't take up arms, we picked coffee beans. As befitted the generation that would give the world the triple grand skinny latte, it was less *A Homage to Catalonia*, more *A Homage to Cappuccino*.

I'd taken a degree in history and politics at the School of Oriental and African Studies. I wanted to get away from parochial matters and to challenge the clichés about the Third World. I wanted, I suppose, to investigate the possibilities of a world that was not the anxious, adversarial one that stood in the shadow of the Cold War. I read Edward Said's *Orientalism* and Benedict Anderson's *Imagined Communities*, and found out what I thought needed to know about imperialism and nationalism. In my final year I wrote a one-eyed and rather turgid dissertation on the US's role in Nicaragua. It was filled with well-earned rage at the Reagan administration and also an unquestioning admiration for the Sandinistas. It featured quotes from Noam Chomsky like 'The US is a one-party state as far as foreign affairs are concerned', and it highlighted the revolution's achievements, most notably the reduction in illiteracy and the redistribution of land.

This was the unambiguous appeal of Nicaragua, it made politics simple. Class, identity, race, crime, culture, sexuality and almost all other issues that made liberal-left politics so complex and intractable in Britain were boiled down in the Nicaraguan dialectic to '*patria o muerte*', the homeland or death. And if into the bargain the Sandinistas could improve the conditions of the impoverished campesinos and cut a few big-time landowners down to size, then all power to the revolution! Particularly as the United States government was doing its utmost, heedless of both international and its own law, to undermine those efforts and destroy the fragile Nicaraguan economy. Everything I knew about Nicaragua's history led me to believe that here, at last, was a politically and morally straightforward issue.

That said, I had no burning desire to go to Nicaragua. I had no technical gifts to offer, I knew nothing about agriculture and I wasn't the kind of person who longed to live alongside the peasants in rugged harmony with nature. What's more, the idea of joining a coffee brigade seemed only slightly more attractive than joining the Scouts. Perhaps one of the reasons I never became a party activist is that, like many people who pay lip-service to the collective ideal, I couldn't stand organised groups. The thought of spending six weeks in the jungle with twenty-five devout believers filled me with anthropological dread. But I had decided that Nicaragua was a cause worth suffering for, and enduring the torment of group activity was a small sacrifice in the grand scheme of opposing Western imperialism and injustice.

There were other reasons too. Like many men of my generation, I was keenly aware that I lived in a part of the world during a period of history that, Cold War nuclear weaponry aside, offered no serious threat to my liberty, life or, come to that, material comfort. I also suspected that this privilege came at the price of others' well-being, that Western freedom and affluence was, as it were, underwritten by Third World oppression and poverty. Reflecting on a youthful year spent in the United States, Louis Carrion, one of the Sandinista leaders, described the nature of the imbalance this way: 'I saw that the relative luxury of a few countries had its necessary counterpoint in the misery and suffering of countries like Nicaragua. Individualism was taken to the extreme of people trying to climb over each other to get ahead. I wanted to try to build some kind of better society, and I decided that my own country was the logical place to start.' In London I felt that individualism was growing ever more competitive and ugly. I was working as a bicycle dispatch rider, a dropout job that nonetheless was Darwinian in its test of fitness. In a way it was quintessential Thatcherite employment – no union, no protection, no benefits – but it was not a career. To build a career seemed to me like a commitment to a society from which I was semi-detached, if not fully alienated. Nicaragua afforded a way out, albeit temporarily, of the cul-de-sac along which I'd been carelessly speeding.

Perhaps the first thing to say about Nicaragua is that it was a textbook example of reactive American foreign policy, almost perfectly designed to create the very thing it was meant to prevent. Right from the start, the Sandinistas were made up of pro-Soviet and pro-Cuban Marxists. And yet it was obvious to even the most casual observer that at no time during the Sandinistas' rule did Nicaragua resemble the communist state of Reagan's propaganda. For a start, you were pretty much free to go wherever you wanted, notwithstanding the geographical impenetrability of large parts of the country. That was not the case early on in the war when the Atlantic coast was off-limits and the Miskito Indians were forcibly relocated by the Sandinistas – another baleful policy for which they would repeatedly apologise in the years to come. But by the mid-eighties, even the most active war zones were not completely out of bounds if you were sufficiently determined. The main newspaper *La Prensa*, it's true to say, was periodically censored and closed down. Given that *La Prensa* was the paper of Pedro Joaquin Chamorro, the brilliant newspaperman whose assassination triggered the protests that led to the revolution, it was a disturbing limitation on freedom of expression. Chamorro's motto had always been '*Sin libertad de prensa, no hay libertad*' – without freedom of the press, there is no freedom. But the Sandinistas could argue that there was a war on. Similarly the Sandinistas' failure to redress the grinding poverty that existed in both the towns and the countryside could also be attributed to the US blockade and the expense of fighting the US-backed guerillas. The shops were empty, the roads were empty, there were food queues everywhere, inflation had reached 34,000 per cent, the black market was effectively the only market, and electricity was in such short supply that Managua sometimes went days without it – but what could anyone expect? There was a war on.

While a nation at war is not exempt from criticism, it's only fair that it should receive the benefit of the doubt. But Nicaragua's supporters had no doubt, or at least few that we were prepared to voice. We read Salman Rushdie's *Jaguar Smile*, a poetically upbeat little paean to the revolution, complete with the politest of rebukes to rescue it from the charge of party propaganda. Even these friendly criticisms we preferred to skip over. There was common agreement that they were not helpful to the cause. (Secretly what annoyed me most about Rushdie's book were not the minor heresies but the constant suggestion that he too, the English public schoolboy, was just another victim of Western imperialism. I'm not sure if this was old class antagonism that refused to be buried or an early sign of my suspicions of the 'me too' victim mentality that was beginning to transform British politics.)

Anyway, if you looked closely it was possible to notice a vital truth about the nature of Nicaraguan society. It was a nation of small-business people: farmers, artisans, bakers, car-repair men, juice sellers. It adapted with spirit and imagination to the American embargo as Nicaraguans turned their talents to making machinery and cars function without spare parts. And it was this creative energy that the Sandinista leadership never really understood or respected. None of this I realised at the time. Indeed, very few Western visitors had any kind of nuanced view of Nicaragua. Either they were for or against the Sandinistas. Nothing else needed to be added. There were one or two exceptional journalists who went out of their way to find out about real conditions and aspirations in the country, and when they did they began to see a picture that was not black and white but coloured by all manner of inconvenient truths. They discovered that the Sandinistas were not always the heroic protectors of the people, and that the Contras were not just a bunch of CIA-sponsored thugs from the Somoza regime. They interviewed trade union leaders who had been intimidated and arrested, and educationalists who had been beaten up and threatened. They found out that some of the Sandinistas' land reforms had proved disastrous for the economy, and that a number of the Sandinistas most staunch early followers and fighters had as a result crossed over to join the Contras. Berman, for example, wrote about these sorts of issues for a variety of American publications including *Mother Jones*, San Francisco's progressive magazine. At the time the magazine was edited by Michael Moore, who would later find worldwide fame as a maker of comical-polemical documentaries. Moore refused to publish Berman's piece because, he claimed, it was anti-Sandinista.

I'm confident that had I heard about Moore's stance at the time I would have supported the big man. Yet it began to irritate me when I came across similar attitudes among the *brigadistas* on my coffee brigade. The brigade I joined in January 1988 was called Margaret Roff, named after a Manchester City councillor and lesbian rights campaigner who had died in a Nicaraguan hotel fire the previous year. We were sent to the region of Matagalpa, the main town in the north, to the Danilo Gonzales cooperative, a coffee plantation deep in the thickly forested hills. The farm had been abandoned by one of Somoza's cronies, we were told, and the land redistributed to landless campesinos.

The brigade was about twenty-five strong and made up of an assortment of hard-core communists, Trotskyists, softish socialists, liberals, Christians and, I suppose, that cast of fellow-traveller that George Orwell famously described as 'every fruit-juice drinker, nudist, sandal-wearer, sex-maniac, Quaker, "Nature Cure" quack, pacifist, and feminist in England'. It was a very 'English' group, slightly uptight and ill-fitting but sensitive to common decencies and good manners. I became friendly with an environmental health officer from Islington, an amiable bloke with a dry sense of humour who liked to refer to himself as a 'rat-catcher'. As time passed the early camaraderie of strangers in a strange land began to fade and the brigade divided quite naturally into various social cliques. Joining me and the rat-catcher in a small subgroup were a couple of communists from Manchester, one of them a fireman, who sang disparaging songs about Trotsky and made well-worn excuses for Stalin (he modernised the country, the kulaks were counter-revolutionaries, the Russian people loved him, etc.). Despite our political differences, the four of us spent many heartening hours discussing the pettiness of some of our comrades in coffee. One of the main targets for our disapproval were the brigade members who had taken it upon themselves to become the 'cultural imperialism police'. These were the people who were unceasingly alert to the corrupting influence of brigade behaviour on the locals. Some of their concerns were doubtless sensible precautions against avoidable tensions and disruptions. But there was also a curious kind of moral puritanism displayed by several of the more guilt-ridden *brigadistas*. They saw us Westerners, with our wealth and decadent social ways, as a form of contagion from which the guileless campesinos had to be protected. So women were reminded to wear bras at all times and men were warned to restrict themselves to just one beer in the local bar. Meanwhile the male campesinos, in all their prelapsarian innocence, would get so drunk that they would regularly fall down on the ground and remain there overnight. Sunday mornings in the local village could look like a scene from a sci-fi movie, with apparently lifeless bodies scattered around in the most unlikely places, as if victims of a sudden emission of a mysterious nerve gas. I once saw a man unconscious from drink hanging almost upside down from the saddle of his horse.

We stayed in the owner's abandoned hacienda that had been stripped clean. Each morning at 5 a.m. we would set out to bring in the coffee harvest. We'd eat a tasteless tortilla and beans for breakfast and rice and beans for lunch. Some days there were no beans. The campesinos were friendly, in an endearingly shy way, and much amused by our clumsy efforts. The idea was that we were there to fill the labour shortage created by army conscription. But lacking the speed and dexterity required to strip coffee bushes, our contribution was meagre if not quite negligible. We could barely fill a basket let alone a labour shortage.

The life of a campesino was tough, and made tougher by army conscription. The conditions on the co-op were extremely basic. There was little understanding of vital sanitary procedures and many of the children had distended stomachs through malnutrition or intestinal parasites. Though they performed much the same work as the men, the women, who also looked after the children, never seemed to figure in decision-making. Domestic violence was widespread in Nicaragua and there was evidence to suggest that the co-op was no exception. The fact is, when it came down to it, we had little to do with the real lives of the campesinos. They were merely the ciphers through whom the story of the revolution's successes and triumphs was told. With their bucolic stoicism, you could project on to them whatever you wanted and most of us preferred to project an image of Sandinista diehards. Some of the *brigadistas*, however, were not content with romanticising the 'Sandinista' campesinos, they had also to demonise the 'Contra' campesinos. Just as 'our' peasants were endowed with virtues of fraternity and bravery so did 'their' peasants embody the vices of sadism and venality.

In reality the situation was a little less simple. The Sandinistas themselves had already had to make some apologetic noises about earlier mistakes with agrarian reform. The extent of the damage wrought by the doctrinaire socialist Jamie Wheelock, the minister for agriculture, had become apparent to all but the most dogmatic supporters. And as much through naivety as ideological intention, all of us on the brigade were prone to factual myopia. The Sandinistas' endless rules and regulations had stifled the peasants, leading many to abandon farming, and decimated production. Wheelock was in many ways a typical revolutionary ideologue, an intellectual who'd become a guerrilla and an exile. In other words, someone who had little or no experience of how the campesinos actually worked. And that was very much the same with the majority of leading Sandinistas. Like all well-trained Marxists, they were concerned with the proletariat. Unfortunately Nicaragua didn't have a proletariat to speak of. The Sandinistas tried to amend the calamitous reforms during my time there but the results were still disappointing. Production declined even as soldiers returned to the land.

Needless to say none of us on the brigade displayed much of an appetite for the small print of agricultural policy. All we needed to know was that the land had been taken from the rich and given to the poor. The other stuff, the complaints and the shortages, could be explained by the war and the fact that revolutions were always messy and imperfect affairs. That was invariably the conclusion whenever such topics arose during coffee-picking debates that took place in the evening over a bottle of Flor de Cana rum. For some brigade members the very thought of questioning the Sandinistas was a betrayal. These were the kind of people who thrilled to every Sandinista announcement and initiative, happily oblivious to their actual effect.

One day towards the end of our coffee-picking stint, we were taken to visit a new prison. I've visited prisons in a number of countries and despite what some hang-'em and flog-'em types like to believe, there is no such thing as a pleasant prison. And if there were such a thing it would be most unlikely to appear in Central America during a civil war. The prison we visited had presumably been prepared for visitors so that it might be seen in its most positive light. Certainly there was little sign of the kind of practices – confinement in darkened closets, threats of death – that I later learned were rumoured to be commonplace in Sandinista detention centres. Nevertheless it was transparently a place in which you wouldn't want to be locked up for thirty minutes. A number of the prisoners we saw, most of them Contras, had been sentenced to thirty years – capital punishment having been abolished by the Sandinistas. Under Somoza, political opponents were tortured as a matter of course and frequently murdered and dumped in the giant refuse holes that are Managua's volcanic lakes. The Sandinista penal system, instituted by the interior minister Tomas Borge, a Somoza torture victim himself, was without question an improvement. All the same, the prisoners were presented to us like animals in a zoo. And the effect was made more distasteful by the way that a number of the brigade gawped and made disparaging remarks, even though they knew no details of the prisoners' crimes. I recall one couple, a timid and unprepossessing pair, who spoke of a particular prisoner as if he were evil incarnate, simply for having had the audacity to stare back at them. They left so impressed by the beneficence of the spare, cramped institution that to hear them talk one could believe they were describing an open prison in the Netherlands.

This willingness to believe the best of one side and think the worst of the other was shared by a number – perhaps the majority – of my fellow *brigadistas*. And it was witnessing this mindset, rather than any revelations about the true nature of the Sandinistas, that made me more sceptical about what was actually taking place in the country. In 'Looking Back on the Spanish War' Orwell wrote: 'But what impressed me then, and has impressed me ever since, is that atrocities are believed in or disbelieved in solely on the grounds of political predilection. Everyone believes in the atrocities of the enemy and disbelieves in those of his own side, without ever bothering to examine the evidence.' Although in terms of indiscriminate brutality the Contras were by far the worst offenders, evidence would surface a few years later that a number of atrocities were also committed by the Sandinistas. It would be very strange if it were otherwise, for there is almost certainly no war in history in which one side was utterly guiltless. Sustained proximity to people who were determined to accept a government monopoly on truth was an excellent lesson in how uncritical support develops into blind allegiance. As would serially prove the case, however, it was a lesson that

I chose not to learn. It was a political fact that placing ideology in front of reality led inexorably to hagiography. But I preferred to personalise the process. I found it easier to think of the most zealous *brigadistas* as simply life's natural sycophants. Which, apart from anything else, made little empirical sense. These were people who would happily call for the whole of the British establishment to be held to account over a single policeman's or soldier's actions, yet they showed no curiosity about the injustices committed in the name of a party-mobilised state. It wasn't authority worship per se that led the brigade to write the Sandinistas a blank moral cheque – though it may have motivated some of my *compañeros*. Rather it was the conviction that to question your friends was by definition to aid the enemy. And by the same token to demonstrate your full opposition to the enemy, it was necessary always to endorse their enemies. This is the same fallacy that haunts the past of progressive politics and has consistently curtailed the development of its future.

One of the most striking aspects of the international brigades that went to Nicaragua was their national character. I came across brigades from Italy, Poland, the Soviet Union, England, Scotland, Ireland and there must have been many others. In the district of Managua near the Plaza España that used to be known in the eighties as Gringolandia, you could meet people from all over Latin America, Europe and North America. And nobody, including United States passport holders, seemed as troubled or tortured by their national identity as those from England. It was as if it was implicitly understood, particularly by the English, that in the global table of victims England was at the bottom, which meant that in the global table of oppressors the English held top spot. But it went deeper than the crude post-colonial apportioning of blame. The English had no idea how to present, much less celebrate, their common bonds. Whereas everyone else had songs, poetry, stories, and even a cuisine that they felt comfortable to offer up as examples of their shared culture, the English had little to declare but our awkwardness and reticence.

There were countless incidents where I either witnessed or demonstrated this self-conscious uncertainty but several stick out in the memory. Before the brigade left the co-op there was a big discussion about how to mark our departure. Some of us wanted to throw a party for the co-op members with lots of food and drink. This was vetoed by the cultural imperialist police, who argued that such a fiesta would warp the campesinos' view of visitors, so that we would be seen only as wealthy benefactors rather than solidarity workers. Some of us suspected that this was merely an excuse for avoiding paying out for a big party. In any case, the party did not go ahead. Some time later, at another co-op, I was invited to a leaving party thrown by an Italian brigade. They cooked spaghetti for everyone, managed to track down some drinkable wine, and sang traditional Italian songs that all the Italians could sing. Not only did they give the campesinos a day to remember but also they gave them a flavour and sense of Italy, which seemed to me something like the necessary basics of cultural exchange. On another occasion in Managua I found myself at a gathering in which the guests were called upon to sing a song from their homeland. All the Europeans and Latin Americans had a wealth of traditional songs from which to draw and they did so with gusto. But as my turn neared, I grew increasingly anxious about what I could sing. I knew of no folk songs of heroic struggle, no romantic numbers that spoke of the beauty of the countryside, both of which the Irish, French, Argentinians and everyone else seemed to possess in sentimental abundance. About the only traditional songs I could recall were 'God Save the Queen' or 'Rule Britannia', which were not likely to elicit the audience's heartfelt appreciation. Eventually I sang a Beatles song – perhaps there is an academic somewhere who has revealed the early Lennon and McCartney oeuvre to be an extended paean to working-class love under the unyielding thumb of Western capitalism. The reasons why the English lack popular forms of national expression are many and various – industrialisation, imperialism, mass immigration – but the fact remains that the post-war generation of the English grew up with the understanding that Englishness was at best problematic and more often dangerous. By the time I reached adulthood Englishness had become in polite circles almost indivisible from fascism – English symbols and flags having become the preserve of far-right parties – and therefore it was seen as a concept that should be ignored, or better still denounced.

But setting aside the issue of how the English could ignore themselves, how could anyone ignore Englishness, that core unit of Britishness, when Britain continued to play a prominent, if no longer dominant, role in the world? And especially when some people took such an obvious delight in equating the sins of the British state with the sin of being English. While I was in Nicaragua a grim series of murders took place in Northern Ireland. They started outside the province with the killing of three IRA operatives in Gibraltar, apparently in cold blood, while they were preparing for a bombing mission. At their Belfast funeral, a Loyalist gunman ran amok, shooting and throwing grenades among the mourners. He killed three and wounded sixty-eight others. In a further funeral held for one of the murdered mourners, two British soldiers drove up to the cortège, by accident or on purpose – neither seemed explicable. They were dragged from the car, stripped, beaten and then shot dead. In revolutionary Nicaragua the sequence of events fitted perfectly into the narrative of imperialism (in this case British) and resistance (Irish). It so happened that at the time an Irish brigade was in Managua, on its way home from coffee picking. A Glaswegian human rights lawyer named Paul Laverty, who would later become Ken Loach's scriptwriter, threw a farewell party for them and invited me along. Unsurprisingly the events in Belfast loomed large in conversation, the standard line being that the British state had behaved with typical brutality, while the British soldiers got what they deserved. One guy from Dublin, in particular, took great pleasure in pointing this out to me, as if I was a member of Thatcher's Cabinet. His hatred for me as an Englishman was visceral. He also made made pronounced references to his IRA connections in such a boastful manner that it embarrassed several of his fellow brigade members. Gloating over the murders of the soldiers, he was jubilant that they had been shot like 'British dogs'. I should have remonstrated with him, said something, and not only because my brother had served in Northern Ireland. I should have done so because the soldiers were lynched. It wasn't people's justice, it was mob justice, and the inhumanity of the scene was duly captured in the photographs of the soldiers' naked corpses that were seen around the world. I should have said something because the truth was the overwhelming majority of English people (perhaps the same could not be said for Scottish) had no desire to maintain a military, much less costly economic, presence in Northern Ireland. It was yet another problem, inherited from Britain's colonial past, to which there was no easy answer. I should have said something because there we were in Nicaragua, a group of multinational internationalists united in a just cause, and yet a guy whose party and country remained neutral in the Second World War, and even entertained the policy of supporting Hitler, was bating me on the basis of my nationality. However, I said nothing. I allowed the Dubliner to carry on insulting the 'lying, two-faced English', rejoicing at the soldiers' sickening fate, because I had accepted the idea that his Irishness gave him some moral right to behave offensively to an Englishman, namely me.

It may seem like I'm making a big deal out of a small scene with an obnoxious character in a far-off country many years ago. But the reason it sticks in the memory is because deep down I knew at the time that my silence was a kind of a lie, or at least an acquiescence to a lie. The lie was that I – or indeed anyone else – was determined and guilty by dint of nationhood. What's more the lie maintained that aggressive nation-hating nationalism was a positive, even progressive stance, if directed at a citizen of a nation like Britain (never mind that it was multiracial, cosmopolitan, secular) by a citizen of a nation like Ireland (which happened then to be uniracial, religious, politically corrupt). The hypocrisies and contradictions in that attitude could only be sustained if they were left unspoken. And that's precisely what happened. In itself that was harmless enough – so what if a few Brits got insulted from time to time, it was not exactly a global crisis. But this obligatory sentiment of guilt, with all its unexamined negations, became the emotional source of the moral relativism that increasingly informed the left's international perspective, and the cultural relativism that would become the basis of social policy for successive governments and local authorities in Britain and across Europe.

When the brigade came to the end of its six-week stint, I stayed on in Nicaragua for a further five months. I travelled around the country working on various projects: on a farm for Salvadorean refugees, building latrines on another co-op, and for a time I lived with a war photographer with the inspired name of Raoul Shade. His wife was a former trainee nun whom Shade had helped rescue from a death squad in El Salvador. They had an epileptic baby, and all of us shared a tiny bungalow in Esteli, a battle-scarred town in the north. Raoul was a stateless European who spoke five languages but had no native tongue. He was the first pro-Sandinista person I met who mentioned his suspicions of the Sandinistas. He'd been an early convert to the cause but in his gloomier moods he would make oblique reference to things he'd seen and claim that the revolution had been betrayed. I had nagging doubts about Raoul but I think they were based on nothing more solid than the knowledge that he admired the poetry of Ezra Pound, whom I knew to be a fascist sympathiser. It wasn't a very sophisticated analysis of his reliability. And my more generous interpretation of his barbed comments was to put them down to his natural anti-authority spirit.

Raoul's pride and joy was a souped-up Datsun on which he had emblazoned the name of his photo agency – Gamma – in large white lettering. But as the US trade embargo made it impossible to get spare parts, all his money was spent on maintaining the car. To earn cash, he would drive anywhere that someone had been shot. However, the roads were so bad that he wrecked his car on the way and would then have to spend whatever he made on repairs.

A couple of months after I arrived in Nicaragua a ceasefire of sorts was agreed and and one of the effects of the falling death rate was a sharp drop in Raoul's income. There were still skirmishes, however, and one day Raoul asked me to accompany him upcountry to where a Contra attack had just taken place. The off-road journey took hours, a costly trip for the Mustang which was destined for an extended stay in the repair shop. But eventually we came to a small village, no more than a cluster of shacks in a jungle clearing. A gathering of grim-faced locals led us into the main hall where three bodies were laid out on the floor as lifeless as stone. I met a number of people who had lost family in often unspeakable ways in Nicaragua but this mournful scene was my closest encounter with the war.

In many ways Nicaragua was a misleading place, and its moment in history a deceptive time. All the huge public demonstrations I witnessed in support of the Sandinistas, the revolutionary spirit that was palpable in spite of the hardships, and the anti-'Yanqui' sentiments that were constantly expressed suggested that what had happened in Nicaragua was an irrevocable social movement. Yet within two years the Sandinistas were handsomely defeated at the polls by a coalition of pro-American liberals and conservatives. After the Sandinistas were voted out of office, Raoul set about investigating a series of graves around the country that contained a number of people thought to have been killed in cold blood by the army. He passed his findings on to the Nicaraguan Association for Human Rights.

Though Nicaragua was never a Soviet satellite, it was in some ways both a victim and, to a lesser extent, a product of the Cold War. The existence of the Soviet Union, with its ability to subsidise failing economies like Nicaragua, as well as pose an existential threat to the United States, appeared to be so assured as late as 1988 that its non-existence was inconceivable. Yet within roughly the same time span as the Sandinistas' demise, the Berlin Wall came down, the Eastern bloc collapsed, and the Soviet Union ceased to be. Such was the speed of the transformation that the Sandinista revolution quickly began to seem as if it was an anachronism, a historical footnote destined soon to be forgotten.

Almost twenty years later, history would play another of its farcical tricks, this time with the return of the Sandinistas. Led by Daniel Ortega, who had been president back in the eighties, the FSLN had come to be almost indistinguishable from the many corrupt populist parties that tarnish Latin American politics. Ortega had reinvented himself as a happy-clappy, God-spouting caudillo in hippy pink. He had entered into a cynical deal with Arnoldo Aleman, the former president and archetypal Third World kleptomaniac, who was guilty of stealing over $100 million from the impoverished state's coffers. Most of the senior Sandinista were either purged by Ortega or they left in disgust at his antics. The single exception was Tomas Borge, the much-feared former minister of the interior and unreconstructed Stalinist. If that wasn't enough, Ortega's new deputy was a former Contra spokesman from whom Ortega, in his less forgiving days, had stolen his vast compound of a home. Nor had Ortega ever convincingly answered the allegations of child sex abuse made in 1998 by his stepdaughter, Zoilamerica Narvaez. Instead, with Aleman's help, he arranged for himself a lifetime's immunity from prosecution. Nonetheless, left-wing commentators like Tariq Ali hailed Ortega's election as part of Latin America's Bolívarian revolution led by Venezuela's Hugo Chavez. When I wrote of Ortega's chequered record, I received letters telling me that none of that mattered. What counted, apparently, was that Ortega remained opposed to American imperialism.

To look back at what took place in Nicaragua in the eighties through the prism of what the Sandinistas and in particular Ortega have become is an ahistorical distortion of events. And just as it was silly to pretend that Nicaragua was a workers' paradise, it's also wrong to discount the Sandinistas' many achievements. The first being that they played the leading role in ending the Somoza dictatorship. Without the heroism and determination of the Sandinistas, it is highly unlikely that Somoza would have been defeated. They also gave the down-trodden campesinos a sense of dignity and purpose, even if their agricultural policies were cumbersome and ill-conceived. Finally, the Sandinistas did make an important and symbolic stand against American domination. These were all beliefs that I held in 1988 and I continue to hold them twenty years later. For the ideologue that's where the debate ends but for anyone interested in thinking about the difference between liberation and freedom, that's where it begins. Nicaragua started a revolution in my head and for many years that's where it remained, buried deep in thoughts and doubts I was too confused and reluctant to express.

5

Guilt

People talk about the culture shock of arriving in a Third World country, but it was my re-entry to England that left me in a state of psychological paralysis. At twenty-six I was jobless, penniless and under threat of being homeless. I was single, suspended in class limbo, seemingly unable to make the economic move upwards and unwilling to accept the social step backwards. My middle-class friends had stopped slumming, their parents having handed them hefty down payments on large houses. And even my working-class siblings had moved into private property in the suburbs. I was beginning to seem like a leftover from another era, an ageing student without the fig leaf of a course to study, one of those people who put a lot of effort into avoiding the conversational enquiry 'What do you do?' Girlfriends no longer found my damp shared flat, with its mushroom-sprouting bathroom walls, quite so irresistibly charming. My carless status was also beginning to lose its idiosyncratic appeal. In short, I looked like a bit of a loser. Of course, no one said as much but it was hard not to notice that a rupture was under way. More troubling still, I had built up a debt in Nicaragua that was considerable, insofar as I had no hope of paying it off. Companies were hardly queuing up to employ twenty-six-year-old history graduates whose only work experience was manual labour and tearing cinema tickets. And few employers were likely to view a six-month disappearing act in support of a Marxist revolution as a mark of reliability. Marx talked about estrangement from 'species being', the alienation suffered, in part, when available labour falls short of intellectual potential. I don't know if that was the nature of the malaise but when my landlord hiked up the rent, my outlook turned darkly Raskolnikovian. Like Dostoevsky's anti-hero, I not only found it difficult to access the world of material advancement, I resented its very existence. In my blackest conspiratorial moods, it seemed that the whole of lawful society was designed to maintain my exclusion. This sentiment was not the product of any socialist yearnings, much less rational analysis. Rather, I think, it was a kind of juvenile nihilistic funk. At any rate, it would be wrong to say that I was burdened with an overdeveloped respect for the law.

And yet instead of murdering my landlord with an axe, I found a job, through a friend, working for a magazine with one of the most alluring titles in the annals of journalism: *Information Technology for Local Government*. Or *ITLG*, as we liked to call it in moments of tie-loosened informality. I was taken on as a trainee news reporter at £7,000, rising to £7,500 after completion of a three-month trial period. Even at the time it was a paltry sum but I didn't have much bargaining power or alternative options. The business – including two other magazines with similarly melodious titles – was run by a surly pink-faced man in his late thirties with the mock-regal name of Phil Windsor. He had long straggly hair that failed to hide his gathering baldness and he would walk up and down the office, like his namesake on a royal visit, with his nose raised at such an angle as to suggest the company of his minions was physically unpleasant. The image that stuck in my head was of one of the pigs in *Animal Farm* – 'A little awkwardly, as though not quite used to supporting his considerable bulk in that position, but with perfect balance, he was strolling across the yard.' Nor did the porcine imagery end there, for *ITLG*'s umbrella company was called the Public Interface Group: PIG to its employees. Most of the day, Phil would sit in his swivel chair, fingers knitted together in deep contemplation, I presumed, of gaps in markets and unique selling points. Should anyone dare to seek his advice or agreement, he would complain that he was far too busy to be distracted by their trifling concerns. Phil would often quote William Randolph Hearst, the American media magnate on whom *Citizen Kane* was modelled and on whom Phil thought to model himself. On his excursions round the office, he would suddenly announce, to no one in particular: 'News is something that somebody somewhere doesn't want published.' I used to think about this definition as I compiled my report on, say, Hampshire County Council's acquisition of a new computer system: 'Hampshire signs deal with IBM'. And after much rumination I would conclude that the only conceivable person who could want the story not to be published was its author: me. I loathed the job. I hated the cynical money-driven operation, its piggyback excuse for journalism and its pretension to national-historic significance. I hated the new Victorian working conditions, the manner in which the lunch break was seen as optional, and the way the option was always frowned upon. I hated that it was necessary to pretend to be working even when there was no work to do. I hated the permanent expression of terror that animated the face of Phil's secretary. I hated the cheap grey carpet, the job-lot furniture, and the drab lifeless atmosphere of the office with its plastic plants and crappy little coffee-making facility. I hated that Phil refused to honour my feeble pay rise after three months, arguing that he wanted to extend my traineeship. And most of all, I hated the mindless soul-crushing monotony of the work, phoning council IT departments to ask if they were looking to upgrade their mainframes. Years later in *The Office* Ricky Gervais would capture the suffocating environment of the vacuum-sealed modern workplace, and that numbing, if quietly tragicomic, sense of time being put slowly to death. The fictional offices of Wernham-Hogg paper suppliers could have been, without the slightest alteration, an utterly plausible stand-in for *Information Technology for Local Government*. The only conspicuous difference was that, in contrast to David Brent, Phil did not appear to rate being liked as one of his major ambitions.

Then one day something interesting happened. I arrived early and noticed that Phil was sitting in a chair, wearing a raincoat but no trousers. He looked like an overeager customer in a disreputable Soho cinema. I glimpsed his secretary's frozen stare, and grew more curious when she refused to meet my eye. For his part, Phil showed no discomfort or embarrassment at his semi-clothed state. His attitude towards my presence seemed much the same as it always was, an indifference that shared an open border with contempt. It took me hours of dogged questioning of the only witness before his secretary acknowledged that Phil had had an 'accident' on the way to work and that he'd given his trousers to her to have dry-cleaned. As soon as I established the sordid details, I wrote and designed my first proper news story on the firm's new desktop publishing software. It was headlined: 'PUBLISHER SHITS HIMSELF'. I then went on to describe in best Hearst yellow-press-style how, owing to a packed schedule, the publisher had relinquished control of his bowels, delegating the dirty work to his secretary. I printed out copies of the piece and passed samizdat versions to trusted co-workers around the office. At last, I thought, my talents were being put to good use. Here was a story that would pass Hearst's news test. Somebody, somewhere, did not want it published.

I felt enthusiastically, if temporarily, re-engaged with the species being, and all because of a being who appeared to be from another species. But for the remainder of my time at the magazine, I was sent round the country to any and every council office that convened a meeting on IT. Anywhere, it seemed, to keep me out of the office. Nowhere was too far to be dispatched if there was a conference with a title like 'Meet the Challenge of Change: Developing Initiatives in IT Project Management'. To get to each sorry town – and Britain, I came to realise, was one great urban apology – I was given company train vouchers that could be used for any journey.

After a few weeks of this enforced exile, I decided I had had enough and I quit. At the same time I also experienced a severe downturn in my romantic fortunes, when my some-time girlfriend dumped me for a contemporary who, entirely coincidentally, happened to have an impressive job, his own flat and a car. I seemed entrenched in failure, incapable of breaking through the pain barrier to a reasonable or satis-fying life. To offset my despair I had taken the precaution of stealing a number of train vouchers before I left ITLG and with a female friend I went on a first-class train tour of Britain, complete with sleeper car and free bar bill. We travelled to Edinburgh, Glasgow and the west coast of Scotland in as much style as British Rail could muster. I ran up over £1,000 in expenses. I also distributed free travel tickets to my friends, who made use of them in a similar fashion. It seemed the perfect way of saying, 'Look, I don't care about your poxy little job or your safe hermetic world and, what's more, there's nothing you can do about it.' The idea was to make it obvious that I was the culprit but not to leave any tangible evidence. And it so very nearly worked out that way, just as so many crimes so nearly do.

A few months later I was arrested and charged with theft from an employer. My case was handled by a detective who took such a Dostoevskian delight in the glacial progress of the investigation, and the psychodrama of my flagrant guilt, that I became convinced he had based his technique on that of Porfiry Petrovitch, the policeman in *Crime and Punishment*. And like Porfiry, he was able, following a series of meticu-lous, threatening and yet cunningly sympathetic interviews, to gain a confession.

Between the far-flung British Rail expedition and my arrest, I also managed to get married to a Turkish air hostess. I'd met a vivacious communist in Nicaragua who needed to get out of Turkey, and she asked if I would marry her. I declined on the suspicion that her interest was not entirely bureau-cratic, but I later regretted the decision. It seemed churlish, petty bourgeois, and, perhaps more pressingly, I could have done with the cash she offered. In London I met up with her again and belatedly accepted her proposal, but she told me that she had already married someone else. Luckily she had a friend. An air hostess. The going dowry rate back then for a fake marriage was £3,000. Being an egalitarian-minded character, I said that £1,000 would suffice. We got married, the air hostess and I, in a grim registry office near Heathrow airport. The only wedding guests were a group of Turkish dissidents, most of them, as far as I could make out, members of the Turkish Communist Party. Like any good nonconformist, I thought the institution of marriage was a fraud, so a fraudulent marriage was by my way of thinking nothing more than a tautology. That's what I told myself, anyway. I laughed inside when I forgot 'our' address during the ceremony. 'You must be nervous,' the sympathetic registrar said, smiling to put me at ease. And I savoured the fact that I had sabotaged a hypocritical bourgeois convention not only in its own terms but also in relation to myself: I could never get married for the first time again. How little I cared for tradition! How liberated and unsentimental! Yet posing for ironic 'kiss-the-bride' photographs afterwards, standing on the concrete steps of the registry office, I recall feeling empty and forlorn in that way that, for maximum depressive effect, requires the celebratory noise of a happy crowd.

Not long afterwards I stood in the dock of Clerkenwell Magistrates' Court feeling a different kind of emptiness. A lawyer friend had warned me that it was a 'toothbrush case', meaning that prison was a distinct possibility. My own solicitor had already shown me various case records in which similar crimes committed by first-time offenders had received six-month sentences – a mere three months with good behaviour, I reassured myself. The first week's always the worst, I would recite by way of preparation. I imagine many people have pictured themselves in court, perhaps in scenes of high drama in which they are able, by way of a tremendous oratorical speech, to prove their innocence. The fantasy, if you can call it that, has countless film scenes to draw on but the reality in my case was more like the fractured, frustrating logic of an anxiety dream.

To begin with, I had problems coming to terms with the knowledge that my barrister, whom I met five minutes before the case, had only just received the case papers. One sort of hopes that they have been studying nothing else for the previous month. The first question she asked me was whether I was employed. A couple of months before I had parlayed my film-watching as a part-time cinema usher into a job writing mini-reviews for a listings company. It so happened that on that day some of them appeared in the *Guardian*. She asked to look at my copy of the newspaper, as if the reviews might yield the key to my liberty. It all seemed like a desperate last-minute scramble, but I calmed myself with the thought that as I had pleaded guilty, the proceedings would be much less adversarial, more a formality. That turned out to be a naive hope. In his grave, almost malicious, address to the court, the Dostoevskian detective, who had previously seemed more a psychologist than a policeman, maintained that I had deliberately obstructed the investigation for as long as possible. He claimed that it was only when they had laboriously assembled a compelling weight of evidence that I acknowledged my guilt. This was untrue, though I had no means of registering that fact. I finally confessed because the detective wanted to interview my flatmate, who would have been placed in a position of having to lie for me. It suddenly dawned on me that the police and prosecution were looking for an example to be set. The cynical view of the criminal court is that the aim is not to establish the facts but to lie in such a way that cannot be proved wrong. Most initiates would probably find little to disagree with in this assessment. That I learned this lesson just at the moment I had decided to tell the truth was perhaps an appropriate irony. After the detective spoke the chance that I would require a toothbrush seemed to grow like plaque.

The fact that she knew nothing of my case only a few minutes before did not prevent my barrister from presenting it as if the study of its details had been her life's vocation. 'My client,' she explained, during a highly spirited defence, 'has recognised his mistake and is filled with contrition. He now intends to build a career as a journalist, to which end he is currently employed writing film reviews for the *Guardian*.' At this point she held up my copy of that day's paper, opened to the page on which my miniscule contributions appeared, and waved it in front of the magistrate like Neville Chamberlain holding the Munich Agreement. 'I would suggest that in the circumstances a custodial sentence would be inappropriate.' The other defendants waiting for their cases to be heard that day were all black and in their teens or early twenties, and, unlike me, none of them was wearing a suit, still less a tie. Possibly unaware of the *Guardian*'s long-standing reputation for supporting penal reform, my fellow lags cast me scornful looks when the paper was produced, as though I had transgressed an unspoken code of decency. Even the magistrate seemed embarrassed by the performance. 'I think you can put the newspaper away,' he said with a raised-eyebrow expression of disapproval, 'I'm not sure what film reviews have to do with this case but I agree that there would be no benefit in a custodial sentence.' Woody Allen once observed that the most beautiful words in the English language were 'It's benign', but the non-custodial sentence sentence takes some beating.

The fine instantly consumed the marriage money and much more that I didn't have. None of the friends who had used the free train tickets offered to contribute anything towards the payback. Instead it was my brother, hardworking and honest, who came through with financial help like a trusty character out of Dickens. By the age of thirty almost one in three British males has a criminal record. That seems to me a simultaneously shocking and reassuring statistic. Shocking, obviously, because it's such a large section of society. And reassuring because, however out of control crime may sometimes appear to be, the large majority of those with a criminal record do not go on to become career criminals. I'd left it rather late in the day to join the ranks of the criminal classes. The few other applications I'd made down the years – stealing books, holiday insurance fraud – were pathetic efforts, easy to commit and even easier to ignore. Now, though, I was a recognised member of the criminal fraternity, albeit the less than heroic white-collar chapter. I had initially persuaded myself that my crime was a statement, an act of protest, perhaps not overtly political, but a personal score-settling dedicated nonetheless to all those faceless souls rotting away in dead-end respectability. All I could see, or all I wanted to see, was the bland corporate edifice that was the victimless target of my crime. The insurance would cover the money lost. No one was out of pocket. No one got hurt. And I justified the fake marriage in the same terms with even fewer moral qualms. But what did I really feel? The answer I think was a little more complicated.

Dostoevsky makes use of utilitarianism and utopianism, Bentham and Marx, in the debate at the heart of *Crime and Punishment*. The book was written at a time when the Russian intelligentsia was exhilerated by radical social theories. One character, Razumihin contends that socialists view crime 'as a protest against the abnormality of the social organisation and nothing more'. This, in essence, is the argument to which many social reformers subscribe, give or take a proviso here and there. And it suited me well enough to go along with its thrust, never more so than in my own case. However, Raskolnikov, whose name derives from the Russian for 'schism', comes nearer an uncomfortable truth in his obscure pamphlet, when he divided society between the 'extraordinary' and the 'ordinary'. Explaining its meaning to Porfiry, he says: 'I simply hinted that an "extraordinary" man has the right . . . that is not an official right, but an inner right to decide in his own conscience to overstep . . . certain obstacles, and only in case it is essential for the practical fulfilment of his idea (sometimes, perhaps, of benefit to the whole of humanity).'

All crimes are to some extent opportunistic but it was the ordinariness of society, not its inequality, that moved me to grab the opportunity. In other words, I awarded myself the right to steal because I thought I was exceptional, that I, in contrast to the mass of drones, recognised the absurd limitations of society. This is the paradox of the revolutionary: egalitarian in aim, elitist by nature. For it is the dearly held conviction of every radical that he is part of an enlightened minority – sometimes as small as one – that understands objective reality. Of course, I also wanted to drink free champagne with a beautiful woman on the first-class sleeper to Glasgow, but a sense of being less ordinary – arrogance by any other name – led me to believe that a) I wouldn't get caught and b) it was the right thing to do.

And I wanted to stick two fingers up to Phil Windsor, the boss who conveniently symbolised all that was cold, uncaring and petty about the world of Thatcherite business. He was strange and ruthless and unsocial and, infinitely more to the point, suffering from adrenoleukodystrophy, a rare and viciously debilitating illness that later came to public attention in the film *Lorenzo's Oil*. He didn't realise that he was dying back in 1989. And nor, of course, did I. Apparently he was not diagnosed until a couple of years later, but his adrenal glands must have been fast degenerating when I worked for him, when I silently rejoiced in referring to him as 'Pig'. The 'accident' about which I'd been so cruel and tasteless was almost certainly a consequence of the neurological disability that would lead first to a wheelchair, then bedridden paralysis and finally to his death in 2000. As the nerve fibres in his brain were stripped of their protective coating, he must have suffered in unimaginable ways. Deprived of the fatty sheath known as myelin, the brain loses control of the body, which then slowly gives way to innumerable corporeal tortures before the eventual release of death. So the target of my little protest, my criminal jape, was not only a man who was guilty of setting up a business that employed a number of people who might otherwise have not had jobs, he was also terminally ill and on the brink of total bodily collapse. Seldom has a rebel had such a pitiful cause.

At the end of *Crime and Punishment*, Raskolnikov, infused with love, has seven years of his prison sentence left to serve. He is at the 'beginning of a new story', writes Dostoevsky, 'the story of the gradual renewal of a man, the story of his gradual regeneration, of his passing from one world into another, of his initiation into a new unknown life'. Raskolnikov found God and a kind of spiritual peace but, if anything, his change of heart was not as extreme as that of his creator. Dostoevsky too started out as a militant radical. He was arrested by the Tsar's secret police for the seditious crime of reading out a letter written by the Russian literary critic Vissarion Belinsky to the Slavophile novelist Nikolai Gogol, which protested at the enslavement of the Russian peasantry. For this he was subjected to a mock execution in front of a firing squad and then sent to a Siberian penal colony. In prison he set out on a political journey that would lead him to embrace the reactionary, Tsar-supporting religious nationalism against which as a young man he had been so violently opposed. This, of course, is the time-honoured path from youth to middle age, from left to right, radicalism to reaction. Equally obvious, it is the route that some readers will be determined to discern in these pages.

My redemption, however, was a little less pronounced. I had not killed anyone and nor was I sent to a forced labour camp in Siberia. The court case, and specifically the vexing proximity of prison, had two distinct effects on me. I grew far more conscious of the consequences of criminality – certainly more appreciative of everyday liberty – and as a result more thoughtful about those who suffer the consequences. And it made me realise that I did not want to be a criminal. I had spent the whole of the decade of the 1980s, which happened to coincide with my first ten years of adult life, wrestling with the contradictory beliefs, ideas, ambitions, lifestyles, experiences, peer groups, identities, cultures, subcultures and accidents of birth that had shaped, in unknowable ways, the person I appeared to have become. The shock of looming imprisonment acted as a full stop on that process. What was the point of waging a low-level attritional war with convention? Whom did it benefit? The margins of society were full enough without me. With the court case, I stopped behaving as if an awkward social position in itself served any great purpose and came to an accommodation with life as it was organised. To put it another way, I began to grow up. This meant developing a career, forming a committed relationship, owning property (even a car), and all the other bourgeois trappings. But to put it in political terms, it also meant that I became a liberal.

Liberalism is an elastic concept which has several distinct forces pulling on it. It's often employed, for example, by the left as a means of demanding rights and liberties that many on the left are only too happy to deny to others. It has been a tactic of the hard left to stretch liberalism to its breaking point, to test its weak points, in the hope of creating the kind of conflicts and chaos from which they have tried to benefit. Thus the repeated accusation made by the hard left against any government is illiberalism, though, of course, were the hard left ever to achieve power, liberalism would be its first victim. Another tradition that lays claim to liberalism is Christianity, especially the turn-the-other-cheek, sin-forgiving, pacifist stripe of Christianity that in the modern era has largely metamorphosed into a secular religion, or a vague sensibility rather than a scriptural faith. There are also what might be called liberation movements – the whole panoply of lifestyle and sexuality issues – that draw on the permissive strand of liberalism. And somewhere buried away beneath all the competing interest groups is the philosophy of liberalism itself, the foundation principles of the Enlightenment –

freedom of speech, social and religious tolerance, the rule of law, democracy. At university, when I read Locke, Kant and Voltaire, and later thinkers like Bentham and Mill, they all seemed rather tame and somehow irrelevant. They were dead white men who failed to come alive. It would not be until much later in life that I began to grasp the enormity of their moral and intellectual achievements and, in particular, the life-enhancing legacy of the liberalism they bequeathed.

In recent years 'liberal' has entered a strong claim to be the most abused word in the modern lexicon. Indeed, it's not just an abused term, it's also a term of abuse. In America the defamation comes from the right, but I use liberal to describe the person I became after my court case in the same way it's used as an insult by sections of the left. I was a confirmed liberal in the vital sense that I respected democratic society. I could see its flaws, injustices and inequalities but I could no longer indulge, even half-heartedly, or flirtatiously, the idea that they could be remedied or improved by mass social conflict or selfish militancy. Since adolescence I had been peddled the comforting idea by a succession of teachers, lecturers and people I admired that the system was to blame, or the government, or society at large. It was time to wean myself off the habit. It was time to accept responsibility.

Reasons

6

Leftovers

The date of 9/11 ought to be one that is celebrated by all free people of the world, for it refers, at least in the British and European rendering of the calendar, to 9 November. On that day in 1989 the Berlin Wall began to be dismantled and with it the dire seventy-two-year experiment of communist dictatorship. Yet although it opened the way to the liberation of hundreds of millions of people, that historic date is remembered by very few people outside Germany and Eastern Europe. As things stand most free people of the world, certainly in Western Europe, would struggle to utter a phrase like 'free people of the world', much less celebrate new members to the club. To the sophisticated ear 'free people' sounds embarrassing and culturally condescending. 'What right have we to say who is and is not free?' a thoughtful Westerner is likely to ask, before duly listing the restrictions on liberty that exist in the West. The answer, of course, is the right of free speech – it's just not an answer that fills many Western hearts with pride.

Two decades on from the event, there remains in Western Europe an ambivalent attitude towards the collapse of communism. Among the wider population, concerned by global instability and Anglo-American interventionism, there is a sense that at least we knew where we were in the Cold War, when there was a superpower counterbalance, a status quo. For the great majority of Western Europeans, not just those on the left, the existence of the USSR as an oppositional entity, a known otherness, was more important than its actual reality. After two world wars no one wanted a third, particularly not a nuclear war. So it was that for almost half a century a fear of mass death and the equilibrium of Mutually Assured Destruction helped a generation or two to ignore or fictionalise the sorry plight of 1.5 billion Eastern Europeans, Russians, Central Asians and Chinese.

There was something else, too, not always articulated but always there: a sneaking sympathy, even admiration, for communist nations, especially among the intelligentsia. The liberal intellectual tradition in Europe (and to a far lesser degree America) tended to give the Soviet bloc and Chinese dominion the benefit of the doubt, while reserving for the United States a relentless and unforgiving scrutiny. The rule, in so many words, was to divert disapproval away from our harmless enemy and in the direction of our perfidious ally. That's why we protested at American nuclear missiles aimed at the Soviet bloc, but said next to nothing about the vast array of Soviet nuclear missiles aimed directly at us. And in this same spirit did Western thinkers dismiss the first reports of Cambodian atrocities. Noam Chomsky, the 'world's greatest public intellectual', wrote an essay in 1977 that chastised those who claimed a genocide was underway in Cambodia and praised a book written by George Hildebrand and Gareth Porter that was a shameless defence of Pol Pot's homicidal regime. Tens of thousands had already been put to death by the Khmer Rouge when the book was written, never mind reviewed, but Chomsky's instinct was to see the very best in what was in reality the very worst.

The same principle applies with the intelligentsia's contrasting judgements of Cold War behaviour. All but the most obsessively hard-line anti-communist grew up in post-war Europe accepting that the political witch-hunts conducted by Senator McCarthy and his acolytes in the 1950s were a severe assault on freedom – which indeed they were. Yet if you took McCarthyism at its most demented and placed it against the

Soviet model at its most liberal – say, for instance, the Khrushchev era – the repression in the East was incomparably more ruthless and extensive than in the West. Almost no one now, except for the most zealous Stalinist, would dispute this fact. Nonetheless the litany of human rights abuses committed by the Soviet state from Prague to Vladivostok never elicited the same invective of intellectuals or protesters in the West. Two books were kept with two totally different methods of accounting. Why?

One explanation for this discrepancy might be that Western protesters felt themselves powerless to influence Soviet policy. The only problem with this analysis is that when it comes to protests the popularity of a cause appears to have no direct relationship with its likely effect. The anti-war demonstrators who tried to storm the American Embassy in Grovesnor Square in 1968 did not seriously think the US would respond by pulling out of Vietnam. And of the millions who marched across Europe in protest at the Iraq War in 2003, very few expected that the US and Britain would call off the invasion. Indeed, you could argue that it was the foregone conclusion, the certain knowledge that coalition forces *would* invade, that brought so many protesters out on to the street. Nevertheless the Soviet invasions of Hungary in 1956, Czechoslovakia in 1968 and Afghanistan in 1979 took place with minimal protests in the West. Students did not take to the streets in their tens of thousands, unions did not mobilise their memberships, committees and action groups went unformed, and angry letters from academics and prominent intellectuals found themselves unwritten, unsigned and unsent. There were exceptions, of course, some principled individuals, predictable right-wing ideologues, a few human rights groups. But on the whole the response to the Soviet Union's aggression was much like the reaction to its implosion: muted.

What did I do when the Wall came down? I didn't race to Berlin to join in the greatest surprise party in history. Nor did I even think to offer help or support, however small or symbolic. I just watched it on TV. And I watched it with a certain semi-detachment born of mixed feelings. I was jubilant at the overthrow of the Romanian despot Nicolae Ceaușescu and pleased that Erich Honecker, East Germany's goon-like leader, was forced to eat the words he'd uttered just eleven months before: 'The Wall will be standing in fifty and even in a hundred years, if the reasons for it are not removed.' But a part of me, a larger part than I was aware, did not want to stare too long or hard at what the fall of communism meant.

The two years leading up to the dissolution of the USSR in December 1991 undoubtedly marked the most dramatic global change of my lifetime. The seemingly indestructible monolith of the communist state rapidly withered away, but not in the way Marx had envisaged. The distance between the illusive dream and stagnant reality just became too difficult to conceal and the people walked out through the gaping hole. And I welcomed them not with elation but a disengaged cynicism. I recall, for instance, making snide remarks to friends about the 'great stonewashed masses', in reference to the East Germans' poor taste in jeans and bad haircuts. It was a sort of ironic protection from having to acknowledge what a real revolution, the greatest uprising of the century, looked like. I even wondered out loud if the whole thing was not really a 'counter-revolution'. Only a year before I'd been actively supporting a revolution that had been supported and aided by the Eastern bloc – the Sandinista interior police had been trained by Bulgarian and East German secret police, the economy existed on subsidised Soviet oil. How could I make sense of a world turned upside down without reference to reliable clichés? It was that same reflexive instinct again that Marx had noted, of turning to the past in order to disguise the new scene in old, familiar clothes.

Without signing up to a manifesto, or joining a party, I had, as I say, become a liberal. It was not a conscious decision, but it was a change in conscience, if not yet consciousness. My brush with the law had proved the revelatory moment at which I came to appreciate the advantages of democratic society. These were advantages that I now wanted to take advantage of myself, and quickly, but I was in no rush to see them extended to people elsewhere in the non-democratic world. I supported Gorbachevian reform in the Soviet Union, a fantasy in which the systemically corrupt party that had brought the nation so low, the party that had governed every aspect of public life, and far too much of private life, would oversee the transition to a more open society. I now understood that any kind of full-bloodied socialism would be a step backwards in Britain. Yet for a variety of reasons I was not ready in 1989, and nor for some years after, to admit that communism was a wrong turn in history, a political, economic and moral dead end. While keen to make my way in Western bourgeois society, I was reluctant to close and lock the door on the old utopian dream, even if like all utopias it had turned out to be a dystopia. As the unreconstructed communist professor in Tom Stoppard's play *Rock 'n' Roll* says: 'From each according to his ability, to each according to his need: what could be more simple, more rational, more beautiful?'

And here we come to a critical question regarding the epistemology of political opinion and, in particular, this book: why should it matter what I or anyone like me thinks or thought? I'm not a politician, a theorist, an ideologue, a philosopher, an activist. At the time of the Soviet break-up I was writing film reviews for *City Limits*, a now-defunct radical listings magazine – not what you would classify as an influential forum for international debate. Even the Kremlin's legendary powers of surveillance and observation failed to stretch so far as to listen into the conversations of inconsequential north Londoners. So why rake over my state of mind fifteen or more years ago when it had no bearing on history whatsoever? The answer, it seems to me, is that it offers an instructive lesson in how prevailing attitudes are shaped and uninformed opinions are formed. 'An intellectual,' wrote Albert

Camus, 'is someone whose mind watches itself.' Camus was a staunch anti-Stalinist in France when it was a lonely position to inhabit on the left. But what of those who watch intellectual minds and forget to watch the world? I did not know how to react to the revolutions in Central and Eastern Europe because I had lived quite comfortably with the knowledge that the Soviet bloc was a miserable police state. In this, I think, I was not unlike a huge number of wishful-thinking left-liberals in Europe and America. We lived in what I would call a state of Gulag denial. It comes in many forms, not all of them conscious, but Gulag denial is the spectre that continues to haunt the revolutionary fantasies of the left. It's the failure to admit what was in our midst, an unwillingness to acknowledge the totality of the repression, that still prevents many on the left from being able to discern the danger in anti-democratic forces. In the age of Hezbollah and Hamas and Iranian conferences devoted to its promotion, Holocaust denial may no longer carry the stigma it once did. All the same, in non-Islamist society it's still an accusation that any civilised person is keen to avoid. Not so with Gulag denial. Overlooking or understating Soviet and Chinese slave camps have never rated as cardinal sins. Gulag denial continues to be the great moral blindspot of the left, a vast and murky territory in which the language of evasion and doublespeak is the preferred means of communication.

If I never achieved fluency in that tongue, it's because I could not quite master the logic of moral equivalence. Though it wasn't for want of trying. What made me rethink the baggy notion that the West and East shared a rough parity in distribution of good and bad, like fractured mirror images of themselves, was meeting Central and East Europeans who had relocated to Britain in the 1990s. These people had lived in both systems and not one of them entertained the idea that there was balance between the two. All of them saw communism as inherently sinister and the Russians as invaders and occupiers. Without behaving like evangelical converts, they made it clear that the freedom we took for granted in the West was immeasurably preferable to the control they had endured in the East. One day I spoke to a Czech friend about an essay I'd read on the similarities between Western advertising and the form of Eastern bloc state-sanctioned art known as socialist realism. It really gave advertising a kicking, this essay, for its ideological promotion of capitalism, drawing a vivid and damning parallel with Soviet visual propaganda. I thoroughly enjoyed the tone of the piece. I thought it was an 'interesting' comparison. 'No,' said my friend firmly. 'There is no comparison. The writer doesn't know what he's talking about and nor do you.' And I didn't. I just wanted to establish that capitalism was far from perfect and that maybe there were some equivalents of the Soviet errors in the West. But my friend never mistook Western capitalism and liberal pluralism as flawless. He just knew through experience that it was far superior to the communist system, and he did not want me or anyone else to pretend otherwise out of a misplaced sensitivity to his background. Thereafter I learned to stop trying to recast communism as a near miss that had many positive features. But it took me until 11 September 2001 before I broke the habit of always looking for the downside in the West.

The French philosopher Alain Finkielkrant has called the Western liberal's appetite for guilt 'penitential narcissism', and angsting over the appropriate response to the fall of communism could, I suppose, also be filed under that rubric. However, a clear distinction must be drawn between the impulse to feel responsible for all the world's ills and the straightforward acknowledgement of historic injustice. One is a twisted emotional reflex, the other a moral and rational duty. However you look at it, what took place in the Soviet Union from 1917 through to 1991, and Eastern Europe from 1945 to 1990, was not primarily the fault of the West. And for a persistent, even dominant, strand of liberal thought, if the West is not the criminal then almost by definition there can be no crime. If we can't blame ourselves, in so many words, then let's not blame anyone else.

For those who see themselves on the left, which is notionally a humanitarian, internationalist place to be, this should be a self-evidently absurd position to adopt. Human suffering is human suffering and those responsible for it should be identified, remembered, held to account. As a character in Milan Kundera's *The Book of Laughter and Forgetting* phrases it: 'the struggle of man against power is the struggle of memory against oblivion'. Soviet-style communism, which is to say real-world communism, was much concerned with erasing troublesome history. The state arranged and demanded amnesia, rubbing out anything or anyone that didn't fit the prescribed version of events. Western intellectuals colluded in this process, sometimes actively, but more often with deaf ears and silence. Jean-Paul Sartre, the godfather of twentieth-century French philosophy, once explained his rationale for sidestepping Soviet crimes against humanity: 'As we were not members of the Party, it was not our duty to write about Soviet labour camps; we were free to remain aloof from the quarrels over the nature of the system, provided no events of sociological significance occurred.' That 'sociological significance' speaks with chilling eloquence of the intellectual indifference to human suffering. Other responses were so unconcerned as to find the very mention of Bolshevik terror in bad taste. As long ago as 1933, when Malcolm Muggeridge reported on the real condition of the USSR, the celebrated historian A.J.P. Taylor complained: 'I really would like to say what terrible grief and pain your late articles about Russia cause your friends, but then what's the good? We all have to do pretty unpleasant things to raise money.' There are countless similar examples which over the years have aided the forces of oblivion. Nearly all of them quietly forgotten.

It's customary whenever a reckoning is made of communist misdeeds to bring up the dismal record of Western European colonialism. The idea is that before we come over all righteous about Stalin and his ilk, let's look a little closer to home. And it should never be forgotten that when Taylor wrote that letter to Muggeridge the British Empire was still very much in operation and the Bengal famine of 1943, which led to the deaths of perhaps 3 million Bengalis, was ten years in the future. And as late as the 1950s, British rule in Kenya was responsible for abuses that were atrocious. However, it's not an either/or situation; one crime does not absolve the other. Colonialism, like communism, resulted in enormous loss of life because, like communism, it subjugated people, denied their rights and turned them into expendable masses. It's very hard, if not impossible, nowadays to find defenders of colonialism working for liberal causes. But it's still common in liberal establishments to come across guardians of the communist flame. The Stop the War Coalition, for example, probably seemed like an exemplary soft-left pressure group to the majority of the hundreds of thousands of protesters who marched under its banner in 2003. The chair of STWC is Andrew Murray, a member of the Communist Party's executive committee. Murray has put on record his and his party's 'solidarity with Peoples Korea' – that's the galling euphemism for Kim Jong-Il's North Korea, a slave-owning dynasty and the most restrictive and repressive police state on earth. Even today this is not a particularly embarrassing position to hold in polite company. It's not like, say, expressing support for the flawed democracy of Israel, which is tantamount in many circles to a declaration of fascist sympathy. I'm regularly told by liberal friends and acquaintances that North Korea is none of the West's business, that America should back off (very few people of my generation seem to realise that it was American, British and allied troops that saved South Korea from North Korea's aggressive invasion, and therefore from the fate of universal slavery). At the same time we see in the liberal press a stream of articles which hail China, a nation with a scandalous human rights record, as the great hope for this century, the longed-for alternative to US hegemony. Martin

Jacques, the former editor of *Marxism Today*, has built a second career as an emcee for the glories of Chinese communist-capitalism, authoritarian state control combined with unflinching free-market exploitation of labour. 'In the 90s, after Tiananmen Square,' Jacques lamented in 2005, 'China was overwhelmingly seen through the prism of human rights and democracy. For a long time it was virtually impossible to start a discussion in the West about China except in these terms, or when this question was a central part of the agenda. This remains part of the western agenda, but a much less important one in the light of China's stunning transformation. The question of western-style democracy remains no closer now than it was in the wake of Tiananmen. On the contrary, the regime has not only survived but prospered to an extraordinary extent over the last quarter-century.' How irritating it is, Jacques seems to be saying, when Westerners get het up about human rights and democracy. Can't we get it into our thick heads that it's just not culturally relevant?

A classic example of communist flame maintenance was given by the *Guardian*'s Seamus Milne in March 2006 on the fiftieth anniversary of Khrushchev's secret criticism of Stalin. Milne was then the comment-page or op-ed editor, the most important opinion-shaping position on a newspaper with the arguable exception of the overall editor. He is the same writer who was so precipitate in his denunciation of the United States the day after 9/11. Here, with far more time to consider the details of Soviet abuses, Milne showed the more understanding side of his nature. First of all he rebuked revisionist historians who, he claimed, inflate the figures for Stalin's victims. He cited archival figures – '799,455 were recorded as executed between 1921 and 1953 and the labour camp population reached 2.5 million at its peak' – that he acknowledged were 'horrific enough', but did not trouble himself or the reader with the full number of the recorded murders for which the Soviet state was responsible. Then he went on to list Stalin's achievements. 'For all its brutalities and failures, communism in the Soviet Union, eastern Europe and elsewhere delivered rapid industrialisation, mass education, job security and huge advances in social and gender equality,' he wrote. 'It encompassed genuine idealism and commitment, captured even by critical films and books of the post-Stalin era such as Wajda's *Man of Marble* and Rybakov's *Children of the Arbat*. Its existence helped to drive up welfare standards in the west, boosted the anticolonial movement and provided a powerful counterweight to western global domination.'

This sounds suspiciously similar to that lamentable old formula, 'Say what you like about Mussolini but he made the trains run on time.' But let's for argument's sake allow that rapid industrialisation, mass education, job security and huge advances in social and gender equality not only took place in the Soviet Union but were desirable in and of themselves. This last proviso is worth considering because the 'new global capitalist order' that Milne went on to deride also promises to deliver rapid industrialisation, mass education, job creation (if not security) and huge advances in social and gender equality. And many on the left, Milne included, now praise movements that resist such developments. Still, if we ignore that little contradiction and accept that the social developments of modernity are beneficial, then a comparative analysis of nations that were part of that 'new global capitalist order' and those that subscribed to the Stalinist plan shows that by all the above criteria the democratic capitalist nations did better. In the same way that studies of separated identical twins can tell us a lot about environmental influences, then an examination of the divided nations of Korea and, until that epochal November in 1989, Germany is tellingly informative. In North Korea, arguably the last Stalinist state in existence, starvation is commonplace, unemployment rife, mass education is nothing more than a system of disseminating virulent propaganda, and equality means the immiseration of the slave camp, where women are treated just as mercilessly as men, and the party officials are awarded the elevated position of prison guards. If that wasn't enough, there is mounting evidence that the earthly hell with which 'peace campaigner' Murray is in solidarity employs two of the Nazis' defining atrocities, gas chambers and eugenics. South Korea is by no means a paradise and it has known extended periods of authoritarian rule, but it has no famine, is hugely more industrialised, infinitely better educated, and there is an equality of basic rights. The state does not kill disabled and mixed-race children at birth, and political prisoners are not held and gassed in concentration camps. The contrast with the two Germanys was perhaps not as stark but it was just as real. West Germany outperformed the East in every sphere with the exception of pumping athletes full of drugs. There was, it's true, marginally better job security in the East, but it was security in jobs that few wanted, making products that even fewer desired. And as with North Korea, East Germany was able to exist only by creating and maintaining a vast network of spies, colleague snitching on colleague, neighbour snooping on neighbour, even brother betraying brother. In any case, when the Wall came down, it wasn't West Germans clamouring to embrace Stalinism. The traffic was all the other way.

These are mostly obvious points. Too obvious, one would hope, to require even this cursory recapitulation. And they are in a sense beside the point. For the point is this: 799,455 executions. How do you get beyond a statistic like that? What length of pause is decent enough before you can move on to the excellent results in tractor production or the first-rate exam scores in Marxist–Leninist thought? And is there any rational argument worth having that takes you from 799,455 executions to driving up welfare standards in the West?

The other point about that obscene figure is that it grossly understates the deaths for which the Soviet state was responsible, not least the millions who died in the slave camps of the Gulag. Anne Applebaum notes in her exhaustive *Gulag: A History* that, unlike German concentration camps, the Russian concentration camp system was 'not deliberately organized to mass-produce corpses – even if, at times, it did'. And how it did. The incomplete archival figures puts the death toll in camps during the Stalin era at 2,749,163. But, as Applebaum points out, the number who died as a result of the Red Terror, the civil war, mass deportations, in the camps of the twenties and between Stalin's death and the eighties is estimated to be anywhere between 10 and 20 million. Stalin, who knew the truth of his words, famously said that one death is a tragedy, a million is a statistic. And 10 to 20 million is not even a statistic – it's a rough approximation that owing to its flexibility stretches easily into the disputed territory of rumour and from there, with a tug or two, into the reassuring realm of fiction.

So to avoid being dragged in that direction by the Gulag deniers, let us just stick with the bizarrely precise aggregate official figures of 3,548,618 state murders.

OK, it lacks the totemic power of the 6 million Holocaust dead. And as Martin Amis noted in *Koba the Dread*, we all know the names of Auschwitz, but how many of us know the name of the Soviet concentration camps? But still: *3,548,618* state murders.

That's what it took – leaving aside the enforced famines, mass resettlements, torture and imprisonment – to get the Soviet Union to the terrorised and subdued state in which it could be policed by party idiots like Brezhnev, Andropov and Chernenko. But of course those are just the murders in the Soviet Union. They don't take into account Eastern Europe or China or North Korea or Cambodia, all of which followed from the Soviet example. And with these cases we find further and more egregious examples of Gulag denial. Despite the exposure of Pol Pot's murderous regime, armed and supported by China, and the growing revelations about the nightmare of North Korea, armed and supported by China, the exotic, dare I say inscrutable, image of China has made Gulag denial still easier and more acceptable. Take the example of Tony Benn, the veteran Labour Party left-winger. In the seventies and eighties, Benn was regularly portrayed in the press as a left-wing lunatic hell-bent on destroying British society. Now he is of the age when he is nominated as the nation's 'political hero' in a BBC poll and even his fiercest critics tend to describe him in sweet avuncular terms. Benn is a serious, committed politician, an active democrat, and a practising Christian who was a hardworking and conscientious MP. What's more he is perfectly sane, rational in debate, and willing to make his case to any audience that will receive him. He also makes a point of emphasising the importance of political movements and playing down the significance of individuals. 'Remember,' he self-deprecatingly told one interviewer when he was put up for another Man of the Year award, 'that progress is always made by political movements, never by guys on white horses.' And yet this is his entry for his diary of 6 June 1996:

> Had a long talk to the Chinese First Secretary at the embassy – a very charming man called Liao Dong – and said how much I admired Mao Tse tung or Zedong, the greatest man of the twentieth century. He said that I couldn't admire Mao more than he did. I asked him how Mao was viewed now. He said Mao was 70 per cent right and 30 per cent wrong; the Cultural Revolution didn't work. He said he had been named after Mao – it was amusing.

By 1996 no one with even a passing interest in China could be unaware of the massive scale of Mao's crimes. Deaths alone for which his autocratic rule was responsible far exceed even those of Stalin, with estimates ranging between 30 and 70 million. Those dreadful figures do not take into account the widespread and summary imprisonment, torture, purges, intimidation, terror, arbitrary cruelty, enforced cult-worship and the wholesale abuse of human rights that were the hallmark of Mao's leadership. And Mao spoke openly about being prepared to lose two to three hundred million Chinese in a nuclear war if the result was the defeat of capitalism. The 70/30 per cent figure parroted by Liao Dong, and recorded approvingly by Benn, was the one Deng Xiaoping, the leader who followed Mao, made up to allow a limited amount of political reform without risking the loss of power. To this day the Chinese Communist Party cannot admit to the extent of the tyranny and madness of the Mao years because it would destroy the myth and pseudo-history on which the party's authority rests. Nevertheless, the deranged pathology of the man became all too apparent following his death in 1976 and beyond question with the publication of *The Secret Speeches of Chairman Mao* in 1989.

It was one thing for my maths teacher, the goth Maoist, to fantasise about a workers' utopia back in the mid-seventies, when Mao's Great Proletarian Cultural Revolution brought death, jail and abject misery to 100 million of his countrymen. But for a well-read politician with international contacts to laud the century's greatest murderer as its greatest man, at a time when the gruesome facts were well established, is much harder to skirt around. Or again, it should be. But no one accused Benn of glorifying mass homicide. His reputation is under no threat, certainly not among sympathisers on the left. Here are the citations for him when he was voted twelfth in the *New Statesman*'s Top 50 Heroes of Our Time last year: 'He recognised the need for dignity in the lives of others, and respected it as much as his own'; 'A tireless campaigner for social justice and peace within a democratic framework. A true hero of the people.' Now how do those noble tributes fit with venerating a dictator who showed no compunction in consigning millions of his countrymen to death? Students of unintended irony will perhaps appreciate the title of the volume of Benn's diaries in which the above entry is found: *Free at Last!*.

It's necessary at this stage to state what should not need to be stated, namely that the Benns and Milnes and Murrays of this world have a perfect right to think what they wish and to write what they choose. Just as newspapers have the same right to publish the results. And these rights must be vigorously protected regardless of the fact that they tend not to exist in the regimes to which the above names like to offer their support. The problem, as far as I can see, does not lie with such people, who, at least in the cases mentioned, are sincere in their beliefs. No, the problem resides with their casual readers or followers, people who adopt second- or third-hand positions for the sake of radical fashion, people who think Benn or Chomsky are somehow, despite their one-eyed obsessions, dedicated to telling the truth, people whose nodding-dog opinions and posturing platitudes form the chorus of complacent leftish-liberal debate, people who sit up and take notice at the mention of the Pavlovian trigger words 'right wing' and 'America' yet close their ears and eyes to the heinous crimes committed in the name of the 'left'. People, that is, like me, or the person I was content to be.

No one has ever exposed this mentality, and particularly its English incarnation, with more clarity and authority than George Orwell. Having taken a bullet to the neck in the Spanish Civil War, fighting for the Republican cause, Orwell was hounded out of Spain by Stalinists, under threat of death. Sick with TB, he expended all his depleted energy in writing his two cautionary masterpieces, *Animal Farm* and *1984*, the latter a book that over fifty years ago anticipated the monstrous reality of current-day North Korea. And he died from the exertion. He was not a secular saint, he was more often than not wrong in his predictions, and his contradictions were many and striking. Yet he described in words a child could understand the lethal dangers to democratic society that so many adults refused to see. The first of these dangers was the threat of totalitarianism from the Soviet Union. One hypothetical question that rabid anti-Americans consistently manage not to ask themselves is what the world would have looked like if the Soviet Union had won the Cold War. Orwell, to his undying credit, had a pretty good idea and he tried until his last breath to let the world know. He also realised that the prevention of that outcome was not helped but hindered by people who put all their critical energy into rubbishing the democratic West while averting their gaze from the totalitarianism in the East.

In these endeavours he was constantly opposed by agents of the Soviet Union both real and unwitting. For example, Peter Smollett, a Soviet agent working at the Ministry of Information, advised Jonathan Cape not to publish *Animal Farm*, while Victor Gollancz rejected the book because he did not want to damage the image of the Soviet Union. Subject to this kind of literary silencing, the hovering danger of mortal silencing from Stalin's thugs (he was only too aware of Trotsky's fate), and his knowledge of the Gulags, Orwell understandably developed strong suspicions about those who were sympathetic to the USSR. And he voiced them accordingly.

In a book entitled *The Betrayal of Dissent*, a writer called Scott Lucas recently argued that it was Orwell, 'the policeman of the "left"', who did the silencing. He did so, apparently, by 'negative' attacks on the left and by 'vilifying' his opponents. One wonders what kind of dissenter is silenced by a solitary tubercular writer who was on his deathbed by the time he gained any fame. It's true that a terminally ill Orwell handed a list of thirty-eight names of suspected communist sympathisers to a friend, Celia Kirwan of the Labour government's Information Research Department. Orwell designated some of the names 'crypto-communists' and 'fellow-travellers', while others were left with just a question mark. The idea, it seems, was to warn the IRD, which was trying to counter Soviet propaganda, which writers and artists could not be trusted. On the list were Smollett, the Soviet spy, and Tom Driberg – 'Usually named as "crypto",' Orwell wrote, 'but in my opinion NOT reliably pro-CP.' Driberg, gossip columnist, Labour MP, High Church Anglican, and legendarily promiscuous homosexual, was in fact later revealed in KGB papers to be a Soviet agent, though, as Orwell suggested, he was almost certainly not a very reliable spy. We can get an idea of how the fiendish British state responded to Orwell's information by the fact that Smollett was awarded an OBE and Driberg was made a peer. There is no evidence that anyone on Orwell's list, which included E.H. Carr, Isaac Deutscher and Michael Redgrave, ever suffered any recrimination at the hands of the state – quite the opposite (Redgrave was later knighted) – but it is possible that they were not approached to disseminate anti-Soviet information. The existence of the list was first revealed in a 1996 news story in the *Guardian* co-written by Seamus Milne. 'The revelation is likely to shock many of Orwell's admirers,' he wrote, 'for whom he is a 20th century radical icon.' And it was a shock, a much greater shock, for example, than the revelation two years earlier in *The Spectator* that Milne's colleague Richard Gott had been a paid informant for the KGB. In resigning from the *Guardian*, Gott denied the allegation, but admitted that he accepted from the Soviet intelligence service expenses-paid foreign trips to meet its agent.

'The significance of "The List",' writes Lucas, 'is not what it says about the 38, but what it offers us about Orwell.' Well, one of the things it offers us about Orwell is that he was right about Smollett. Another is that as Stalin ruthlessly ensnared Central and Eastern Europe, and was rhapsodised in fashionable London circles, Orwell was determined that his supporters and apologists should be made known to British propagandists. Whether Orwell was wrong to do this is, I think, a difficult question to answer, though I suspect many on the left would find it easy to answer if it was a list of Nazi sympathisers. But in 1949 Nazism was dead, while Stalinism was working overtime, slaughtering, imprisoning and enslaving.

On the cover of my copy of Lucas's book there is a quote from Peter Wilby, then editor of the *New Statesman*. It describes the work as 'completely fearless'. What fear, the reader is bound to ask, is it that Lucas has had to overcome? Fear of the secret police? Of imprisonment? Torture? Or is it fear of losing tenure at Birmingham University? Of course none of these fears exist in the open democratic society which Orwell spent his last days working to maintain, though they very definitely would have been legitimate fears had characters like Smollett had their way. Perhaps, then, Wilby means fearless in the sense that Lucas had nothing to fear, which seems a curious application of the word. In any case, Lucas's argument is that any kind of criticism of left orthodoxy, even if it targets those who cosy up to dictators and tyrants, is by definition a betrayal of dissent because it coincides with the interests of the state. It's a simplistic thesis which reduces the complex and often antagonistic components of the democratic state to a single ideological standpoint. It also assumes that this (largely fictional) standpoint is again by definition wrong. Whether it would continue to be wrong if an orthodox left-wing government had complete control of the state Lucas neglects to say. Perhaps because his main concern is to insist that Orwell and those journalistic heirs who invoke his name – Christopher Hitchens is fingered as the prime culprit – have tried to 'shut down dissent'. Did an Orwell sympathiser from the government warn Lucas's publishers not to go to print? Has an Orwell acolyte prevented Lucas, who boasts of his regular contributions to the *New Statesman*, or anyone else from voicing their dissent? Given that the dissent that most concerns Lucas is the opposition to the war in Iraq, the answer would have to be a resounding no. Countless books have been published opposing the Iraq War, newspapers like the *Guardian* and the *Independent* have been filled with anti-war voices, who have also gained a considerable hearing in the *Daily Mail* and *Daily Telegraph*. The same can be said for radio, television and, indeed, cinema. So by any tangible measure Lucas is talking the most paranoid nonsense. But that isn't the strangest part of his argument. The strangest part is that many people agree with him.

I don't mean that lots of people bought his book – he was

silenced only by a lack of readers – but that many on the left believe, or like to believe, that they are assailed by establishment forces. And as they have been so brave as to stand up to these ruthless if invisible forces, they expect the full loyalty of their comrades. Unfortunately this brand of group-think runs right through radical politics. Anyone who dares to bring attention to the diaphanous line of clothing the group has taken to wearing is condemned as a sell-out, a lackey, a counter-revolutionary. Increasingly you see this same dynamic of control characterises ethnic, cultural and religious politics. There is almost no political forum in this country at which it would require the slightest courage to get up and denounce Tony Blair or George Bush, nor any in which there would be deleterious repercussions. But there are plenty of environments in which it would take a stiffened resolve to speak out against, say, a community leader or a religious ideologue. Few want to risk being tagged as an 'Uncle Tom' or, more intimidatingly, an 'apostate'.

It is around this kind of communalist politics that much of the old anti-West left now gravitate in the hope of encouraging discontent and recruiting new blocks of support. Some of these groups, like George Galloway's and the SWP's Respect Party, still harbour the fantasy of the unified collective. But while loud and accomplished in protest politics, they are small and of limited significance. A more pervasive theme shared by the old left, and the new multiculturalist left, and seen in local government, academia and some areas of the media is the old loathing of Western society and humanist values that blinded a previous generation to the horrors of communism. The anti-Westernism no longer takes the rigid form of pro-communism but instead the more protean shape of cultural relativism. The job now is to overlook the abuse of women and homosexuals, to legitimise superstition, deride secularism, pour scorn on Enlightenment values, and recast religious terrorism as a simple function of Western brutality.

This form of denial may not be as extreme or ambitious

as Gulag denial but it does stem from the same instinct, the guileless preference for any group or idea that stands opposed to liberal democracy. It therefore behoves anyone who is a liberal and a democrat to think about how much encouragement and support they want to extend to such people and ideologies. For there is little doubt that separatism is being actively fostered by anti-liberals, many of whom were once Soviet apologists, and cultural ghettos are beginning to take shape. In cities across Britain and Europe the wall-builders are once again at work.

7

The Cult of Multiculturalism

One of the many unexpected effects of the 9/11 attacks was to make multiculturalism a topic of urgent debate. For a number of years, at least in polite circles, multiculturalism had been beyond discussion, accepted as much a part of modern Western society as sexual equality and gay rights. But it was not long after the smoke began to clear over Manhattan that commentators started to ask if multiculturalism was in some way to blame. At first it seemed a strange choice of suspect because, in the most obvious sense of the word, multiculturalism was the victim. There was, after all, no more multicultural city in the world than New York. Representatives of every class, race, sexuality and culture perished in the World Trade Center. Multiculturalism, it could be legitimately argued, was not the cause but the target of the terrorists.

But the concern of those who questioned the role of multiculturalism was that the people who planned, organised and carried out the attack on the WTC and the Pentagon were products of a culture – radical Islam – that was vehemently opposed to 'Western' culture. Therefore, they asked, was it sensible or possible, in the name of cultural diversity, to support and encourage cultures that sought to attack the host culture. They pointed to the Hamburg cell, the group of 9/11 terrorists who formed around Mohammed Atta in Germany. They were students who had reaped the benefits of Western education, were accustomed to Western lifestyle and yet remained dedicated to its destruction. Moreover, they were in contact with a whole continent-wide network of Islamists who took advantage of Europe's tolerant political and social atmosphere to ferment hatred of political and social tolerance. It seemed only natural to ask how they could have gained from Western freedoms and yet resented the existence of such freedoms. And from asking that it was only a short step to wondering if a multicultural society could or should incubate cultures that rejected the liberal principles on which multiculturalism rested. The question that would be repeatedly posed was whether tolerance by definition necessitated the acceptance of intolerance.

Then as the weeks and months passed it became clear that the apologists for the terrorists rejected the idea that the pluralist liberal democracies of the West were in fact multicultural. To those who sought to explain the motivation of the suicide killers in sympathetic terms, the multi-ethnic, multinational, pan-sexual profile of those slaughtered in the World Trade Center was more properly representative of a monoculture culture: Western culture. And behind Western culture's claims of diversity and tolerance was a controlling ideology: capitalism. What is more, in this reckoning, the perpetrators of the atrocity represented a culture that had been stifled and oppressed by Western capitalism. Thus 9/11 – like the other massacres that would follow – was an expression of an alternative culture whose voice had been suppressed in the global dialogue. Indeed, the very brutality of the crime paid testament to the weight of that suppression suffered by the culprit. Two and a half years after 9/11, John Pilger responded to the bombing of Madrid commuter trains by Islamist terrorists with these words: 'The current threat of attacks in countries whose governments have close alliances with Washington is the latest stage in a long struggle against the empires of the west, their rapacious crusades and domination. The motivation of those who plant bombs in railway carriages derives directly from this truth.' This, in essence, was the 'satisfactory picture' that Frederic Jameson had suggested that we should wait to see emerge.

119

What seems significant to me about Pilger's claim was that the people who blew up over two hundred Spaniards in Madrid were based in Spain. They worked, lived and took part in Spanish culture, which though not as multicultural as that of other Western nations was far more open and tolerant and diverse than the culture from which its attackers originated. Had multiculturalism created the conditions for its own destruction?

The process of changing one's mind is seldom a conversion of Damascene rapidity. There's usually too much intellectual pride, and too much social or professional investment suddenly to dispatch long-held ideas to the conceptual waste bin. Even when we can no longer persuade ourselves of an argument's validity, there is often a reluctance to abandon a discredited position because to do so would amount to deserting our ideological tribe. It seems disloyal, a betrayal of a shared vision. Such was the case for me with multiculturalism. For a number of years I had thought of multiculturalism as akin to what the philosopher Kwame Anthony Appiah calls 'cosmopolitanism' – a sort of 'we are the world' outlook derived from the classical meaning of cosmopolitan: 'universal citizen'. If I had had to articulate what I meant by the word, I would probably have come up with something woolly and idealistic like 'the free exchange of different cultural perspectives'. To put it more simply, I subscribed (and in fact still do) to the belief that cultural diversity was not only beneficial but preferable. By the end of the 1990s, when it had become more or less a moral principle and strategic policy of most Western European governments, multiculturalism seemed as inseparable from liberalism as to be virtually synonymous.

The origins and specific meaning of multiculturalism are subject to disagreement but it's safe to say that its main antecedent was the civil rights movement in the United States. Whatever else multiculturalism was about, it was concerned to protect minority rights in majority cultures. To be in favour of multiculturalism, then, was to support equality and liberty.

To be an opponent was to be racist, xenophobic, prejudiced. It wasn't a difficult choice. But what did the choice mean in practice? By the turn of the millennium, my home city of London had become one of the most cosmopolitan places on earth. Only American cities could rival its diversity. But whereas America was founded by immigrants and became home to the world's huddled masses, London's historic role has been very different. As the capital of the world's first industrialised nation, it had its own masses, drawn from throughout Britain and Ireland. Up until the end of the Second World War, there had been no need to import labour. The workforce had always comfortably (which is to say uncomfortably) outstripped available work. Like any large city, and especially one that was the centre of a vast empire, London naturally drew inhabitants from across the planet. But they made up a tiny minority of the populace, small communities of Italians, Jews, Chinese and Poles, for example, that gathered in self-sufficient neigh-bourhoods and made limited claim on the capital's identity. As late as 1950 the overwhelming spirit of the city was Anglo-Saxon. It was also, after the toll of two wars, exhausted.

Mass immigration in the second half of the twentieth century not only helped revive London but reinvented it as a global city. It now houses people from every nation on earth. A 2001 census found that over a quarter of Londoners were born outside the UK, and two-fifths of all Londoners were non-white British. What's more, this extraordinary transfor-mation took place with scarcely any of the ethnic tensions that played such a defining part in shaping, for example, New York's sense of self. Never before in peacetime had a city received so many and so varied a number of foreigners with so little communal conflict.

Working as a journalist in the nineties there were occa-sions on which I would turn a blind eye to cultural practices that were problematic or difficult to reconcile with a liberal outlook. For example, when writing a long magazine article about police and crime in east London I decided to omit one officer's comment to me regarding the high incidence of forced marriages and domestic violence among the local Muslim community. It seemed unnecessarily targeted and I feared that, even if I reported it in such a way as to reflect the officer's own attitudes, it might be construed as anti-Muslim. There were other similar cases of negative cultural images that I steered clear of, none of which amounted to much in the grand scheme of things, but taken together might perhaps have been seen as a double standard. Had they concerned groups from the indigenous culture I very much doubt I would have hesitated to make reference to them. But I reasoned that members of more recently imported cultures had enough problems to contend with without receiving any extra pressure from the liberal press.

Still, my first serious doubts about the direction of multiculturalism predated 9/11. They actually took root the year before with the publication of a book called *The Future of Multi-Ethnic Britain*, said to be the most comprehensive review of British identity and race relations of its time. A kind of blueprint for how to manage cultural diversity, it was produced by a commission of eminent cultural theorists, social policy types and some prominent liberal journalists. In keeping with the mainstream make-up of the commission, the report was not particularly extreme. Many of its suggestions were in fact constructive and based on sound practical sense, even if they were written in the tortured prose of politically correct committee-speak. Yet there was a certain tone of contempt towards the established or 'majority' communities, an implicit understanding that the burden of cultural adjustment was overwhelmingly their responsibility, that wilfully failed to take account of how societies have historically operated. The idea that in the give and take of cultural exchange newcomers were obliged to take stock of local customs and values was treated almost as uncouth racism. Indeed, the report went so far as to conclude that the very word British 'has systematic, largely unspoken, racial connotations'. Its answer was to envision a loosely formed state with minimal social solidarity, a so-called 'community of communities' in which separate groups maintained their own culturally derived systems of morality.

The chair of the commission was Bhikhu Parekh, a Labour peer and former deputy chair of the Commission for Racial Equality. Underpinning Parekh's vision of multiculturalism was the belief that morality was culturally specific, that no culture should be judged by the terms of another. A communalist who saw cultural identity as inherited rather than freely chosen, he emphasised group rights in favour of individual rights. Parekh, that is to say, was a cultural relativist. And his book helped me to understand that I was not.

In my conception of multiculturalism all cultures had something to contribute and gain, not least the dominant culture. Only a myopic bigot could look at the indigenous tendency towards drunkenness, random violence, snobbery, disrespect for the elderly, by way of a small sample of Britain's less appealing habits, and think that the established populace had nothing to learn from newer arrivals. Coming from a background of narrow-mindedness that was suspicious of change, I appreciated the innovation and improvements that other cultures had brought to London life in areas as disparate as gastronomy, literature, music and street life. And I noted the irony of how those who made triumphal noises about 'British culture' often knew so little, and cared even less, about the history – great works, artists, philosophers and writers – from which it was formed. In the same way that so many illiterates took to burning *The Satanic Verses*, the archetypal British nationalist's major cultural references were football and the pub.

Yet notwithstanding those observations, a major thrust of the British story over the centuries has been emancipation: religious, political and, increasingly in the last century, social and sexual. As a result of this protracted and sometimes bloody struggle, British culture, however it is divided and defined, is both reflected in and a reflection of certain rights, liberties, responsibilities, protections and opportunities. It's not perfect, and progression and adaptation should be integral to any living culture, but I had to acknowledge that I thought these principles and the attitudes they fostered preferable to the petty corruption, sexism, homophobia, tribalism and patriarchal authoritarianism that were characteristic of many traditional cultures in the Third World.

No doubt that sounds rather harsh given the obvious cultural richness that exists in the Third World, but I'm referring to the sort of practices witnessed in the Birmingham postal vote fraud of 2004, what Salma Yaqoob, head of the Birimingham Stop the War Coalition and national vice chair of Respect, attributed in the *Guardian* to 'Biraderi politics – loyalties based on clan or kinship links' in South Asian Muslim communities. I'm also thinking of the experience suffered by a professor who left England to go to Baroda University in India. He received death threats from students who demanded degrees without exams, and his wife was told that she would be sent a bag containing her husband's bones. The professor, understandably, soon returned to the more sedate environment of British academe. His name was Bhikhu Parekh.

The Parekh report avoided that kind of comparison, restricting itself to anecdotes that exposed the racism, small-mindedness and ignorance of British mainstream culture. Its argument was that all cultures had their plus and minus points, but its recommendation was the need to focus on the minus points of the majority culture. That was a healthy and necessary process, while drawing any attention to the negative aspects of minority cultures was seen as dangerous and counterproductive.

The report approvingly quoted Ben Okri: 'Stories are the secret reservoir of values: change the stories individuals and nations live by and tell themselves and you change the individuals and nations . . . If they tell themselves stories that are lies, they will suffer the future consequences of those lies. If they tell themselves stories that face their own truths, they will free their histories for future flowerings.' But the report intended this truth-telling to be directed at British myths, not the stories that other cultures are built upon. Those were to be respected. Parekh and his commission wanted to see a full and frank debate about British identity and the imperialist history, racist myths and political fallacies on which it was based, the better to accommodate other and newer cultures that had been marginalised from the story. And it simultaneously argued that the minority community cultures were fundamental to identity and were therefore not up for discussion.

I presumed, though I didn't dare articulate the thought out loud, that one of the reasons that such large numbers of people moved halfway across the world to live in Britain, and one of the reasons why an even greater number wished to do the same, was in some sense out of sympathy with its values. Put simply, they wanted to take advantage, in the innocent meaning of the phrase, of its freedoms and the rule of law. It also seemed to me that cultural ideas were competitive and their wider authority was contingent either on strength of numbers or strength of argument, but not because they were notionally representative of a defined cultural group. So when it came to a conflict between, say, freedom of expression and religious belief, and the dominant sympathies were in favour of freedom of expression, then the case for religious belief needed to be more compelling than just 'cultural respect'. For Parekh this was a liberal misnomer.

The Parekh report got me thinking about multiculturalism, about Britain, about identity, common values and social cohesion. I sensed that these were destined to be defining issues of the new millennium and, as a journalist, I wanted to find some way of writing about them, partly to find out what I really thought. But what right did I have to talk about multiculturalism? I was white, now middle class, and male. These biographical facts seemed to disqualify me from comment, at least from a liberal perspective, and therefore I decided to let the issue pass. It felt better and easier to hold on to a vague, unproblematic appreciation of cultural diversity without following through on what it actually entailed.

I had taken much the same silent, 'nothing to do with me, guv' stance during the controversy over the publication of *The Satanic Verses* back in 1989. In the Parekh report *The Satanic Verses* affair is described as an example of discrimination and marginalisation. According to Parekh the discrimination and marginalisation were not aimed at the book's author, Salman Rushdie, who was threatened with death and forced into hiding, but at the Muslim community at large. As Parekh commented at the time, shortly after the fatwa was issued by Ayatollah Khomeini, and in defence of the book-burning mobs who took to the streets of Bradford in celebration of the fatwa, 'Religion requires a greater degree of sensitivity.' Not for religion the myth-exploding treatment prescribed by Parekh for nationalism. Religion was a special case that required protection from the insensitivities of rational and even fictional discourse.

In fact, *The Satanic Verses* affair represented a vital juncture in the multicultural experience and, like far too many people, I failed to grasp its significance until much later. I found it hard to take the whole drama very seriously. It seemed a bit of a joke, almost like a fictional story itself. Some bearded fanatic thousands of miles away entices pious bibliophobes to murderous rage. And what date does he choose to send his message of hate? Valentine's Day. Then there was the imperious-looking Rushdie, with his mandarin sneer, darting between secret hideouts and London literary parties. Surely there was nothing to get too hot under the collar about. Was it not the ideal occasion on which to deploy the famous British sense of humour? Granted, there was that unfortunate incident in 1991 when Hitoshi Igarahi, the novel's translator in Japan, was stabbed to death, and also the Italian translator, Ettore Capriolo, was badly wounded. And, yes, in 1993 William Nygaard, the Norwegian publisher, was shot and gravely injured. Also, in the same year, thirty-seven

Turkish intellectuals were burned to death in an Islamist arson attack in an attempt to kill Aziz Nesin, the Turkish translator. Oh, and twelve people died in anti-Rushdie rioting in Bombay. But, really, had anything grievous taken place in Britain?

Yes. A British citizen was placed under mortal threat in his homeland, forced to live with round-the-clock police protection, because an Iranian cleric – a man who had written on such weighty issues as in which conditions it was permissible to have sex with a goat – declared that the novelist should die for having written a fictional dream sequence in his fiction. If British citizenship meant anything, if British freedoms were not to fold when put to the test, and if British culture and society had developed since William Tyndale was burned at the stake in 1536 for translating the Bible, then people like me, people who earned their living writing words and spent their leisure time reading them, should have made the clearest stand in solidarity with Rushdie. He should have received the protection of not just the police but the public at large. Together the British people, and in particular its intellectuals, ought to have sent out the most uncompromising message that tyranny, superstition and religious censorship were not part of modern Britain.

In the event it did not work out like that. A number of Rushdie's fellow authors, such as John Berger, John Le Carré and Roald Dahl, decided that Rushdie was the author of his own travails. And with a minority of stalwart exceptions, the general response of the liberal intellectual community was to plant its flabby buttocks on the nearest fence at hand. Everyone had a right to their opinion and this was a matter of opinion, not a principle of historic importance. On the one hand, you had people who believed literature was boundless and no one was under any compulsion to read it. And on the other, you had people who thought a suitable punishment for imaginative prose was death. In a multicultural society, it seemed, you had to accept that neither was right or wrong. To grant the two positions notional equality was to tolerate not only the intolerant but the intolerable. Alas, that is precisely what happened.

'It was a seminal moment in British Muslim history,' the Muslim Council of Britain spokesman Inayat Bunglawala later told me. 'It brought Muslims together. Before that they had been identified as ethnic communities but *The Satanic Verses* brought them together and helped develop a British Muslim identity.' It's easy to let the words of sentences like that slip by like well-dressed gatecrashers, without checking their credentials. 'Ethnic', 'communities', 'identity': the guilty liberal instinct is to nod them through on sight. But in effect Bunglawala was saying that burning books and intimidating authors was central to Muslim identity. It's not, of course. But that was the kind of offensive idea with which community leaders were happy to libel hundreds of thousands of people in an effort to co-opt them into an imagined community.

Nor was Bunglawala some street-corner crank, ignored by the powers that be. For several years he and the MCB had the ear of the British government as the main spokespeople for British Muslims. One of the leaders of the anti-Rushdie protest was Iqbal Sacranie, who would go on to become head of the MCB. At the time of the fatwa, Sacranie proclaimed that death was 'too easy' for Rushdie. Bunglawala explained to me that Sacranie's formulation was in fact a piece of nifty semantics. 'He had to somehow put across the view that he did not support the fatwa without also distancing himself from ordinary Muslim opinion' (the implication being that ordinary Muslims wanted Rushdie dead). When I asked why Sacranie had to pretend to hold a view, just because others from his faith held it, Bunglawala told me that Sacranie's priority was his community. And for putting his community first – before the interests, for example, of a fellow citizen sentenced to death by a foreign tyrant – Sacranie was later awarded a knighthood by the British state.

People like Sacranie were not the only ones to treat Islam

as a pseudo race. In circumventing racial hatred laws, the far-right British National Party had begun to speak of 'Muslims' in the same derogatory language it had once used to describe 'Asians'. I went to interview Nick Griffin, the leader of the BNP, in 2002. A Cambridge law graduate with a history in far-right politics dating back to his childhood, Griffin is a naked but canny opportunist. He shifts political tack often and at will, but he sensed a change of wind in the post-9/11 era and he wanted to reposition his party to take maximum advantage. 'The tendency within the nationalist movement,' he told me, 'is to think within terms of multiracialism, but the debate will be about multiculturalism.' And in the multicultural discourse he was beginning to see ideas that he could appropriate for his party. For a start, there were a number of rhetorical touchstones – race, culture, identity (the BNP's magazine was called *Identity*) – that the nationalists and multiculturalists shared. But most promisingly for Griffin, if the logic of multiculturalism was one of distinct ethnic and cultural communities represented by community leaders, then he wanted the BNP to audition for the role of representatives of the 'white community'. The irony was that a number of those who presumed to speak for the BNP's new enemy – 'the Muslim community' – shared Griffin's views on several issues, not least Holocaust denial and homosexuality. Multiculturalism may have been anathema to the BNP but in practice multiculturalism favoured monoculturalists.

As the Nobel Prize-winning economist Amartya Sen noted in his book *Identity and Violence*:

The vocal defence of multiculturalism that we frequently hear these days is very often nothing more than a plea for plural monoculturalism. If a young girl in a conservative immigrant family wants to go out on a date with an English boy, that would certainly be a multicultural initiative. In contrast, the attempt by her guardians to stop her from doing this (a common enough occurrence) is hardly a multicultural move, since it seeks to keep the cultures sequestered. And yet it is the parents' prohibition, which contributes to plural monoculturalism, that seems to get most of the vocal and loud defence from alleged multiculturalists, on the ground of the importance of honouring traditional cultures, as if the cultural freedom of the young woman were of no relevance whatever, and as if the distinct cultures must somehow remain in secluded boxes.

After 9/11 those boxes appeared to grow larger and more secluded. In Britain and the rest of Western Europe many young Muslims began to perceive 9/11 as an empowering experience, something which enabled them to reconnect with their cultural identity. As one Muslim correspondent to the *Guardian* wrote, explaining his daughters' decision to adopt the hijab: 'Since 9/11 however, they will not relinquish the "headgear". It would be a sign of defeat. Whilst worn, it symbolises resistance.' Religious dress and fundamentalist opinions gained greater popularity, especially following the overthrow of the Taliban in Afghanistan in November 2001. This growth in Islamic identity and militancy was portrayed in liberal circles as a reaction not only against Western imperialism in Afghanistan, but also the increased prejudice and policing Muslims suffered post-9/11 at home, a show of defiance in the face of a coordinated global and domestic campaign of Islamophobia. But I couldn't help but wonder if multiculturalism, and its emphasis on difference and separateness and communal identity, hadn't played a part in making a difficult situation worse.

The year before I saw Griffin, and a few months before 9/11, a number of mill towns in the north of England were convulsed by riots. Pitched battles were fought between gangs of South Asian youths and gangs of white youths, and against the police. Shops and cars were burned, and severe damage was done to community relations. If they were in some sense a protest, the riots did not appear explicitly Muslim in character, though they involved men who were largely from a Muslim background and some reports suggest that rioters in Bradford targeted only non-Muslim-owned (including Hindu) shops and businesses. By and large news coverage at the time preferred the description of 'Asian' or 'Pakistani and Bangladeshi', though many Asians now defined themselves, as Bunglawala had hoped, in terms of religious affiliation rather than geographical or national heritage.

The first riot took place in Oldham a few weeks before the general election held in June 2001. In that election the BNP registered its best result in the country in Oldham West, where Griffin took 16 per cent of the vote. It was commonly agreed that the BNP had provoked confrontation in Oldham. Tony Blair attributed the blame to the 'bad and regressive motive of white extremists'. And no doubt the BNP did its worst. But the story was more complicated than that. Not long before the riot, it was announced that there had been 572 race-related crimes in the Oldham area. It was a grim figure that captured local headlines, not least because in 62 per cent of these crimes the victim was recorded as white. The BNP naturally used this statistic to maximum divisive effect. In response, it was claimed that South Asians were less likely to report racial abuse or attacks because they had less confidence in the police. Either way it pointed to a fault line whose troubling depth and breadth were detailed in a report that was written by Lord Ouseley on Bradford, a town with similar problems to Oldham and which had also suffered race riots. Ouseley described communities that lived completely separate lives, segregated schools in which 98 per cent of the pupils were Asian or white, estranged neighbourhoods, a belief on both sides of the cultural divide that the local council favoured the other community, and a police force that was afraid to tackle ethnic minority crime for fear of being labelled racist.

I visited Burnley, the scene of yet another riot, where the BNP had scored its second highest general election result.

The story was much the same. Two communities with nothing in common except their proximity to each other in a doleful post-industrial town desperately in need of regeneration. It didn't need a major effort of investigative journalism to see that white racism was a factor in creating division and tension in the town. But it could not be said that it was the sole, or even most significant, polarising force. There were also testaments of violent Asian drug dealers, of town-hall favouritism towards Asians, of Asian attacks on whites, of white women being insulted and threatened for their immodest dress. It was possible, if one was of a mind, to dismiss these tales as further evidence of white racism. After all, many of those who made these claims were to be found in pubs, covered in tattoos, pushing prams and pulling ferocious dogs. And if there was one section of society about whom it was acceptable to be untrusting and disdainful it was the white working class in all its tracksuited, binge-drinking horror. However, the people who told me these stories seemed no less sincere than those who told me about violent white drinkers, white attacks on Asians, the town-hall favouritism towards whites, and the threats and insults levelled at Asian women in hijabs and niqabs. In short, it soon became apparent that the white and brown communities of Burnley were rent by mutual antipathy, distrust and suspicion. And far from growing closer together over the years of living side by side, they had retreated into their own exclusive neighbourhoods, the better to nurture hostility towards the other.

The more I spoke to people, the more it seemed that they had taken to their separate communities because they lacked a shared sense of belonging. In Burnley, a town with dwindling self-confidence, a struggling football team, and falling church attendance, one of the only abstractions to hold on to was 'Englishness' or 'Britishness'. But the symbols of English or British patriotism had long been abandoned by schools, local government and workplaces, and, by default, had become the preserve of the extreme right. To wave a

St George's Cross flag or a Union Jack was tantamount to a profession of racism. At the same time, South Asian communities in these northern mill towns were not only encouraged to celebrate their differing national identities – Pakistani, Bangladeshi, Indian – they were also drawn in growing numbers to the unifying and distinguishing forum of the mosque.

In Burnley I met the Labour MP Shahid Malik, an affable Lancastrian who came to public attention when trying to calm anti-BNP demonstrations in the Burnley riots. For his efforts he was beaten and handcuffed by the police, and the scene was captured on TV. With his strong local accent and open manner, Malik was able to move between the Asian and white communities with comparative ease. He described an upbringing of mixed friendships and a dual but integrated lifestyle. The dominant trend in Burnley, however, was in the other direction. The system was producing fewer individuals like Malik, who felt at home bestriding both camps. One of the main indicators of communal interaction are so-called 'mixed marriages'. Over the passage of time, mixed-heritage relationships are expected to increase in heterogenous societies. But in towns like Burnley and Oldham they still formed a tiny percentage of marriages. Social pressures on both sides mitigated against 'intermarriage', but there were also specific cultural reasons within the Asian community that made such marriages unlikely – chiefly the practice of importing arranged spouses from the subcontinent. In this respect multiculturalism, with its preference for group culture over individual rights, supported the status quo of division.

The difficulty I found in expressing this heresy, or even acknowledging it to myself, can be seen in the tentative conclusion I came to on this issue in the piece I published on Griffin in the *Observer*:

There are obviously economic solutions to the problems that beset places like Burnley, but perhaps more challenging are the cultural questions that also accompany them. At present, multicultural society has more than its share of inconsistencies, hypocrisies and contradictions. It's an idea that isn't sure how to become a reality. That's why it is often discussed in terms of vague generalities and hopeful platitudes. So far no one has come up with a post-imperial identity for Britain that is broad enough to be inclusive but relevant enough to want to be included in. There remains an uncertainty about how to embrace cultural diversity without succumbing to cultural relativism.

By the time the piece was published I was working on a journalistic assignment as a driver for a west London minicab firm. The idea was to write about the plight of the transient, ghostlike characters who did the kinds of jobs that no one else wanted to do. Randomly selecting one of the innumerable minicab calling cards routinely dropped through my letter box, I got a job in west London with a small company run by a Pakistani from Luton. I didn't need to show a driving licence or get insurance, and I soon learned that many of the other drivers had not bothered with either formality. All the other drivers were from Afghanistan or Iran. I was the only non-Muslim. In one of those natural ironies of which feature writers dream, the cab office was located in a sort of annexe of a particularly raucous pub.

No one knew that I was a journalist, and so no one spoke to me as if I was there to document their complaints. Instead what I learned about my co-workers emerged in unselfconscious conversations between job designations. A picture began to form that once again did not square with the approved image of cultural diversity, community relations or, indeed, asylum seekers. Most of the drivers had been granted or were seeking asylum, and the rest had been turned down. The standard liberal line on asylum was probably best exemplified by the Stephen Frears film *Dirty Pretty Things*. Here we saw a furtive world of plucky Third World workers relentlessly pursued by ruthless white officials from the Home Office. A few years later, it would be revealed that the Home Office had neither the manpower nor inclination to trace individual asylum seekers and that, in any case, such officials as there were came from many ethnic backgrounds.

But it was not the complacency of the failed asylum seekers I worked with, the complete absence of fear or concern about being 'caught', that most contradicted the prescribed version of the asylum experience. It was the cold contempt with which those granted asylum regarded their new home. The fact that their rent was paid by the state, their children had school places, and they had free access to the National Health system in no way softened their resentment of the country that had given them right of abode, the country they had traversed one and a half continents to make their new lives in. If anything, this beneficence seemed just another decadent aspect of a society – Western – for which they had little or no respect. Their attitude was that London was a city in which they could earn some money, but beyond that economic function the place meant nothing to them. Some of the drivers were Taliban sympathisers, some were admirers of Ayatollah Khomeini, but none were pro-British. Indeed the opposite was the case: being the only obvious 'Englishman', I was constantly reminded of the shortcomings of my country and its culture. The virulence of the anti-British sentiments sometimes embarrassed the Pakistani owner, who had lived in England for twenty years. Aside from the minicab firm, the owner maintained businesses in Pakistan, and was a skilled and seasoned tax avoider. Having had his own rent paid by the state for two decades, he was at least appreciative of what Britain had to offer. 'But these asylum seekers,' he announced with something close to exasperation, 'they think Britain owes them everything.'

Almost none of this I chose to report. There was a liberal way of telling a story and a reactionary way and I was a liberal of the left. Noble talk about 'objectivity' was all very well but in reality the journalist confronted choices of selection and focus. I was an *Observer* writer, and a *Guardian* contributor, the newspaper I'd always wanted to work for. I'd turned down a lucrative offer from the *Daily Mail* a couple of years before because I didn't like its politics, so why would I write anything that could be construed as a *Mail*-like attack on a minority? I knew that sensationalist reporting had played its part in worsening community relations in Oldham. Just prior to the Oldham disturbances a white World War II vet was mugged and badly assaulted by a group of Asians. The *Mirror* ran the story with the headline: 'BEATEN FOR BEING WHITE: OAP, 76, ATTACKED IN ASIAN NO-GO AREA', while the *Mail on Sunday* flagged the story: 'WHITES BEWARE'. This was just the kind of irresponsible troublemaking that I wanted to avoid. In the decade that I had been employed by the *Guardian* and the *Observer*, I had always known my targets. When I wrote about British society it was to criticise the Metropolitan Police or lament the racism that ethnic minorities faced.

So instead I picked out the few positive remarks I heard and put the best spin on the few negative comments I relayed from the group conversation that I had on 11 September 2002. It was Mossad who were behind the attacks the year before, I was confidently informed by all my co-workers, as proved by the fact that no Jewish workers went to the World Trade Center that day. Osama bin Laden could not possibly have organised such a complex and devastating plot, they all agreed, though simultaneously a few spoke of the pride that they felt for bin Laden's achievement. Princess Diana was killed by the British secret services because she was pregnant by a Muslim. I skipped over the irrational thinking, paranoia and conspiracy theories in a couple of paragraphs and, in a traditional coda played on the heartstrings, I made an appeal on behalf of the invisible people we prefer not to see.

I'd performed my liberal duty but the truth was I had seen close up the chasm between the wishful thinking of multi-culturalism and its unhappy reality. Married together were the most libertarian instincts of free-market globalism and blind cultural relativism to father a 'community of communities' whose only bond was economic necessity. It was possible, of course, that the minicab firm I worked at was an exception, and that elsewhere asylum seekers were filled with a common sympathy for modern British values and way of life. But if that was the case then it wasn't because British values and way of life were promoted by liberal society. Rather the progressive line was more in keeping with a comment I read by the cultural commentator Darcus Howe in the *New Statesman*. Speaking of Idi Amin's expulsion of Asians in the mid-1970s, Howe wrote: 'Just like their present equivalents – the asylum seekers – the Asians from Uganda came to what can only be described as the most inhospitable place on Earth.' He meant Britain, of course. Logic means that by this definition Britain, the country that took in, housed and educated the Ugandan Asians was more inhospitable than the country, Uganda, that had just confiscated their property, seized their money and ejected them under threat of death. And many people on the left would instinctively agree.

Similarly, asylum seekers were clinging to the bottoms of 150-mile-an-hour trains to get to Britain from France. No one had ever been caught taking the same risk on the return journey. Yet the Islamic rap artist Aki Nawaz echoed Howe's sentiments when he wrote in the *Guardian* of the 'pathetic and repulsive racism that is inherent in this [British] society'. Howe and Nawaz were strident but not lone voices. The view that new arrivals owe nothing to Britain but their disgust has been common enough on the left for many years.

Without a shared sense of purpose, the question remains, how could a society work that was dependent on the shared burden of welfare? This was the question I asked myself when I read Parekh's report. One example cited in the book was a complaint from a Somali organisation that health and social services offered little or no budgetary provisions for translators. With an estimated three hundred languages being spoken in London, a comprehensive translation service would place an insupportable financial liability on health authorities. Translations would eat into the budget of transfusions. In effect a non-English-speaking patient would require more money spent on him or her and, by the same token, reduce that spent on an English-speaking patient. Lee Jasper, one of multiculturalism's leading theologians and race adviser to the Mayor of London, once said that 'you have to treat people differently to treat them equally'. That's a difficult enough concept to sell at the best of times, but what if the patient has no intention of learning English or is discouraged from doing so by family members? In such a case citizens who invested least in society would gain most from its central pot. Common sense suggested that, in the long term, this was not a viable approach but ever since Marx exposed it as a ruling-class construct, common sense has not enjoyed a good reputation in left-wing circles.

Not until David Goodhart published a long essay in early 2004 in *Prospect* magazine did anyone describe the tensions between solidarity and diversity with intellectual rigour. '. . . the laissez faire approach of the postwar period,' concluded Goodhart, 'in which ethnic minority citizens were not encouraged to join the common culture (although many did) should be buried. Citizenship ceremonies, language lessons and the mentoring of new citizens should help to create a British version of the old US melting pot. This third way on identity can be distinguished from the coercive assimilationism of the nationalist right, which rejects any element of foreign culture, and from multiculturalism, which rejects a common culture.' It was a reasoned and thoughtful argument and for his pains Goodhart was predictably accused of racism. One of the members of the Parekh commission, Trevor Phillips, the chair of the then Commission for Racial Equality, compared Goodhart to Enoch Powell and Nick Griffin. What really bothers 'xenophobes' like Goodhart, suggested Phillips, was 'race and culture'.

Just two months later Phillips announced that multiculturalism was dead. It 'suggests separateness', he informed *The Times*. 'We are in a different world to the 1970s.' And presumably a different world to the one in which the Parekh report was produced only four years before. A couple of years later Phillips himself was accused by Ken Livingstone, the mayor of London, of moving so far to the right that 'soon he'll be joining the BNP', after he made a speech in which he said some parts of Britain were 'sleepwalking to segregation'.

Whenever you hear the word multiculturalism, someone, it seems, is bound to reach for their gun. The fear of the racism accusation has narrowed the debate, often with legitimate reason but increasingly to the point of unreason. Like all faiths, multiculturalism had constructed its own theology of irrational ideas and the stupefying effects of relativism have allowed those ideas to spread without informed debate. The outcome has been a corruption of identity politics. What started out as a means of liberating women, gays, blacks and assorted minorities from the tyranny of male or majority prejudices has, taken to its multicultural conclusion, imprisoned individuals in group identities. The promotion of faith schools, the rise of unelected leaders who presume to speak for whole communities, and the constant readiness to define people by their skin colour or religious heritage are all examples of this new approved repression. And the actuality of multiculturalism is that celebrating difference has become a means of enforcing group conformity. For a liberal society, that's not just an irony, it's a blatant injury.

8

The never-ending race

If a Martian stood outside my local train station and watched the passengers emerge in the evening, he would notice a striking division of movement. A disproportionately high number of people with black or dark skin turn right out of the station exit, and nearly everyone who turns left has white or light skin.

Does this parting of ways matter, and if so what can be done to break the pattern? These are questions that in varying forms are replicated up and down the country, across the Continent, the United States and many other parts of the world. The most obvious problem, in my local example, is to do with money. The neighbourhood directly to the south of the tube station is made up largely of subsidised local authority housing. The shops are boarded up, the petrol station that used to be there, run by an Asian family, was secured like a bank vault but nonetheless repeatedly held up by robbers. At night only young hooded men dare walk the dimly lit streets, and even during the day few use the thoroughfare on foot unless they have to. There is high unemployment among the young and a large number of families recently arrived from Africa, particularly the disintegrated state of Somalia. Social problems are rife and police cars pay frequent visits. A few years ago the grey council tower blocks gained brief national notoriety when a man grew fed up with his screaming baby granddaughter and threw her off a twelfth-floor balcony. This area has a high percentage of inhabitants with dark skin.

To the north of the station is a series of tree-lined and well-maintained Victorian terraced streets. There is an active residents' association, the main street features pretty cafés, a farmers' market, a fine delicatessen selling expensive European cheeses, a number of busy restaurants, a swanky boutique and a general air of satisfaction and well-being that, if one were feeling unkind, could be described as smug. This is where the people with light skin live.

So in one sense the divide is strictly socio-economic. It's the old cliché of the other side of the tracks. On the south side of the railway bridge the neighbourhood is working class, and on the north it's middle class. And if we left it like that we could say that the two areas simply reflect the uneven distribution of wealth that is the often unpleasant reality of all industrialised societies. After all, there are plenty of white people who live on the south side. But the conspicuous nature of skin colour, and the manner in which its distribution is so closely linked to low income, means that the direction people take each night from the station is not just a matter of class. Therefore if class is removed from the equation, then whatever remains – the complex tangle of biology, history, culture, bigotry and prejudice – is what is commonly referred to as race.

Race is the ghost in the social machine. Everyone knows it's there but no one, despite relentless efforts, can quite pin it down, much less 'deal' with it. A shape-shifter with a diabolical gift for evasion – one minute it's a cosy Benetton ad, the next it's hiding in the darkest recesses of the unconscious – race is the shadowy issue that stalks contemporary political debate, from the international corridors of power to the local school gate. A clue to its fiendish elusiveness is the way in which it constantly refashions language without ever being contained by words. To take just one example. It used to be that people now referred to as African hyphenates (African-American, Afro-Caribbean), and colloquially and still semi-officially known as 'black', were called, as a polite alternative to 'Negro', 'coloured people'. Nowadays that term is universally seen as offensive. But at the same time, the approved expression for non-whites is 'people of colour'. Squeezed between those essentially reversed phrases is a twisted tale of lexical uncertainty. And no one has proved more contorted and confused about race than the well-meaning Western liberal (who, just to further complicate matters, tends to have white skin).

Here are some statements on race:

Race is a biological fallacy.
There is only one race, the human race.
All races are equal.
Different races require different levels of support to redress the inequality they suffer.

Most liberal-minded people would probably agree with each of the individual points above, at least to some degree, but taken together they seem intellectually inconsistent. Does race exist or not? And if race does exist, are all races equal or not? These are just the beginning of the contradictions and anomalies that form the basis of contemporary racial discourse. Hardly any intelligent person believes that there is a uniform group of humans that are 'black' and another that is 'white'. Yet we routinely describe people in these terms. Indeed, governments and employers often demand that we define ourselves in this way. And frequently the most hard-line racial determinists are avowedly anti-racist. Here, for example, is a passage from the Parekh report, which, it's worth reminding ourselves, was meant to 'propose ways of countering racial discrimination'. It's taken from the 'Dealing with Racism' chapter: 'White men perceive Asian men as effeminate. Stand-offs between white male police officers and black youths on the street, or between white male teachers and black pupils, are imbued with a combination of sexual rivalry and racism.' Note that there are no qualifiers like 'some white men', no exceptions to the cast-iron rules of race.

In fact, as genetic markers go, skin pigmentation is neither particularly informative nor reliable. To say that someone has 'black' skin (which can mean anything from coffee-coloured through to dark brown but never black) tells us almost nothing about their genetic make-up. And to further complicate matters, people from mixed-heritage parents are by convention described as 'black'. All of which is enough to suggest that categories of racial group definitions are close to useless.

Race is a human invention twice over. In the first instance it's likely that what are loosely termed racial differences emerged through human migration, wherein different conditions encouraged different selection priorities. Thus minor genetic variations were established in distinct regional populations. But owing to an overdeveloped ability for visual classification, we have historically tended to read too much into differences that are largely skin-deep. As a result we invented race anew as a system of differentiation that was way out of proportion to the difference. The renowned geneticist R.C. Lewontin put it this way: 'It is clear that our perception of relatively large differences between human races and subgroups, as compared to the variation within these groups, is indeed a biased perception and that, based on randomly chosen genetic differences, human races and populations are remarkably similar to each other, with the largest part by far of human variation being accounted for by the differences between individuals.'

In its innocent manifestation racism is little more than a misleading urge to classify, what Richard Dawkins called the 'tyranny of the discontinuous mind'. But racism has also formed the scientifically approved rationale for slavery, colonialism and genocide. The fact is, though, that all things being equal, a random healthy child from one race is likely to achieve roughly the same in life as a random healthy child from another race. But all things are not equal, and the question continues to be: how can we create equal opportunities? The liberal consensus for the past half-century is that racism is

143

the main cause of inequality. Remove racism, the thinking goes, and equality will thrive. The problem with this analysis is that experience suggests otherwise. One obvious case in point is the academic performance of Afro-Caribbean boys in British schools. By most criteria and indicators racism has dropped dramatically in British society in the past few decades. The kinds of attitudes that were ubiquitous thirty years ago are sufficiently rare as to be shocking. Anti-racist initiatives and diversity awareness have been standard in schools and local authorities for a number of years. African and Asian faces at least have enough representation on television nowadays as to pass without notice, and popular culture is heavily populated with non-white idols. Even the police force, once a bastion of whiteness, is now multicoloured. Yet despite the apparent decrease in racism, Afro-Caribbean boys have consistently underachieved, particularly when compared to the academic performance of boys from other ethnic groups, such as Indian and Chinese.

According to the anti-racist analysis, the explanation is simple: racism has not diminished. It may be more subtle and nuanced but it's just as institutionally pernicious. The anti-racists, by which I mean those observers whose first instinct is to shout 'racism' and then construct a supporting argument later, cite the lack of black teachers as a key reason for the poor performance of black pupils. Yet the lack of black teachers does not explain why Indian and Chinese boys manage to perform so well with a corresponding shortfall in Indian and Chinese teachers. Nor does it explain why boys from African backgrounds outperform boys from Afro-Caribbean backgrounds. Or why children of Pakistani and Bangladeshi heritage trail a long way behind those from Indian heritage. Racism in the traditional sense of the word cannot account for these discrepancies. Racists, after all, are not known for their ability to distinguish from which part of the subcontinent a child comes. For anti-racists, the answer is to update the definition of racism. No longer is racism a matter of discrimination.

Instead, treating an Indian child the same as a Bangladeshi child, or a black boy the same as a white boy, is what now falls under the heading of racism. It has become racist *not* to discriminate.

Again, the origin of this approach is the United States and its affirmative-action programme of positive discrimination. Quite why a nation that was built on slavery and maintained racial segregation long into the second half of the twentieth century is seen as a model for race relations is a topic that never seems to have made it on to the political agenda. The implicit understanding is that racism, alone among social phenomena, transcends cultures, or 'white' cultures. It is the same wherever you go. While wars on abstract nouns like terror are ridiculed by the intelligentsia, the 'fight against racism' is not only accepted as a just and winnable cause, but its tactics and strategy have been imported and agreed upon with scarcely any public debate. So it is that the duty of society is not to examine how and why Indian boys thrive academically and seek to encourage non-Indian boys to adopt similar behaviour. That would suggest that Indian culture was in some respect superior to other cultures. Instead, society is charged with ensuring that Afro-Caribbean boys attain equality through attention to specific Afro-Caribbean needs. In Lee Jasper's formula: treat people differently to treat them equally. It's only the fact that Bangladeshis and Afro-Caribbean boys are not being treated differently enough that is holding them back. Inherent in this conception is the notion of discrete racial identities, a core of 'blackness' or 'Indianness' or, increasingly, 'Muslimness' that needs to be maintained against the dominance of 'whiteness'. Racial identity, we are told, is compromised by integration.

In which case I should presumably be relaxed about the racial division at my local tube station. Yet I'm not. When I see the racist Nation of Islam standing outside the station selling their message of racial segregation, I can't help but think that a form of segregation has already taken place,

145

without the help of the NoI, right on my doorstep. And living in a part of London with 60 per cent non-white inhabitants, I ask myself why so few of my friends and neighbours are non-white. Is it because I am sensitively refusing to impose my whiteness on members of ethnic minorities? Or is it, as cynics will doubtless conclude, because I'm an unreconstructed racist? The fiendish beauty of the charge of racism is that it can't be disproved: certainly not with the claim that 'some of my best friends are black'. The truth is I'd no more avoid friendship with someone because he was black than I would befriend someone else because he was white. Or vice versa. The friends I have that happen to be Afro-Caribbean, African and Asian are people that seem to be about as conscious of their racial identity as I am of mine, which is to say, hardly at all. I don't walk around thinking of myself as first and foremost white and I'd prefer not to think the prime characteristic of anyone I know is their blackness.

A couple of years ago the poet Benjamin Zephaniah said something that stuck in my mind. 'Race,' he said, 'is an important part of my identity but I wish it wasn't.' His contention was that racism, in the form of police stop-and-searches and the like, had made him acutely conscious of his race. Obviously that kind of negative attention is, alas, an integral part of the identity equation but it must be hoped, as we become a less racist society, a declining part. In any case it's not the only part. As the American academic Shelby Steele wrote: 'The greatest problem in coming from an oppressed group is the power the oppressor has over your group. The second greatest problem is the power your group has over you.'

An Afro-Caribbean friend of mine named David Matthews made a three-part series for the BBC a few years back entitled *The Trouble With Black Men*. It was polemical and provocative and intended to generate what he thought was some much needed debate within the black community. Matthews set out to explore how black culture in Britain was complicit in creating and maintaining black stereotypes. He was informed by his own experience – as a teenager he sought affirmation in street gangs, crime and violence – and motivated by a desire to look at the attitudes and assumptions that, in his opinion, were at the base of a spiralling drug and gun culture. He wanted to look at why black males did less well in school, why they were six times more likely to go to jail than their white counterparts, and why they were less likely to play an active part in bringing up their children.

He interviewed teachers, pupils, drug dealers, DJs, community leaders, commentators and educationalists and many other black voices and he found that racism, while still an issue, was not the main factor that held black youths back. Absent fathers, for instance, were a more significant negative influence on the development of black boys. The offspring of all those abandoned 'baby-mothers' from when I was young were too often left to gain their idea of male adulthood from gang members and drug dealers. Older black people, Matthews found, frequently had low expectations of younger black people, especially in terms of academic and professional achievement. And Matthews was also critical of the casual homophobia and misogyny that he saw as endemic in certain aspects of black youth culture. But the programme was full of articulate, successful black men and, perhaps more impressively, it recognised the potential in the drug dealers and gang members Matthews interviewed, drawing out their intelligence and humanity rather than simply demonising them.

Matthews certainly drew a response but it was mostly accusation rather than the debate he had wanted. He was denounced in the black media. A typical reaction came from Lee Jasper, race adviser to Ken Livingstone. 'The trouble with David Matthews,' he said, 'is that he has internalised racism, and that makes him an excellent gift to the British National Party and the leader-writers for the *Sun* and *Mail*. There has always been a tradition of the mainstream media offering opportunities for black people who appear to validate racist thinking. David Matthews firmly belongs in that tradition.'

Three years later Jasper attacked Tony Blair, after the then prime minister suggested that the black community needed to address knife and gun crime that was killing black youths. 'For years we have said this is an issue the black community has to deal with,' said Jasper. 'The PM is spectacularly ill-informed if he thinks otherwise.'

If racism is undermining black youth, then to an increasing degree it's racism from within the black community and within black individuals themselves. It's the racism of low group expectations, and the racism that sees any individual's attempt to break free from those constraints, or even to bring attention to them, as somehow a betrayal of group identity. Naturally there will be those who see such an assertion as another case of blaming the victim. But I remember well the pressures exerted on black children, especially black boys, by other black boys at school not to act 'white' – by which they meant, not to study or even to pretend to study (which is the most that teachers expected in my school). The very few black kids who stood up to the social pressure and applied themselves academically were very tough characters. And they had to be. The situation has, if anything, got worse since I left school. Back then the drug economy and its accompanying violence had yet to arm teenagers with knives and guns. Nowadays the supposed attributes of male blackness as constantly celebrated in black and mainstream culture – physical prowess, disrespect for authority, a readiness to react violently at the merest provocation, real or imagined – have become synonymous with urban survival. The pressure today is on white and Asian kids to act 'black'.

At this stage any self-respecting liberal will feel compelled to make mention of the myriad historical, political, social and economic influences that go towards shaping and constraining the average black youth's (indeed the average urban youth's) dreams and ambitions. Also, for good measure it's obligatory to throw in a reference to the hysterical scaremongering of those who complain about violent, homophobic and sexist rap imagery and lyrics. And just to make sure both sides are covered, we can add a swipe at the 'white'-controlled record industry that exploits negative images of 'black' culture for its own material gain. Very well. But what concerns me is the question of how society and the broader black community combine to define blackness, and how unnecessarily limiting that concept has become.

The subtle way in which a constricting perception of blackness is maintained is illustrated, I think, by something I wrote a decade ago. It was a brief profile of an obscure political aspirant by the name of Derek Laud. Laud was by any standards an unusual character. An enthusiastic fox-hunter with a camply posh accent, he favoured fine tailored clothes that were almost Edwardian in style and he enjoyed a number of friendships with Tory politicians on the right wing of the party, including the then heir apparent, Michael Portillo. Furthermore he was the only black member of the Monday Club, the right-wing Tory group that, among other things, promoted the voluntary repatriation of immigrants. I met Laud, which rhymes with 'fraud', in 1997 when he was the prospective Conservative candidate for the constituency of Tottenham, the run-down north London suburb with a large black population whose long-time MP was the black Labour politician Bernie Grant. It was here that the Broadwater Farm riot and murder of PC Blakelock had taken place.

The incongruity between Tottenham's gritty streets and Laud's haughty persona could not have been more pronounced. And it would have taken a writer with far greater circumspection than I possessed to ignore the comic possibilities. I duly went to town with Derek, mocking everything about the man. It was a job he made so easy that it was all I could do to keep a straight face during the interview, which took place in his Pall Mall gentlemen's club. The joke, of course, was that Laud did not realise he was black. He behaved – oh the merriment – as if he were a white man, as if his skin was not dark, as if his family did not originate from a colonised people, and as if he felt no pain for the slavery suffered by his ancestors. He lacked race consciousness to a degree that would have been tragic had it not been so funny. Especially as he was up against Bernie Grant, veteran of the Socialist Campaign Group, the man who famously said the police had been given 'a bloody good hiding' after Blakelock was hacked to death by a machete-wielding mob on the Broadwater Farm estate. Now *there* was a man who knew about black suffering, a man who was firmly in touch with his people and his roots. A black man.

And then, well, Laud was obviously gay, outré but not then quite 'out'. As a good liberal I was not going to say anything derogatory about his sexuality but I did drop large ironic hints as to its orientation because gayness, especially a decade ago and particularly in Britain, had only the merest Venn diagram overlap with blackness. There were no James Baldwins in the Black British story. But viciously homophobic reggae singers, like Shabba Ranks, did enjoy popularity. It was yet another element of Laud's flamboyant character that seemed to be a bald-faced renunciation of his racial identity. At one point I asked him about being black. He replied that it had the same significance to him as the fact that he wrote with his right hand. I suggested that it must have taken an act of will to maintain that attitude in the racially homo-geneous environment of his gentlemen's club and the Tory Party.

'This is your problem,' Laud told me. 'You clearly think of me as being black.'

It was with a certain mirthful confidence that I pointed out that he was indeed black.

'I never wake up in the morning and look at my face and think, "Gosh, I'm black,"' he retorted. 'It never strikes me that way. It's only a label that the white middle classes tend to engage in. It's certainly good sherry talk in Hampstead. The real point is to overcome this ridiculous stereotyping. Most black people don't actually go round thinking of themselves as being black, most black people think of themselves as being ordinary, decent, law-abiding members of society.'

How could someone be in such self-erasing denial of their own oppression? I recall thinking. Not for a moment did I consider the fact that whiteness played no conscious part in my own identity. I didn't walk around thinking I was white, except of course late at night in black areas, like Tottenham or Brixton, when it was customary to congratulate yourself on your fearless embrace of otherness – 'Yeah, honestly, I was the only white guy in the club . . .' But that was different. I was white. I wasn't fighting my own racial oppression. For there was only one way to combat racism and that was to stick with your own kind. Everyone agreed that the way to liberation from racial prejudice was to 'get in touch' with your racial identity.

Laud was deliberately vague about his private and professional background, and it seemed he had a lot to be vague about. He was part of a discredited consultancy culture that made its wealth by linking unscrupulous firms with compliant politicians. I wrote that Laud was 'a "political consultant" with a PR firm called Strategy Network International, whose major clients included South African Chamber of Mines and other agencies connected to the apartheid regime'. That seemed to do the trick. When the piece was published several left-wing colleagues took the trouble to let me know how much they enjoyed what I'd written, which, I'm afraid, was not an everyday response. Not long after, and through no efforts of mine, Laud resigned his candidacy and he disappeared off the media radar. He only started bleeping again in 2005 when he turned up as a contestant on the reality TV show *Big Brother*. By now his campness honed to a provocatively acerbic act, he quipped of a fellow contestant: 'He is the first black person to make me want to support the BNP.' Predictably, many observers chose to believe that Laud was speaking seriously. 'Derek Laud is a prime example of cultural disinheritance,' stated Ligali, the British African pressure group, claiming that 'the gay pseudo intellectual . . . expressed a public desire to join the British National Party in order to expunge young African Britons from the UK.'

But has Laud betrayed his racial heritage? Or has he, in his guise of the gay, camp, intellectual aesthete, done more than most to break down the well-policed confines of black identity? Which is not to say that Laud himself is some kind of example to follow, only that he challenges a number of the notions of blackness that we are all, black and white, liberal and conservative, guilty of enforcing.

A couple of years later another race issue was played out on *Big Brother*, this time on the 'celebrity' version, a distinction that is largely academic. It's curious to think that a TV show peopled by chronic attention-seekers could be the subject of an international diplomatic crisis, ministerial intervention, the largest protest campaign in television history and feverish public debate, but that is precisely what happened with *Celebrity Big Brother* 2007. The cause was the treatment of a Bollywood actress named Shilpa Shetty by two tabloid vixens, Danielle Lloyd, a former 'Miss England', and Jade Goody, a veteran of the non-celebrity *Big Brother*.

According to protesters – of which there were some 50,000 who made complaints to Ofcom, the broadcasting regulator – Lloyd and Goody bullied Shetty in such a way that was racist. Though no overtly racist epithets were used, it was said that Lloyd and Goody behaved in a racist manner. For example, Goody told Shetty: 'You're a liar and a fake. You're not in Neverland here, you're not no princess here. You're normal. You are normal, Shilpa, and learn to live with it. You need a day in the slums. Go in your community and go to all those people who look up to you and be real.' And Lloyd confided in Goody that she thought Shetty 'should fuck off home'.

Interestingly, a black woman was on the wrong end of a far more savage attack in the previous year's *Celebrity Big Brother*. On that occasion Traci Bingham, an American actress, was insulted and shouted at by a white man, Pete Burns, while another white man, the politician George Galloway, watched in complicit silence. Yet there were no protests, no ministerial admonishment, no international incident. This may have been because Burns was a transvestite – therefore from an oppressed minority – and Galloway has gained a reputation as a defender of Arabs and Muslims – therefore an anti-racist. Yet it remains a fact that neither Lloyd nor Goody produced the kind of loathing and vitriol that Burns heaped on Bingham.

There was some discussion as to whether the aggression of Lloyd and Goody stemmed from class hatred (Shetty spoke with an immaculate accent and the exaggerated, slightly snobbish, grace for which Indian high society is justly renowned) or racism. To the culture secretary, Tessa Jowell, the woman who decades before had lectured my mother on racism, there was no doubt. 'I think this is racism being presented as entertainment, and I think it is disgusting. My personal view is that this has caused enormous offence not only abroad but to the Indian community here.' Trevor Phillips, the chairman of the Commission for Equality and Human Rights, who had himself been accused of racism by hard-core anti-racists, was quick to agree. He lambasted Channel 4 executives and called on Jowell 'to step in and ask if this is the board that is capable of holding a public asset in trust'.

Of the many things that could be said about the reaction to Goody and Lloyd, sensible and restrained were not among them. The moment at which I realised an ostensibly progressive campaign to oppose racism had become mired in absurdity and hypocrisy came during an interview on Sky News with Hamant Verma, the editor of the Asian newspaper *Eastern Eye*. He said that Channel 4 was to blame for the controversy because it had invited 'illiterate chavs' to appear on television. It's doubtful that anything Lloyd or Goody said was as offensive as the phrase 'illiterate chav' – chav being the pejorative slang for the white working class. Yet the Sky News presenter merely nodded his head in sober agreement. Goody is a painfully incoherent and ill-informed young woman. On the earlier *Big Brother*, her bullying manner and snub-nose earned her the tabloid nickname of the Pig. There is apparently almost no insult, if aimed at the white working class, that is deemed unacceptable.

The kinds of seething social hatreds generated in any dynamic society are by and large repressed in a multicultural society that insists on the respect of difference. The exception to the rule, the single pressure valve, is the 'chavs', whose vilification is commonplace across the media and middle classes. In this sense Goody, the product of a broken home and drug-addicted parents, is the perfect receptacle for the pent-up revulsion and scorn that can find no other approved outlet. Her father, Andrew Goody, impregnated Jade's mother when he was just sixteen. A career criminal and sometime pimp, he left when his daughter was five and died in 2005, aged forty-two, of a heroin overdose. Jade's mother was a petty criminal who used her daughter to pass stolen cheques. Goody's childhood was a story of violence and school expulsion. In other words, she was a member of that group which is often referred to in polite society as 'white trash' or 'white scum'.

True to their calling, the tabloids, which had done so much to promote her, set about demolishing a contrite Goody, leaving her reportedly on 'suicide watch'. Nor were they the only voices of moral outrage. The *Guardian* columnist Jackie Ashley wondered if the 'Jade Goody episode [was] symbolic of a new rottenness [in Britain's public culture], a failure of New Labour?' And elsewhere in the *Guardian*, Omar Waraich concluded that the 'filthy taint of racism only manages to pollute *Big Brother* because it also pollutes Britain'. So the child of two junkies, a young woman with no education, who had earned her peculiar and tenuous position in British life on the strength of her aggressive manner and ignorance (she thought Cambridge was in London, that 'East Angular' [*sic*] was located outside Britain, and that Saddam Hussein was a boxer), was the symbol of societal racism because she was rude to a beautiful, articulate upper-middle-class woman who came from India.

Racism, in this reading, is a kind of original sin, an evil cancer metastasising in the very marrow of society – specifically 'white' society. So deep does it run that no amount of diversity awareness and anti-racism initiatives can remove its filthy taint. Like penitent self-flagellators, all we can do is shout 'racist!' as loudly and often as possible, preferably at some monster from the urban id. Even this demonstrative purging, this screamo-therapy, is futile. To the race-obsessed anti-racist there is no escape for a white person from their racism. Whites are racist: to deny it is itself proof of the racism. This witch-finder attitude was most revealingly demonstrated by Joseph Harker, an assistant editor on the *Guardian*'s comment pages, in a piece he wrote for the newspaper in 2002. 'White people,' he explained, 'need to accept that, no matter how many anti-racist demos they've marched on, they inevitably make assumptions, however subconscious, which are influenced by a racist society and which help to form their views and opinions. To refute this is to be in complete denial.'

Not much room for debate there. To deny your racism is only to confirm its hidden depths. 'The acknowledgement of personal racism,' he continued, 'is simply a prerequisite before anyone can begin to eradicate its pernicious effects.' Well, actually, not just anyone, it seems, only white people. For Harker went on to say that his suffering was not only from the prejudice of others: 'As a black man, I admit I am bound to suffer from prejudices of my own. I cannot be racist, however, because in the global order I do not belong to the dominant group.' To summarise, all white people are racist, whether or not they acknowledge their racism, and no black person can be racist. This may seem a particularly crude Marxist understanding of the relationship between black and white, a colour-coded system of class struggle and consciousness, but Harker's analysis was not exceptional, for it essentially forms the basis of guilty liberalism's take on race. Shelby Steele described the American version of this mindset: 'Under this stigma white individuals and American institutions must perpetually prove a negative – that they are not racist – to gain enough authority to function in matters of race, equality, opportunity. If they fail to prove the negative, they will be seen as racists.'

Harker cited the example of a train crash in Tanzania, in which two hundred people died, that only made it into *The Times*'s 'In Brief' column. 'What impression,' he asked, 'does this give about the value of black life?' It's a fair point, though what's known as the 'calculus of affinity', rather than naked racism, could equally account for the limited coverage. A major train crash in, say, Slovakia is unlikely to make front-page news in Britain, though it might do if several black Londoners were on board. And was the Paddington rail crash a big story in Tanzania? A much better example would be the war in southern Sudan that accounted for two million civilian deaths between 1983 and 2005. However that conflict is dressed up, a Muslim Arab government laid murderous siege to black Africans, predominantly Christian and Animist. Was there any racism involved in that genocidal butchery? And if so, what was the appropriate response of Europeans, white or otherwise? To protest and call for intervention to stop the slaughter? Or to decide it was a national reordering of colonial legacies and that it was none of our imperialist business? Similarly, was Idi Amin's expulsion of Ugandan Asians an act of racism? And if selecting a section of society on the basis of race, confiscating their property and throwing them out of their home is not racism, does the word have any meaning other than as a handy accusation to lay on anyone whose skin happens to be white?

The idea that a black person cannot by definition be racist is in the end just another means of maintaining racial inequality. It places black people indefinitely in the position of hopeless victims, not fully responsible for their thoughts or actions. In effect, it robs black people of their individuality. The wealthiest, most powerful white-hating separatist and the most assimilated un-race-conscious humanist are forcibly merged in a unitary block of blackness for so long as Africa remains underdeveloped. In Harker's words: 'If I were to mistreat a white person, no matter how low in social status, the weight of this country's white power structure would come down against me. As Stephen Lawrence's parents found, this force does not come to the aid of black people.'

Here is the other myth of racism – that a monolithic white regime is systematically determined to suppress black people – that continues to hold credence despite a preponderance of contrary evidence. To accept this line of thought it's necessary to ignore or at least downplay every progressive step that society has taken. In the case of Stephen Lawrence, the black student who was stabbed to death in an unprovoked attack by a gang of racist white youths in south London, it's certainly likely that racism was partly responsible for the bungled police investigation, though of course plenty of police investigations are bungled without racism. But then to imagine an uncaring 'white power structure' you would have to skim over the creation of the Macpherson Inquiry, ordered by the home secretary, and one of the most far-reaching investigations of state practice ever to be staged in public. You would have to neglect the subsequent report, its recommendations and their widespread and ongoing implementation. You would have to sidestep the massive media campaign, which included the *Daily Mail*, aimed at bringing Lawrence's killers to justice. And it would also be helpful to forget that such was the public disgust at his murder that Stephen Lawrence became a household name. By way of comparison, let's look at the murder of Paul Kelly outside a pub in Bath in the first few minutes of 2007. Kelly, a white man, was repeatedly stabbed by a young black man in front of twenty-five or more witnesses, most of them Afro-Caribbean, in what was said to be an unprovoked attack. The police knew who committed the crime, yet no witness would name the murderer. The reason given was that Bath's black community did not trust the police. 'There is a history of apprehension among older members of the community that has impacted on the younger generation,' Rosco Jones, director of Bath and North-East Somerset Racial Equality Council, told the *Observer*. In an interview with Radio 4's *Today* programme, Chief Superintendent David Tucker of the 'National Community Tension Team' acknowledged that the police needed to increase what he called 'customer focus' as 'some people are choosing not to be our customers'. In translation that meant Kelly's murderer was free to walk the streets of Bath because members of his 'community' preferred to harbour a killer than deal with the authorities. Similarly, very few people outside of Glasgow will recognise the name of Kriss Donald, the fifteen-year-old boy who was stabbed, tortured and finally burned to death by a gang of racist Asian thugs in 2004. His killers, unlike Lawrence's, were caught, found guilty and imprisoned, but it's surely significant that they have not joined a cast of infamous or demonised villains – hardly anyone knows their names or recognises their faces. That is as it should be. Rather than stirring up racial tensions, the media and the police and the courts – 'the white power structure' – acted responsibly. Even Donald's own mother refused to allow her grief to be appropriated by racists and the far right.

Contrast this measured response with the treatment of the suspects in the Lawrence case. By all accounts they were unsavoury characters, and seemingly unapologetic racists. Nevertheless, for a number of reasons – police incompetence and racism among them – they were not found guilty of any crime. Yet due process, innocence until proven guilt, environmental mitigation, the belief in reform: all of these established principles were abandoned by the popular press and liberal media alike. Civil libertarians went suddenly quiet as newspapers portrayed the suspects as both evil and guilty and crowds gathered at the public inquiry to scream and throw missiles at them. As Michael Collins wrote in his book on the white working class, *The Likes of Us*: 'It was the kind of behaviour identified with those small crowds of largely white working-class women who sometimes gather when a child murderer within their neighbourhood has been convicted, to pelt the police van that protects the killer with eggs, and scream abuse. The same journalists who frown on such illiberal behaviour, who dismiss such activities as worthy of "the mob", failed to apply such disdain to the unruly crowd outside the Lawrence inquiry, where apparently the public opinion of the crowd rather than the populism of the mob was making itself heard.'

It was as if abusing the suspects, or at least tacitly endorsing the abuse, in some way proved your anti-racist credentials. 'Look, I'm not like them! See how passionately, how violently, I hate them!' In a less serious, though no less symbolic, fashion the same principle applied with Goody, the whiter than white baddie. She was both a representative of white society and also its sacrificial offering – in her own much-mocked malapropism an 'escape goat' (which is actually the original phrase from which scapegoat derives). The more vitriol aimed at her, the more distance her accusers thought they put between themselves and racism. Yet it is the Goodys of this world, despite their ignorance and suspicion, who are the people most likely to be involved in breaking down racial barriers. The highest incidence of mixed marriages is not between middle-class liberal whites who have acknowledged their incurable racism and racially aware blacks and Asians who are willing to fraternise with their oppressors. It's between races from Goody's social class – the one she emerged from before she became a millionaire freak show. Indeed Goody herself, supposedly white racism incarnate, is the granddaughter of a West Indian who came to Britain to work for London Transport. This interracial mixing is partly attributable to the fact that, unlike other classes who have greater choice about where and next to whom they live, the poorer end of the white working class lives cheek by jowl with all ethnic minority communities. But it's also because at the bottom end of the class system social breakdown has also loosened group restraints on the individual.

In the end, if we think that race is of negligible biological significance, then the aim must be to live in a society in which it has minimal social significance, a post-racial society where race is a neutral description rather than a loaded issue. For ultimately racism will only disappear when our preoccupation with race fades. Nothing happens overnight. All progress is a process. But we appear to be getting nowhere fast, the ideal no closer.

We have to break out of the mental ghettos we inhabit before we can start dismantling the physical ones. Somewhere along the line we have stalled on race and allowed racism to dominate and determine the debate. While racism has declined, the response to it, anti-racism, has increased. And a major component of that anti-racism is the communal enforcement of racial identity. A provisional means of combating a false biological division has itself become an indefinite social division. The solution has metamorphosed into the problem.

What will really demystify race, rob it off its atavistic mistrust, is shared experience, in particular the shared experience of living and working together. More black people need to turn left out of my local station, more black people need to make an impact right across society, and in particular in positions of influence and power. That's a symbiotic process and one that is currently moving too slowly. What may help both the black community and society at large in speeding things along is if we all stop placing such an emphasis on race.

There are, however, plenty of signs that attitudes can and do change, though some of them are so small and symbolic that they would escape the notice of a Martian. My mother was born in 1930 in north London in a white community in which foreigners came from Ireland. She died in 2002 in a cancer ward in south London surrounded by people from across the globe. In the bed next to her a black Christian woman was sung to her death by a mournful choir of evangelical Africans. It was a noisy and crowded ward but my mother felt the strength of its community and turned down my offer to get her a room of her own. The last words she said to me were in response to the Afro-Caribbean woman of her own age dying in the bed opposite. 'She has the most friendly and beautiful face,' she said. Two women from two different places heading with mutual respect and appreciation, at last, in the same direction. In the end race wasn't important. Nor should it be at any other time.

9

Crime scenes

One warm-scented summer's evening in 2005 I pulled up outside a Thai restaurant to collect some takeaway food for my family. It was that relaxed time of the day, after work, the sky still light, that promising hour when the night ahead seems to hold unlimited potential. To drink in these soft London evenings from a pavement café or bar is one of the more civilised pleasures of city life. That's precisely what a number of people were doing in Maida Vale, a smart neighbourhood in north-west London, ten minutes' drive from my house. All that spoilt the scene was the sound of loud female voices piercing the calm some way up the street. It took a few minutes to pick up and pay for the food and when I came out I heard the noise again, this time interrupted by screams. I drove to the corner of the street, where a gang of about ten teenage girls was involved in some sort of scuffle outside an off-licence. A single girl was being kicked and punched and having her hair pulled by the rest. I wound down my side window and barked: 'Hey, stop that!' At the sound of my voice the gang eased off and looked up momentarily then, having satisfied themselves that I was of no concern, set about their quarry once again. Now I could see that blood was pouring from the victim's face onto her white school-uniform-like shirt. I jumped out of the car, uncertain of what I was going to do, and headed straight for the gang, shouting as loudly and authoritatively as my strangled vocal cords could manage. Whatever strange sound was emitted seemed to do the trick. This time they let her go and, with theatrical reluctance, stepped back. The ringleader proudly inspected her work and received high-fives from her companions. A large thick flap of skin hung from the cheek of the beaten girl, like a sole that had come loose from a shoe. I asked her if she was OK and told her I was phoning an ambulance. She was about sixteen or seventeen and she was shaking in shock. She had been stabbed in the face with a broken bottle.

Her attackers casually sauntered off, chatting and laughing, as if they had come out of a lively film at the cinema. If they felt in any danger they did not show it. I called the police and gave a description of the gang and clear directions on where it was heading. As I tried to comfort the girl, she was surrounded by several helpers. These people were spectators a few seconds before but now the attackers had gone they snapped into loud Samaritan mode, shouting at each other and me to stand back as they led the girl into the off-licence. Where had these caring voices been before when the teenager was undergoing a lifetime's disfigurement? The attack had lasted for five minutes, they had plenty of time to intervene. I looked around. There were perhaps ten adults standing by, men and women, mostly in their thirties, and further along, easily within plain view and earshot, were at least twenty more. Anger began to rise in me. I noticed one stationary onlooker with a smile on his face, a sort of amused smirk. He was standing no more than five yards away, a well-built, reasonably fit-looking man in his mid-thirties. His clothes – faded jeans and T-shirt – and general demeanour – unshaven, unruly hair – suggested that he did not earn his living as a stockbroker or corporate lawyer. He looked like he worked in the arts or some creative field, though of course looks can be misleading. In any event, he conformed to nonconformist style and I wouldn't have fallen over in surprise if I learned that his sympathies were anti-authority, pro-underdog, leftish, liberal.

'What's so funny?' I asked him. 'She's a young girl. How could you stand by and watch that happen to her?'

'Don't have a go at me, you pompous prick,' he replied, full of belated aggression. 'Why should I get involved? It had nothing to do with me.'

On reflection I probably did seem like a pompous prick, possibly because I was acting like a pompous prick. There I was, the have-a-go hero, admonishing harmless strangers for their inaction. I must have come across like Rod Taylor in *The Time Machine*, chastising the Elois for responding to the Morlocks' pillaging with pacifist detachment. I'm sure self-righteous indignation animated my every gesture. For I was saying in so many words: 'Why couldn't you be more butch and fearless, like me?' No wonder I was put in my place. And yet I meant it. I was appalled not so much because adults had failed to do what they should do but because a shared understanding of what to do in such circumstances does not exist. A society that places great emphasis on respecting others has next to nothing to say about protecting others.

A few weeks before that incident, my stepdaughter was set upon in a busy high street by a gang of teenagers in an unprovoked attack. Scores of adults looked on and not one of them did or said anything to help. When she described how grown-up faces turned away from her as kicks and punches flew, I could only conclude that everyone was waiting. They were waiting for society to change, for it to become less unfair, with more equitable wealth distribution so that street violence would miraculously disappear. They were waiting for schools to improve, and more youth centres to be built, and better housing. Or they were waiting for the police, the police who ought to be everywhere at all times but who should also maintain a low profile. Or perhaps they were just waiting for somebody else, anybody but themselves.

Community is a word that we hear a great deal about these days. There are community leaders who occupy an exalted position combining the authority of priest, tribal chief and village wise man. Politicians, local authorities and police advertise how they are working 'for the community'. The media anxiously seek the opinion of the 'community', which often comes with an implicit religious or ethnic meaning. Everyone is agreed that we live in communities and that communities are good to live in. But what kind of community turns its back as a teenage girl is stabbed in the face? What values bind us together if we feel that the protection of our most vulnerable citizens is not our personal responsibility?

Here's the strange thing. Most people I spoke to more or less agreed with the man I argued with after I broke up the attack. Leaving aside my pomposity, they could understand why he thought it wasn't his business to get involved. 'What if you got stabbed?' was a common response. Ten years before, Philip Lawrence, the head teacher of the nearby comprehensive school, was stabbed to death only a few yards from where the girl had been set upon. Lawrence was killed because he intervened to prevent one of his students from being attacked by a gang. He could have waited for the police to arrive but instead he placed himself between his young pupil and the thugs who were intent on violence. And for assuming this position he was murdered. At least he knew the boy he defended, and his protection could be said to have been part of Lawrence's professional duty. But to be murdered for defending a stranger, who wants to risk that?

'Just call the police,' was the most popular refrain of my friends. Well, I did call the police and the gang had long disappeared before they arrived. The standard liberal view of the police is a complex and sometimes mystifying affair. By convention they are perceived as the enforcers of a conservative status quo, Little Englanders in blue, restrictive, authoritarian, abusers of the poor and minorities, defenders of 'them' rather than 'us'. That image has changed a little in the post-Macpherson era but a good liberal still errs in favour of not trusting the police. We want them to back off, we don't want them to stop and search, we don't want them to carry arms, and most of all we want them to be there instantly to deal with any situation that threatens physical danger.

The rationale for this apparent contradiction is that while the police may be a long way from perfect they are better than vigilantism. In theory, the power of 'citizen's arrest' exists in British law under section 24 of the Police and Criminal Evidence Act (1984), but in practice it's not a right that is much discussed or encouraged. British liberalism tends to retain a patrician suspicion of its citizenry. In some nations there are 'bystander laws' which, notionally at least, oblige citizens to intervene if they are witnesses to a crime. In Britain the idea of the public 'taking the law into their own hands' is seen by the liberal establishment as a disastrously illiberal development that should be deterred.

In recent years this consensus has been challenged by a groundswell of opinion focused most sharply on the right of homeowners to defend themselves from intruders. As the law stands, homeowners are entitled only to use 'reasonable force'. As a result some homeowners have been charged with serious crimes for injuring burglars. A Norfolk farmer named Tony Martin was jailed for life in 2000 for shooting dead a sixteen-year-old burglar. The sentence triggered a national debate on the rights of burglary victims. In 2004, BBC radio's *Today* programme, British liberalism's home on the airwaves, was discomfited when, in a competition to suggest a new law, its listeners voted to allow homeowners to use 'any means' to defend themselves against burglars.

Martin, whose conviction was later reduced to man-slaughter, had been repeatedly burgled on his isolated farm, where the police could afford him scarcely any practical protection. So he waited up each night armed with a shotgun, ready to greet uninvited visitors. Then one August night in 1999 three burglars arrived and Martin opened fire, killing Fred Barras, the son of an armed robber, and wounding Brendan Fearon, a thirty-year-old serial thief. Fearon was later awarded legal aid to sue Martin for injury, though the case was eventually dropped after Martin threatened to counter-sue.

The *Today* programme vote was an exceptional result but it failed to impress politicians. As the deputy prime minister, John Prescott, said at the time: 'I'm afraid that's the kind of vigilante law that I don't think Parliament would agree to.' Prescott was probably quite wise. The proposed law taken to its logical extreme meant that homeowners would have been within their rights to shoot a child stealing apples from a garden. By falling prey to a vigilante accusation the campaign failed without ever quite articulating the vital issue at its centre. How should individuals and communities as a whole confront crime, and in particular armed crime, in the absence of police? It's a conversation that has gone unspoken for at least two generations. Most people go through life with no idea of their rights much less their duties in these matters. Which is curious given that in large areas of Britain the likelihood is that you will be a victim of burglary or robbery or assault.

In 2006 the prime minister, Tony Blair, gave a speech in which he outlined the problems facing the criminal justice system. He pointed out that the number of crimes reported to the police was fifty-seven times higher in 1997 than it had been in 1900. The detection rate was 47 per cent in 1951, but only 26 per cent by 2005, and conviction rates were down over the same period from 96 per cent to 74 per cent. He argued that the criminal justice system had been fighting twenty-first-century problems with nineteenth-century solutions. In addition he said that 'it is also a miscarriage of justice when the guilty walk away unpunished, as it is when the innocent are convicted'. Blair's figures seemed to suggest that the frequency with which the guilty went unpunished had increased the attractiveness of crime. It's an obvious conclusion but in liberal politics the obvious is often dismissed as 'populist'. One prominent criminal expert, Richard Garside, director of the Centre for Crime and Justice Studies, did just that. He called Blair's comparison 'an attempt to subvert the liberal notion of the miscarriage of justice'. 'Subvert' is a telling word to use. It suggests that Blair was determined to undermine liberal justice, and that liberal justice was concerned with defending the innocent but much less concerned with prosecuting the guilty. One wonders if Garside felt a miscarriage of justice took place when Stephen Lawrence's killers went free.

New Labour's answer to escalating crime and social disorder, in Blair's most famous phrase, was to be 'tough on crime and tough on the causes of crime'. The causes of crime are a subject of warmed-over if not heated debate. Poverty is the most often cited but it's a slippery concept. I know from my own experience that I turned to crime less out of economic desperation than social alienation, though the two are not entirely unrelated. I broke the law not because I had to but because I could. What made it that much easier in my case was the sense that white-collar crime didn't really matter. For a growing minority of young people, in particular, other forms of crime, including violence, are also seen to carry no moral weight. In any case government social policies have had limited effect on groups and classes in which crime has become entrenched. Instead it's in criminal policy that New Labour has showed most appetite for reform. Aside from an increase in police numbers and extension of security measures such as, for example, CCTV cameras, there has been a significant expansion in new laws. By some reckoning over three thousand new criminal offences have been made into law during New Labour's terms in office. The creation of law appears to have been confused with the maintenance of social order, as if changing the laws somehow automatically changed attitudes. Criminalising behaviour, however, does not necessarily discourage that behaviour. Indeed, the opposite may in fact be true. The more laws there are, the more the criminal authorities have to work to enforce them. Conversely, if they fail to enforce the law, the less respect there is both for the flouted law and the law in general. The rule of law is therefore not always best served by its extension.

Yet how else is government to influence behaviour? Education, campaigns, speeches and so forth are tried and trusted means. But these tend to be couched in idealistic rather than practical terms, with discussions about what values need to be asserted instead of how to assert them. And in this respect liberalism seems to offer little help. We may hear a great deal about 'empowering communities' but few self-respecting liberals would want to spell out what that power should actually mean. Even a scheme as tame as Neighbourhood Watch, in which residents report suspicious activity to the police, runs counter to progressive thought. In the liberal imagination it brings to mind small-minded snoopers and busybody curtain-twitchers, insufferable suburbanites hostile to strangers and young people. Among sophisticated people it enjoys the image of a sort of petty bourgeois Stasi. Though of course the kind of people who sneer at Neighbourhood Watch tended not to ridicule the real Stasi.

This squeamishness about crime prevention conceals an unwillingness to grapple with the central issue of public intervention. At the moment citizens are encouraged to take a completely passive role with regard to crime. The police advice is simply never to intervene. In theory, this directive has the virtue of upholding the rule of law and preventing unnecessary civil dispute and injury. However, such a narrow conception of civic responsibility helps foster a sense of social detachment and places a heavy burden on already stretched police resources. And that has several negative consequences. For a start it fails to present a communal challenge to criminal attitudes and behaviour. Nor is it very effective in terms of policing or deterrence. The reason that those girls walked slowly away was because they knew from experience that it was unlikely the police would arrive quickly enough to apprehend them. Relying exclusively on the police is usually a means of guaranteeing that the culprit escapes capture.

Another problem, which doesn't show up on figures or charts, is that while non-intervention may leave the passive bystander physically unharmed it nonetheless exacts a psychic toll. He is made to accept his own impotence and that's seldom a cheering experience. Unchallenged violence has an unseen but crushing effect on the spirit of the individual and community at large. Also, leaving the police to respond to every threat, no matter what the circumstances, turns civic space into a battle ground between antisocial and criminal elements and the law, in which the former enjoy the advantages of greater numbers, opportunism and surprise. Effectively it cedes the streets to the violent, for without a strong collective disincentive, the violent become more confident, more intimidating and more violent. Finally group passivity makes a mockery of the social contract of a community. But then, it has to be said, our contemporary ideas of community do much the same.

Evidence both statistical and anecdotal suggests that in a community of communities there is not enough social glue to create a sense of shared responsibility. Studies show that bystanders are less likely to come to the aid of someone from a different race to their own. The girl I saw stabbed was of Asian appearance. Her attackers were Afro-Caribbean. And nearly all the onlookers were, for want of a better phrase, white. Difference is all very well but it is with sameness, a common humanity, that we most pressingly need to reconnect. A sixteen-year-old girl is a sixteen-year-old girl in any culture and she deserves the protection of adults from all cultures. What was meant to be an embracing live-and-let-live acceptance of difference has hardened, over years of soft thinking, into a live-and-let-die indifference.

When I was a child growing up in Kentish Town I always thought of high streets as safe places because that's where adults congregated in large numbers. In difficult situations the adult world represented security, sanctuary, protection. Nowadays children are less inclined to see adults as protectors. And when it comes down to it, that's because adults are scared of children. Adults are increasingly unwilling to confront aggressive or threatening teenagers. They avoid them on public transport and in the streets and as a consequence some teenagers have gained a heady sense of their own intimidating power. You can feel the atmosphere cool when a group of teenage boys, all hoods and attitude, board a bus. Adults try to disappear within themselves, the better to escape the attention of the youths. It's as if jackbooted officers had got on a train in some dread police state of the imagination. No one wants to stand out. Eyes are lowered, or redirected at the suddenly fascinating scene outside the bus. Do not make eye contact! The full bus is now a collection of isolated, atomised individuals hoping that they won't be the one who is selected for closer inspection. The only solidarity in this community is silence. And then someone, some mad fool, politely asks one of the boys if he could put out his cigarette or joint or – for I have seen it done – crack pipe. There is a collective intake of breath. 'Why cause trouble?' the bus is thinking. Let them do what they want, smoke what they like. Let them urinate on the floor if it pleases them. Just don't provoke them. One of them is bound to have a knife. Then what? Going by conversations with countless friends, people I know and near strangers, this kind of risk analysis seems to be an everyday mental process for people travelling on public transport.

Empiricism and emotion are never more uncomfortable bed partners than in the matter of crime. For one thing crime statistics are notoriously unreliable and open to huge differences of interpretation. Figures in London and Britain as a whole, for example, suggest that crime is going down but at the same time the chance of being a victim of crime appears to have gone up. Also crimes that directly affect people, the kinds of incidents that dramatically change our perception of danger, like rape, street robberies and gun crime, have been increasing. In the ten years between 1995 and 2005, serious woundings rose by 50 per cent in England and Wales. And it is estimated that up to 70 per cent of violent crime goes unreported. Perhaps this is because victims have little confidence of gaining justice, as the conviction rate for these crimes has been falling. According to Home Office figures for 2006, only 9.7 per cent of all 'serious woundings' reported to the police lead to a successful conviction. For robberies the figure is 8.9 per cent and for rape, it's 5.5 per cent. In any case, few would dispute that there is an increased anxiety about crime and much of it, I think, is a reflection of waning communal relations, seen most starkly, but far from exclusively, between adults and youths.

The scene outside the off-licence shocked and depressed me. Violence happens in all big cities and it is always shocking and depressing to witness. Or at least it should be. What made me feel particularly low, however, was the effortlessness and extremity of the attack, the apparent absence of compunction, the offenders' lack of fear of censure, their obliviousness to social constraint, and the compliance, almost conspiracy, of the silent onlookers. Not only was it a savage assault on a young girl but on civic decency as well. Yet the more I thought about it – and I thought about it a lot – the more I realised that there wasn't an 'appropriate' response to what had happened. There wasn't a liberal vocabulary with which to describe the situation. Indeed, even a phrase like 'civic decency' sounded fuddy-duddy, uptight, somehow right wing. There *was* a liberal way of talking about the culprits. It involved referring to their poor education and difficult home lives and the poverty they suffered. To have done so would have meant ignoring the expensive clothes and mobile phones that all of them had, or it would have been necessary to explain that these were signs of superficial wealth, the desperate avarice of the marginalised and underprivileged in a nakedly materialist world. But I had no appetite for that brand of reasoning. It blamed nebulous society and excused not just the individuals but also the community of which they were a part. Thus the problem was not local, communal, immediate, it was national, multifaceted, the result of innumerable political mistakes made by the powers that be. In other words, it was inevitable and effectively incurable. We were all powerless: the girl, the onlookers, and the culprits who had been led by great social forces beyond their control to stick a broken bottle in a young girl's face. There was nothing anyone could do aside from vote for a new government and hope that the implementation of the correct policies would in years to come discourage teenage girls from resolving disputes with improvised lethal weaponry.

For some days after the stabbing I thought about the impulse to blame the government. Of course the government had a role to play. Yes, funding for after-school projects could be increased – though it has to be said that the stabbing took place yards from a large and subsided recreational park with high-standard sporting facilities and community programmes. Schools also needed to be improved (not an easy job to do when reforming headmasters were murdered in the street). And no doubt in some general sense policies that placed less emphasis on corporate profit and more on communal pride would be helpful. Equally, of course, the government could be accused from a right-wing position: not enough police, too many immigrants, too much welfare dependency, the weakening of traditional values and so forth. But when it came down to it, the girl was stabbed because her assailants felt able to do it. The ringleader was inhibited neither by the community nor her peer group. In the first instance, the community turned away, and in the second, her peer group joined in the assault. These were problems of attitude that were not simplistic functions of environment. Had the assault taken place in a war zone then the traumatised and desensitised argument would have made some sense. But what was the point of speaking of economic deprivation when a bejewelled gang of teenage girls in a relatively wealthy neighbourhood in one of the world's most affluent nations brutalised another girl for no material gain whatsoever?

Then, a couple of weeks after that attack, Richard Whelan was stabbed to death on a bus in north London. It was another story of random violence witnessed by a large number of people. The grim details amounted to a kind of moral fable, a nightmarish scene of community disavowal, the lawless law of a western played out in the urban claustrophobia of a double-decker bus. A young man on the top deck of the number 43 had been throwing chips at other passengers. Reports said several passengers left the top deck to avoid a confrontation. But Whelan, a twenty-eight-year-old from my old neighbourhood of Kentish Town, and his girlfriend stayed, along with a number of other passengers, and Whelan asked the chip thrower to stop throwing chips at his girlfriend. The chip thrower took umbrage and attacked Whelan. According to a witness account published shortly afterwards, Whelan's girlfriend shouted out: 'Oh my God, what's going on?' The answer was that the chip thrower, a twenty-year-old by the name of Anthony Leon Joseph, had taken out a knife and thrust it into Whelan's heart. He then left the bus. Again, slowly, smiling, in no rush. No one pursued him or shouted after him. The community did not act.

The murder took place just a few weeks after the 7 July bombings, when most commuters were still very nervous about travelling on public transport, still restively aware of potential danger. In those weeks there had been plenty of time to think about what to do in life-and-death moments, how to come together to combat murderous aggression. Certainly Whelan would have had opportunity to think about such matters, as his close friend Ciaran Cassidy had been murdered by one of the Islamist bombs on 7 July. There was also the 21 July failed bombing campaign, when all of the perpetrators were able to escape from packed tube trains. Some brave individuals gave chase, but the vast majority of passengers ran away. If you think about it, that's not the best comment on the much trumpeted strength of London's community spirit. Islamists had declared war on British society and only two weeks before had slaughtered over fifty people, and injured many hundreds more. Yet four homicidal Islamists made a determined bid to rip life and limb from men, women and children, and not one of them was apprehended by the mass of their intended victims.

Only a couple of passengers came to Whelan's aid. Most left the bus, and a mere five bothered to give a statement to the police that evening. As Whelan bled to death, male onlookers refused to give up their jackets to cover the shivering and sweating man. Apparently they didn't want to get blood on their clothes. Perhaps that was a job for the police and the emergency services as well. It had nothing to do with them.

There is a body of opinion that likes to remind us that, statistically speaking, London is not that dangerous. These kind of freak incidents happen from time to time and the chance of them happening to us is extremely small. And of course a sound mathematical grasp of probability is invaluable for a rational outlook on life. But this kind of cold number crunching neglects the corrosive effect such murders have on our lives and in particular on our feelings towards our fellow citizens. They help ensure that a thousand other less grave crimes, which are nonetheless damaging to the social fabric, take place with minimal reaction from the watching public. They remind us not to make eye contact, to remain invisible. They tell us in the most unforgiving fashion not to get involved. They diminish us as social and moral beings.

Intervention has become a matter of bravery rather than social conscience or moral responsibility. To advocate public action is seen as macho, grandstanding, and ill-judged. And the news reports of the many individuals who have been murdered in recent years for daring to confront gangs of youths tend, in their morbid sensationalism, to endorse this attitude. There is Steven Nyembo-Ya-Muteba, the east London maths student who had the audacity to ask a gang of teenagers on his doorstep to be quiet. They stabbed him to death. Or Peter

Woodhams, the twenty-two-year-old father who was shot dead outside his home in Canning Town, having spoken to a gang of youths who some months earlier had stabbed him. These are just two stories from London that happened in recent years but there are countless others around the country and their combined effect is to confirm that the best option is to do nothing, stay indoors and call the police, even if it's likely they will arrive somewhere between late and never.

Not all these crimes were committed by teenagers, and obviously most teenagers are not violent criminals, but many boys, and indeed girls, are involved in the kind of escalating violence that scares adults. If the relationship between adults and children is in a crisis of sorts it's partly because neither are sure what that relationship should be. Adult responsibility for children, other than their own, has declined over recent decades and at the same time children's awareness of their rights has increased. On the street this shift has led to a mutual distrust that comes perilously close to mutual contempt. This much is notorious. A few years ago I saw a couple of kids around twelve or thirteen spray-painting graffiti on a garden wall in my street. It was not urban art. The pair was not aspiring Jean-Michel Basquiats or Banksys. They were simply defacing a wall. What to do?

Since the early eighties there has been debate raging in criminologist circles on the efficacy of the so-called 'broken windows' theory. The idea was first popularised by George Kelling and James Wilson, a couple of American criminologists. They argued that neighbourhoods that seem neglected or uncared for are more likely to fall prey to crime. In the words of Kelling, criminals are 'emboldened by the lack of social control'. Therefore police were advised to target antisocial behaviour – graffiti, abandoned cars, the eponymous broken windows – in an effort to prevent the creation of, or graduation to, major crimes. Zero tolerance was another name for the same policy. It was seen at the time as a conservative approach to policing but its adoption in various American cities, most notably New York, caused or coincided with, depending on your opinion, a massive drop in crime, especially serious crime. A number of liberal academics have devoted a great deal of effort to debunking 'the broken windows' thesis. They see the criminalisation of antisocial behaviour as the criminalisation of poverty. In Britain the creation of the ASBO (antisocial behaviour order), a preventative order with the power to keep people away from certain areas at certain times, is often described in this way by its critics, who argue that ASBO powers are too broad and ill-focused.

There are persuasive cases on both sides of the argument but in my case, with the graffiti kids, they were largely irrelevant. My local police station, a red-brick fortress of a building, does not go in for zero tolerance. Drunks gather outside the station to share strong lager and panhandle because they know that they won't be hassled in that location. I've seen fights take place on the station steps without drawing the curiosity of those inside. But some citizens do know how to go about attracting the attention of the occupants. When a gun battle broke out in the street, one of those wounded in the exchange drove his car through the police barrier straight into the car park at the back of the building. *Then* the police did come out. So my local police, it's fair to say, are not in the business of responding to calls about prepubescent spray-can louts. In terms of dealing with the problem, I would have no more thought of calling them than I would have thought of dialling the number of my local bookshop. Instead I went out and politely asked the pair to stop what they were doing.

They didn't run away. They didn't stop. They just ignored me, as if I were a minor irritation, like a recorded message. When I repeated the request, they told me to 'fuck off'. These were not the toughest of the tough, they weren't veterans of paternal beatings and drug deals. They were just a couple of average kids who had almost no conception of adult authority. As I stepped closer, one of them told me that if I came anywhere near him he'd call the police and have me arrested for assault. The other laughed, and they both carried on spraying. What I did was to threaten to hit them and take my chances with the law. I didn't feel good about this. I'm over six foot and these boys were just kids. It was an imperfect solution but I didn't see what other option I had. They walked off cursing me but didn't return. For many people, especially women and the elderly, this course of action is not only imperfect but implausible.

Linda Walker, a middle-aged woman in Urmston, Greater Manchester, was subjected to a campaign of intimidation and vandalism around her home. Nuisance callers threatened to rape her, and her gay son was targeted with homophobic abuse. One night in August 2004, Walker, a special-needs teacher, cracked after a minor incident with her son's car. She phoned the police and told them what she was about to do and then took an air rifle and shot it at the ground near a group of teenagers she believed were behind the vandalism. One of the gang had convictions for burglary, theft and criminal damage. Walker, who had no previous criminal record, was arrested and sentenced to six months in prison. She also lost her job. As the judge told her: 'The courts discourage two things, firstly vigilante action, and also the use or discharging of a firearm in a public space. There is no excuse whatsoever for what you did that night.'

The judge was employing classic liberal rhetoric: two wrongs don't make a right, and if we allow them to then we create a vendetta culture. And where will that end? But is there anything else that liberals can say with regard to Walker's plight? Some mitigation, perhaps, or even defence? She was middle class and white so the usual stuff about economic reform, redistribution of wealth, the elimination of poverty and racism, though fine as far as it goes, has little direct bearing on her case. What can be said to a hardworking, tax-paying woman in a stressful job who feels embattled and isolated, intimidated by local thugs, unsupported by the police and local authorities, and fearful for the well-being of her family? Is there a liberal-left line, an explanation or advice, that can reassure someone in Walker's position? If there is, we certainly don't hear much about it. Where are the community leaders who speak for the Walkers of our world? Well, there might be a residents' association, but such prim bodies cannot possibly represent communities, or to put it another way, any community that has a residents' association is not a 'community' that the well-meaning are in any hurry to recognise. No, liberals have little to say to Walker. We can leave her to the *Daily Mail* to worry about. She can be a heroine for the right-wing property-owning classes. We left-minded liberals would prefer to pass over her predicament in awkward silence.

Yet contrary to what guilty liberals may think, the majority of crime victims are relatively poor. Even burglary, a crime that is sometimes thought of as an unofficial tax on wealth, is mostly suffered by those who can ill afford the loss – very often single mothers. In fact, as wealthier citizens invest in an expensive armoury of crime-prevention measures (dead-locks, window locks, house alarms, private patrols) – a move which, incidentally, is chiefly responsible for the drop in burglary – so do those who cannot afford these protections become more vulnerable and more targeted. Nowadays I never go to bed without double-locking the whole house. It's taken three burglaries to teach me that the laidback approach to home security is in effect an invitation to burglary. On the last occasion my house was broken into, our cat awoke me in the middle of the night. As we shut our cat in the kitchen, there were two explanations for her presence on our bed at 4.30 a.m. on a Sunday morning. Either someone had forgotten to shut her in, or someone had let her out. If it was the latter, then logic suggested that person was a burglar. I went downstairs half dressed and half asleep with my fist clenched, ready to meet an intruder. I passed my two-year-old daughter's bedroom and looked inside. She was asleep and no one was in there. I did the same with the rest of the rooms and came finally to the sitting-room, by which stage, convinced that the cat had simply not been locked in the kitchen, I had begun to feel ridiculous in my pyjama bottoms and I unclenched my fist. Having checked that the sitting-room windows were not open, I walked sleepily back out, neglecting to look behind the open sitting room door, and returned to bed. The burglar, of course, was behind the door and once I was back asleep he cleaned the house out and stole our car. I've often wondered what would have happened had I pulled back the door.

Perhaps I would have had the experience of Will Riley. A Londoner in his early forties, he fought with his intruder, overpowered him and called the police. Some time later he was called to prison to take part in a 'conference' with the burglar, a career criminal and drug addict who had spent eighteen years of his life behind bars. He was named, with poetic literalism, Peter Wolf. The conference was part of a 'restorative justice' experiment set up by Professor Lawrence Sherman, a criminologist at Cambridge University. The idea was to bring victim and offender together so that the latter could see what his actions had wrought and the former would have the opportunity to express his pent-up feelings of anger. As Riley told a Radio 4 reporter, the burglar initially began to rehearse a 'social worker spiel' that he had learned off pat during his many years of incarceration and perfected presumably in the course of the countless failed efforts to reform him. Riley listened patiently until Wolf made mention of when they 'met'. At this point all of Riley's frustrations and rage came to the surface. 'For me,' he said, 'it was like a fire hydrant opening up. Jesus Christ, we didn't meet at a cocktail party in Islington. You broke into my home!' In the ensuing outpouring of emotion, the recipient, Wolf, had an epiphany. He realised that he didn't like what he had done to another human being. Despite all the meetings with social workers, it was only this howling confrontation with his victim that finally made Wolf realise the error of his ways. He made a commitment to go straight, came out of prison, got married, got a job and began to contribute to society. A happy ending.

Or would I have ended up like Robert Symons, another London man in his forties, like me, and a science teacher at the secondary school a few hundred yards from my house? Symons had left a well-paid job in IT and become a teacher 'to give something back to the community'. One night in October 2004 he was awoken by a sound downstairs. He had two small children in the house, so he got up to check what was happening. On the stairs he was met by Yousef Bouhaddaous, a career burglar and crack addict who was out on licence from prison. Bouhaddaous plunged a knife into Symons's heart with such force that it broke one of the teacher's ribs. He died shortly afterwards in his wife's arms.

The first time I was burgled the police told me that the culprits were likely to be a gang of Kosovan asylum seekers who were operating in the area. One officer explained that these refugees had been damaged by their experience of war and it was understandable that they were having problems adjusting to life in Britain. Rather than react with anger, he seemed to suggest, I should respond with sympathy. The second time I was burgled by a local crack addict who, the police told me, was well known for terrorising the area. He lived in a kind of halfway house paid for by the state with a number of other seasoned criminals in their twenties. They had turned the building, large and enviably located, into a crack house. There were regular and violent disputes outside the house and neighbours were too frightened to complain directly. But there had been 250 complaints made to the police. To no avail. The residents continued to live there, including my burglar, who was bold enough to leave our car, which he had stolen, in the front driveway of the house. Eventually, after eluding the police in a car chase, he trashed and dumped the car. The police told me that it was unlikely they would be able to make a charge stick against him. The third time I was burgled I became, like Riley, angry. But unlike him, I did not catch my man. I felt invaded and abused, and my thoughts were filled with violent fantasies. The following day I went out and bought a baseball bat. I decided that if I was to meet a burglar in future I'd like to be holding something a little more protective than my bunched fingers.

Not long after, on a visit to a friend's house, I noticed that he had the same make of baseball bat in his bedroom as I had in mine. I guessed he hadn't suddenly developed a taste for American sports. He too bought his bat after one too many burglaries. In the most recent, in the previous summer, a burglar had gained access to his house through his two-year-old daughter's bedroom window. He climbed over the little girl's bed as she lay asleep. Because it was such a balmy night my friend had left his daughter's window slightly open. When I heard this, my first thought was, 'How could he have been so slack?' So adjusted had I become to the need to turn one's home into a fortress that I found it unnatural to allow air into a stuffy room. That an intruder would climb in I took, by contrast, as utterly normal. The burglar managed to steal a few items before my friend heard a noise and woke up. In his rushed exit, the burglar dropped the eight-inch kitchen knife he was carrying. My friend is an old-fashioned lefty, someone who sincerely believes that it's social injustice that causes crime, and he was a little red-faced when I brought attention to the baseball bat. But he admitted that he hadn't been sleeping too well in the months following the break-in. It wasn't the worry about losing a VCR that was causing his insomnia. Like any father, he was troubled by the thought that an armed stranger had been in his daughter's bedroom.

Over breakfast a few days later, I came across a comment piece in my daily paper, the *Guardian*. It was entitled: 'Thieves take stuff, that's all'. The writer's argument was that non-aggravated burglary was, in narrative terms, uniquely uninvolving. 'It lacks tension, pace, humour and, well, aggravation,' she wrote, 'and egregiously seeks to unearth pathos from the loss of inanimate objects that probably belonged to Radio Rentals anyway.' Part of the job of the columnist is to provoke, to rile, and on this occasion the writer, Zoe Williams, performed that task with an uncanny awareness of where my goat was located and how to get it. OK, losing a TV was irritating, but no more. Ditto the video, the DVD player, the CD machine. Insurance would cover them, though it would make the insurance more expensive. Oh well. In my case, I was slightly more annoyed about the coat I'd just bought. I'd spent a long time looking for that particular make and it was no longer stocked. And, yes, not having a car was an inconvenience we could have done without. But none of those vexations came close to explaining the visceral fury I felt about the burglary. It wasn't about 'stuff'. Williams was actually making a sensible case, that prison did not seem to work with burglars, and that locking up first-time burglars was not only draconian but inefficient. I think this is true. Burglary is an attack on the community and therefore why shouldn't convicted burglars be obliged to work for the community rather than the community pay for them to extend their criminal contacts in prison? However, Williams went on to conclude: 'it's unpleasant to have your space invaded; it's grim when they make a mess; it's a bummer if you're not insured; but it's only stuff. And this is all pretty cool. It's when people stop worrying about their videos that revolutions start.'

It was only one piece, written in a sense to spark a reaction, and one should be wary of hungrily taking the bait. But it was echoing an old idea. Burglary as egalitarian wealth redistribution is a near relative of the 'all property is theft' school of romantic thought. Of course no one much believes in that kind of fantasy radicalism any more and yet in some ill-defined way it still plays to liberal guilt. There's at least a vague agreement among progressive people that if you live in reasonable accommodation you are asking for trouble. To occupy a decent house, after all, is to provoke the less fortunate. In reality this is a double insult to the less fortunate. First, it assumes that their means of addressing inequality is criminality. And second, it overlooks the fact that it is the less fortunate who are more often burgled. In any case, the crude materialist understanding of burglary is a nonsense that denies the most natural instinct in humans: the desire to protect our family. The same desire runs throughout the animal world and fundamental to it is the integrity of shelter. Protection of the home is hard-wired into our brains.

Burglars can be many things but anyone who breaks into your home in the middle of the night is unlikely to be someone with whom you would entrust the well-being of the people you love most. What burglars are most often these days is drug addicts – which is possibly not the kind of person you want creeping around your house and your child's room at 4.30 in the morning. Around half of all crime that warrants a prison term is drug-related and I think that any serious attempt to reduce crime would seriously need to look at legalising drugs. Governments do have powers to influence society and the importance of government action should not be underplayed, but people also have the power to change attitudes, rather than simply be their ventriloquist's puppets. And an attitude that could do with abandoning is the acceptance of burglary as a function of poverty. It lends the crime a morality the criminals have done nothing to earn. The fact is, with the exception of the car, which was abandoned anyway, the resale value of all my stolen possessions would have amounted to about a hundred quid. Like most people I know, the kind of people that are guiltily aware of their advantages, my family and I own nothing that's worth anything. We have some books, some art that's not exactly collectible, a large mortgage and that's about it. The TV, DVD, CD stuff would get you, in street prices, a few rocks of crack at the local second-hand stores where stolen goods end up. So much for a wealth tax.

All of this ought to be nothing more than a restatement of the blindingly obvious. But at the moment personal crime – street violence, mugging, burglary – is a reality from which liberals prefer to turn away. Such delicacy would perhaps make some strategic sense in an authoritarian state. In a liberal society in which the main threat to civil liberty is violent crime, it's a fundamental dereliction of intellectual responsibility. We need to talk about protecting each other, reclaiming social space, and trying to build a world in which a summer night's breeze is no longer a forewarning of the cold steel of an intruder's knife.

10

Islamophobiaphobia

Located a few minutes walk from my house is the Islamia school, Britain's first state-funded Muslim faith school. The school is strictly religious and hugely oversubscribed. Many of the mothers of the pupils dress in full face veil and black djellaba, lending a graphic symbol of difference to the everyday business of the school run. On its website, the Islamia school details its ethos. 'The aim of the School,' runs a statement under the heading Admissions Policy, 'is to produce total Muslim personalities through the training of children's spirits, intellect, feelings and bodily sense. Education at Islamia caters for the growth of students in all their spiritual, intellectual, imaginative, physical, scientific and linguistic aspects, both individually and collectively, motivating all these aspects towards goodness. The ultimate aim of Islamic education is the realisation of complete submission to Allah on the level of the individual, the community and humanity at large.'

The man behind the school is informally known as the artist formerly known as Cat Stevens. Yusuf Islam, as he has been called for twenty-five years, set up the Islamia nursery school in 1983 and soon added a primary and secondary school to cater for the then largely unrecognised, or undeclared, demand for Islamic teaching. Islam is a convert, or revert as devout Muslims prefer to phrase it, because to become a Muslim is, according to Islamic doctrine, to revert to the natural state of man. The son of a Greek Cypriot father and a Swedish mother, he was brought up in Soho in the Greek

Orthodox tradition but attended a Catholic school. Having become a pop star at a youthful age, he embarked on something of a spiritual quest in the seventies, trying out different religions and fads, including Zen Buddhism, Taoism, numerology, astrology and Est, before finally settling on Islam.

Back in 1997, long before the world had heard of al-Qaeda, before London became known as Londonistan, I went to visit Islam at the Islamia school. I found him both charming and troubling, at once solicitous and sinister. He felt that his religion was not only misunderstood but misrepresented. I spoke to him about the faint sense of unease at the growth of Islam within the largely secular culture of Britain. 'There is a fear,' he said. 'That's what I overcame when I began to look deeper into Islam and not at the phenomenological appearance of it. It's not curry. It's not terrorism.'

He didn't put a name to the fear, perhaps because at that time the name was hardly used. But it subsequently entered common usage as 'Islamophobia'. Nowadays it's almost impossible to avoid the word. Say or write anything critical about a Muslim organisation, no matter how deserving of criticism that organisation may be, and the charge of Islamophobia will invariably be made. When a 2005 BBC *Panorama* investigation into the Muslim Council of Britain revealed that some of its affiliates were openly calling Jews and Christians 'sick and deviant', the programme was denounced by the MCB as 'Islamophobic' and many liberal commentators rushed to agree – one called the documentary 'McCarthyite'. Two years later a Channel 4 *Dispatches* documentary discovered that in supposedly 'moderate' British mosques preachers were delivering sermons in which they called for women who did not wear hijabs to be beaten, gays to be thrown off mountains, and expressed hatred of all non-Muslims. Despite film and taped evidence to back up its claims, the programme was again accused of Islamophobia. There is in fact a website devoted to making accusations of Islamophobia. It's called Islamophobiawatch. I've been cited on it a number of times.

Once for praising the journalism of the above *Panorama* programme. Another time for pointing out that the influential cleric Sheikh al-Qaradawi, a regular on al-Jazeera TV, honoured guest of London mayor Ken Livingstone and favoured Muslim preacher for a number of British liberals, said that death was the correct punishment for homosexuality. The mayor himself wrote a letter to the *Guardian* accusing me of swallowing Zionist propaganda from the 'notorious' Middle East Media Research Institute. In fact, I had obtained al-Qaradawi's fatwa on homosexuality from his own website, Islamonline, where he stresses that though capital punishment may seem cruel for the crime of homosexuality, it is 'to maintain the purity of the Islamic society and to keep it clean of perverted elements'. Could there be a more clear-cut case of homophobia? No matter. For drawing attention to it, I was an Islamophobe.

In 1997 I didn't know I was an Islamophobe. I had read the Koran at university, travelled a bit in Muslim countries, and didn't find a literalist interpretation of the Koran to be any more or less sensible than a literalist interpretation of the Bible. In one respect I was in sympathy with Yusuf Islam. I couldn't see why other faith schools – Christian and Jewish – should gain state backing but not Islamic schools. As a secularist, I was not in favour of faith schools, but if you were going to have them then I felt that it was unfair and wrong to exclude Muslims from the arrangement. But there was something about the former Mr Stevens, who was christened Steven Dimitri Georgiou, that did cause me to wonder what kind of joyless medieval world he would like to live in. For a start, he told me that he intended to no longer have anything to do with musical instruments because he preferred to follow the strictest interpretation of Islam, for it was with the strictest interpretation that he felt 'safest'. He defended the practice of stoning to death adulterous women, reminding me that 'four live witnesses' were necessary, which meant that the adulterer must effectively confess. Leaving aside the depressing question of how such a confession might be gained, I told him that I thought it was a frightening idea. 'Yes,' he nodded, 'I agree, it's frightening. That's the purpose. Not to cause pain, but to safeguard society from one of the greatest ills: jealousy and war between men fighting over women.'

It was the same formula as al-Qaradawi's explanation of why homosexuals should be killed – it's not nice but it's necessary. Islam also told me that he thought Salman Rushdie should be extradited to Iran, the country that had issued the novelist with a death sentence. All of this he said in a friendly, engaging fashion, as if he were talking about the need for school uniform or good discipline in class, rather than the torturing to death of a woman for sleeping with a man, or the murder of an author for writing fiction. His image of himself was of a peaceful, reasonable man, at one with God and the natural harmony of the world. Though he was dressed in robes and wore a clerical beard and glasses, he was nothing like the ranting monomaniacal preachers that show up from time to time on television, calling for the end of decadent Western society. It was confusing to speak to someone who held such extreme views but voiced them in such an apparently moderate style. I asked him what was so dangerous about blasphemy that warranted a death sentence.

'Look at it rationally,' he replied without a note of irony. 'It's not the breaking of one law, it's the thin end of the wedge whereby all that is held sanctimonious can be demolished.' I don't think I've ever heard a more appropriate malapropism than Islam's 'sanctimonious'. That was exactly what literature had been attempting to do since the Enlightenment and, indeed, before: demolish the sanctimonious. In my dictionary 'sanctimonious' is defined as 'making a show of being morally superior to other people'. That, in a word, is the history of religion. It's not the only history, of course, but it is a consistent one. It's the process by which someone can justify prejudice, torture and murder as morally necessary actions. And ridiculing that process, exposing it for the self-serving cant and hypocrisy that it is, is a threat that any authority that lays claim to total truth cannot tolerate.

Had Cat Stevens become a Christian fundamentalist, I would have severely criticised him in print, like any conscientious liberal journalist, for his illiberal attitudes. But he became an Islamic fundamentalist, and therefore I knew I had to tread more carefully. As a Muslim, Islam's views were embedded in a minority culture, not the culture he was born into, perhaps, but one that meant he could no longer be judged on his own terms. As such, his views were afforded special protection in the liberal discourse. At its most satirical, this kind of moral exemption resulted in the knighthood for MCB leader Iqbal Sacranie, the man who organised protests against *The Satanic Verses*. And at the more extreme end of Islamic opinion, preachers of hatred, who encouraged terrorism and murder, were systematically ignored, not out of some libertarian belief in absolute freedom of speech, but because they were Muslims, and therefore the standards of social responsibility expected of other religious figures were in some sense not relevant or applicable. This same kid-glove approach was also seen on university campuses where Islamist separatist groups like Hizb ut-Tahrir began to gain a hold on Muslim students. The liberals and left-wingers, who would have made a stink had these virulently anti-Semitic groups been white nationalists, muffled their opposition to racism for fear of appearing racist.

Yet the accusations of Islamophobia only multiplied. The more that government, local authorities and the liberal media attempted to accommodate the conservative and often reactionary opinions of Muslim spokespeople and representative groups, the more Islamophobia was cited by those community leaders and groups. But what is Islamophobia? The literal meaning of the word is an irrational fear of Islam. And that in turn begs the question, what is Islam? Is it an ideology, a culture, a people, or an inextricable combination of all three? If the meaning of Islamophobia was restricted to a fear, a prejudicial fear, of people who identified themselves as believers in the Islamic faith – namely Muslims – then there would be no shortage of Islamophobic behaviour, some of it violent or threatening, that could be rightly termed Islamophobic. A good example would be the case of a woman in Oxford who was made to feel unwelcome at a fitness club when she donned a 'burkini', a five-piece swimsuit designed to preserve her modesty. Why should it matter to anyone what style of swim-suit an individual chooses to wear in a swimming pool? To voice objection is to demonstrate a prejudicial intolerance based on nothing but the most pathetic and narrow-minded hatred. And it goes without saying that the intolerance becomes far worse when violence or the threat of it is involved, as it often is. There have been plenty of examples of Muslim women abused in the street, taxi drivers beaten up, and families terrorised. This kind of communalist intimidation actually has nothing to do with disagreeing with someone's beliefs, and everything to do with disagreeing with their right to go peacefully about their lives. It's patently vital that such malign attitudes and behaviour are opposed by all liberal-minded people.

And that's why Islamophobia is a grave charge. No reason-able person would wish to be associated with bigots and racists. Unfortunately that's exactly what happens because Islamophobia has been employed as a blanket term that covers not just a multitude of sins, but also a range of important rights and freedoms. For instance, imagine that a school's expressed intention was 'to produce total capitalist person-alities' or that its ultimate aim was 'the realisation of complete submission to the market on the level of the indi-vidual, the community and humanity at large'. Well, you wouldn't need to be an anti-capitalist to find those senti-ments a little disconcerting. But it's very likely, if not certain, that you would be deemed an Islamophobe if you objected to the Islamia school's wording in which 'capitalist' was 'Muslim' and 'the market' was 'Allah'. And yet at the very least there is legitimate cause to ask if it's the state's place to fund this kind of indoctrination of children. Even so, few liberals, or anyone else, would dare to pose that question in our increasingly fragmented political culture. The Islamophobia accusation conveniently serves as a 'keep out' sign to the community at large.

It has also been recruited to a campaign to unify Muslim identity by universalising a sense of embattlement and entitlement. One consequence is the widespread belief among many Muslims that what took place on the September morning in 2001 was less an attack by Islamists on the West than an excuse for the West to attack Islam. It's common for young Muslims to speak of being 'radicalised' by 9/11, as if they were the real victims that day. And in liberal circles it was accepted as reality that there was a concerted backlash against Muslims. In the weeks after 9/11 the Home Office minister John Denham spoke of the need to cut out the 'cancer of Islamophobia' in British society. In fact, there was very little evidence of 'reprisals' or a significant increase in violence against Muslims. Kenan Malik, the author of *The Meaning of Race*, collated available information on Islamophobic attacks in the wake of 9/11. He cited one study by the European Union that found that there were a dozen serious assaults on British Muslims in the four months after the destruction of the World Trade Center. As Malik remarked: 'That is certainly a dozen too many attacks but it does not speak of a climate of vicious Islamophobia.' He also exposed as a myth the idea that Muslims were exclusively targeted by the Terrorism Act. Sir Iqbal Sacranie claimed that '95–98 per cent of those stopped and searched under the anti-terror laws are Muslim'. Malik discovered that the true figure was actually between 7 and 15 per cent, depending on how 'Asian' was defined. And Malik found that in general police stop-and-search actions, Muslims and Asians were selected roughly in proportion to their population size. Black people were five times more likely to be stopped than Asians (and therefore most Muslims). Nevertheless one or two high-profile incidents involving wrongful arrests, and some overheated news reporting, have been enough to maintain the idea, repeatedly endorsed by religious and community leaders, that Muslims are under siege.

Back in 1997, when I met Yusuf Islam, a youth and community centre in my neighbourhood was put up for sale by the local council, though locals were not made aware of its availability. It had been the only such centre in the area and it really had catered to the community. In the event the centre was bought by Yusuf Islam, whom the local authority viewed as something of a community leader. His plan was to turn the building into an Islamic community centre, even though there were hardly any Muslims in the immediate community. Initially Islam's proposal was to convert the youth centre into a mosque but the building did not possess the necessary planning rights. When Muslim councillors discovered this detail they stormed out of a council meeting protesting Islamophobia. Once Islam took possession of the former youth centre, he boarded it up and left it unoccupied for ten years. It didn't do much in that time either for the real community or a notional Islamic one. When he finally submitted plans, just before the deadline on development, the renovation included the building of a large tower that prompted widespread objections from the local community. Yet local councillors did their utmost to facilitate planning permission. Even though the stated philosophy of Islam's school was that the community should submit completely to Allah, few residents cared about the religious implications or otherwise of the new design. They simply resented that what they considered to be unsightly and out of context was to be foisted upon them in the name of a notional community in which they appeared to have no voice. And they were also bothered by something far more mundane and practical: traffic.

For a number of years there have been chronic traffic, parking and congestion problems around a nearby mosque, which happens to be located at the end of my street. During festivals, thousands of visitors come and go into the early hours of the morning for up to two weeks at a time. In addition there are noise and litter issues and, occasionally, youth gang fights and public urinating. Which is to say, much like the problems generated by a football stadium or pub or rock concert venue. The difference in this case was that very few residents, myself included, were prepared to make a complaint for fear of seeming Islamophobic. We were, I suppose, Islamophobiaphobics. In practice this meant that the desire to sleep at night, to live in clean streets, and park in the bays that we had paid for was somehow anti-Islamic. By any reckoning this was madness but a madness to which a surprising number of my neighbours and I were prone. And with good reason.

The residents who did complain found that their concerns *were* perceived as Islamophobic. And the more they protested that their complaints had nothing to do with religion, the more Islamophobic they appeared. One representative of the mosque went so far as to argue that to address the problems caused by the worshippers without acknowledging the significance of their worship was in itself a criticism of Islam.

I held no animus against the mosque, which I knew to be a pretty enlightened institution, as religious institutions go, but eventually, after years of a deteriorating environment, I did protest. What prompted me to do so was the decision by my local council to lift parking restrictions, or rather to cancel parking payments for visitors to the mosque. The idea was that if there was free parking, they might be encouraged to park legally. This, I felt, was a novel approach to traffic management. Certainly my own experience of being fined when my resident's permit was one day out of date did not tally with this new initiative. To say that Brent Council is against car travel is rather like saying Hamas is against Israel. No resident of Brent is left in any doubt that the car is a destructive force that needs to be discouraged at every turn. The council is committed 'to making new and existing neighbourhoods and residential areas more sustainable, safe, attractive and cohesive places to live' and to 'reduce car travel', to 'encourage the use of public transport' and to 'protect the environment'. And yet here it was offering free parking in a neighbourhood already overwhelmed by car traffic. How could this make sense?

Like a lot of local authorities, Brent is dedicated to multicultural and anti-racist policies, and as such acutely sensitive to any possibility that its actions might be seen as Islamophobic. It is the bureaucratic face of Islamophobiaphobia, institutionally geared to avoiding the Islamophobia charge, even if that means contravening other policies on, for example, traffic control. The mosque had grown used to treating residents' complaints as evidence of Islamophobia, and the mere mention of the word paralysed the council. Though the problem had been building for many years, with most residents reluctant to make a fuss, it finally took over four years of intense resident protest before the council, facing a tight election, acted on behalf of the residents – which simply meant enforcing its own traffic restrictions. Given that track record of political appeasement, it was no surprise that residents near Yusuf Islam's development were concerned about traffic.

From any kind of wider perspective – even from a few streets away – these are embarrassingly local issues. Yet they are precisely the sort of disagreements that, replicated around the country, build up a sense of division and discord. One of the problems mosques face is the difficulty of gaining planning permission for places of religious worship, not least because of the problems of transport and traffic. Too many mosques are ad hoc affairs, run above shops or out of whatever small hall can be used. There needs to be a proper open debate about how best to address the shortage of mosques, but it's a debate in which the word Islamophobia should only be reached for as a last, never first, resort.

The signs, however, are not good. Hysteria tends to drown out rational discussion. It is often suggested, for example, that Muslims are the new Jews, and their position in Europe today is analogous to that of Jews in Europe in the 1930s.

And not just by Muslims. A number of educated secular liberals have made the same ahistorical comparison. The writer A. L. Kennedy had this to say to the *Berliner Zeitung*: 'When I look at the UK, it reminds me of the Nazi era. Blair is a deranged war criminal, and I have little hope that Brown is any better. And again, we are stigmatising one individual religious group, this time it is the Muslims. A section of our society is being marked out as criminals.'

Another author who made similar comments was the columnist and novelist India Knight. 'It's open season on Islam,' she wrote in *The Times*, 'Muslims are the new Jews.' Her column was a response to Jack Straw, who in October 2006 admitted that he asked women visitors to his constituency surgery to remove their face veil known as the niqab. Knight was upset that 'the white, male former foreign secretary' had said the veil was a 'visible statement of separation and of difference'. But this comment was surely a statement of fact, even if it was made by a white male. The veil *does* signify both separation and difference, first and foremost of the sexes.

Knight went on to say: 'I am particularly irked by ancient old "feminists" wheeling out themselves and their 30-years-out-of-date opinions to reiterate the old chestnut that Islam, by its nature, oppresses women (unlike the Bible, eh?) and that the veil compounds the blanket oppression. In their view all Muslim women are crushed because they can't wear visible lipstick or flash their thongs. Does it occur to these idiots that not necessarily everyone swoons with admiration at the fact that they have won the freedom to dress like 55-year-old slappers? That perhaps there exist large sections of our democratic society, veiled or otherwise, who have every right to their modesty, just as their detractors have every right to wear push-up bras?'

There are a lot of contradictory attitudes and confused assumptions cleverly packed into this passage. Opinions derived from thirty years ago are out of date, while a dress code dating from over 1,300 years ago is the latest thing. If the Bible oppresses women, does that mean that Islam does not? But perhaps the most subtle sleight of hand is the conflation of modesty with the concealment of identity – which is what a niqab does, and it's not an insignificant issue. There are known cases of both terrorists and criminals using the authorities' reluctance to check niqab wearers, out of religious sensitivity, to evade detection. It is believed that Mustaf Jama, a murder suspect, fled the country under cover of a veil, using his sister's passport. Similarly, Yassin Omar, one of the 21 July attempted bombers, escaped from London behind the veil.

And, contrary to Knight's implication, democracies do set limits on acceptable dress codes. Try walking around naked and the chances are you'll be arrested. There are also many buildings, settings and institutions which one would not be allowed to enter wearing inappropriate clothing, from jeans and trainers in a nightclub to a thong in a supermarket.

But the question was not whether Muslim women had a right to wear a veil. The question was whether Straw had the right to make a polite request that a constituent show her face while in his office. For Knight the answer was clearly that he did not. She thought it was as if he were to instruct an autistic person to look him in the eye. 'I'm sorry to equate Islam with disability,' she explained, 'but I am doing so because an observant person's religion is as integral a part of them as their genetic make-up.'

Even with the apology that equation does not add up. People do change their religious beliefs as a result of rational observation, but never their genome. Nevertheless it's a complex question, which is related to but quite distinct from the debate held in France over whether religious symbols like the hijab should be allowed in schools. For better or worse, France took a hard-line secularist position, which insists on a neutral space for all schoolchildren. Straw was not arguing for anything so extensive or obligatory. He was simply requesting that as a matter of courtesy he might be able to see the face of the person with whose problems he was supposed to be dealing. It's a very long step from that request to the gas chambers.

A few months before Straw made his view public, a Channel 4 survey produced some disturbing findings. Nearly a quarter of Muslims polled thought that the 7/7 bombings were a justified response to British foreign policy. Nearly half thought 9/11 was a US–Zionist conspiracy and almost one in five thought the Holocaust was either invented or an exaggeration of what took place. At the same time over half felt that hostility towards Muslims had increased after 7/7, though over three-quarters had not suffered hostility, and the hostility that the overwhelming majority of the remainder cited was verbal. Almost half of those polled believed that the police targeted Muslims but only 3 per cent knew of anyone who had been stopped and searched. Put together these figures formed a picture of a Muslim identity fed by myths and rumour and a siege mentality sustained by an inflated perception of Islamophobia.

And it was difficult, not to say impossible, to remove the meaning of the veil from this context. There was no doubt that the growing use of the veil coincided with a strengthening of Islamic identity that was itself informed by a militant sense of grievance. The interesting thing about the veil is that it was a statement of group identity that removed individual identity. All uniform does that to a degree but none so completely or effectively as the veil. The year before Straw entered the fray, I had set out to gain a better understanding of the veil. I had noticed that an increasing number of mothers visiting the Islamia school, as well as mothers at my daughter's non-denominational state primary school along the road, had taken to wearing full face veils and head-to-toe black capes.

One day my daughter, who was five at the time, asked me why some women in the schoolyard dressed like witches. She meant the mothers who were totally obscured in black. I told her that it was their religion and they were not witches. She said that they scared her. There was nothing to be afraid of, I insisted, they were just like everyone else under their clothes, and they were just clothes. But while I said that to my daughter, I strongly suspected it was not true. They were not just clothes. They were clothes with a specific message and that message was 'Don't talk to me', certainly as far as it concerned men. And to that extent my reassurance rang hollow with my daughter because she could tell that I had nothing to do with these women, whereas I smiled, said 'Hello' and chatted to other mothers in the playground.

'A comfortable multicultural society is not made in Whitehall, but on the street, in the school,' wrote the columnist Madeleine Bunting, 'in the myriad of relationships of friends, neighbours and colleagues. That's where new patterns of accommodation to bridge cultural differences are forged; that's where minds change, prejudices shift and alienation is eased.'

But how was it possible to forge new relationships and build bridges with someone who announces in their very clothes that they do not want to talk to you, and that it is offensive of you to try? Trying to make sense of this question, I wrote a column for the *Guardian* in which I suggested that many veil wearers had probably adopted the niqab out of a sense of cultural solidarity rather than religious conviction. I based this conjecture on the fact that many of them were young, and the young often like to feel part of a clearly defined movement, be it musical, sartorial or religious in nature. And I was also guided by noticing that many niqab wearers wore fashionable Western footwear, and hung out with immodestly dressed young men in gangsta-style clothes, which indicated that Koranic direction was far from the only factor involved. A number of correspondents asked me how I dare presume what went on in a Muslim woman's mind. My feeling was that the presumption stemmed from observation of human beings, but I took the point.

So I went in search of a veil-wearing woman whom I could

speak to. I checked the etiquette on a Muslim website. It outlined the requirements of niqab-wearers. 'Do not engage in social conversation with persons of the opposite sex,' ran the instructions. 'This is simple, just don't do it. When a kaffir [infidel] of the opposite sex asks you, "Did you have a good weekend," look down and say nothing in return . . .' Talking to another member of the community, therefore, could jeopardise community relations. So that ruled out walking up to one of the veiled mothers in the schoolyard.

Next I tried a few women accompanied by their husbands in the street. The husbands did the speaking as their wives remained silent and passive at their sides. The husbands confirmed that there was no chance that I could speak to a woman in a veil. If I wanted to find out why women wore the niqab, one husband informed me, I should speak to a male cleric at the mosque. It did not seem like an ideal female perspective but it was all that was on offer. I went to London's central mosque in Regent's Park, where an imam informed me that some scholars thought it was 'obligatory' to wear the niqab while others thought that it was only 'preferable'. 'Except,' he added with a note of grave jurisprudence, like a magistrate reiterating a substantive piece of law, 'if she is very beautiful, because then she may be liable for people to attack her. She is more safe with the niqab.'

Safety, the same priority that informed Yusuf Islam. That seemed to contradict the neo-feminist line that the niqab was simply a religious expression, a woman taking control of how she presented herself. Instead, in the imam's considered view, the niqab was there to protect the wearer and, more significantly, the male observer. For if a man could not see beauty, he could not be tempted by it. I could find no niqab-wearing woman, beautiful or otherwise, who would feel safe with me. Everyone I tried either turned me down outright or prevaricated indefinitely, until finally, after many weeks of searching, I managed to persuade a niqab-wearer from Leicester to see me. Her name was Rahmanara Chowdhury. She told me that she had adopted the niqab as a means to remind herself that she was a Muslim and to get 'closer to God'. We met in a public space at Loughborough University, where she worked as a sport and education development officer. Her main job, however, was as a teacher in a nearby secondary school. Her subject? Communication. She taught teenagers 'interpersonal skills, teamwork, personal development' and did so with the part of the human anatomy designed for universal communication – the face – entirely hidden, except for her eyes.

A friendly woman with self-deprecating charm, Chowdhury told me that she had received nothing but support from her workmates. I liked Chowdhury, though I found it frustrating that I was unable to put a face to the disembodied voice, but I was doubtful that she could teach communication as well as a teacher who showed her face. It was rather like a science teacher who was unable or unwilling to perform experiments. There was a major practical disadvantage that her students were expected to be burdened with so that she could exercise her right to religious expression – an expression that meant concealing her expression. You could make a case that Chowdhury's students were victims of secularphobia, or that Chowdhury was the recipient of her employer's Islamophilia but it was difficult to discern Islamophobia. The following year, Aishah Azmi, a Dewsbury teaching assistant, was suspended when she refused to take her veil off in class. Many of her pupils were learning English as a second language and the school argued that they needed to see the teacher's mouth. Azmi was awarded £1,100 at an employment tribunal and was subsequently dismissed by her employees. She then went to an appeal tribunal which found that she had been the victim of indirect discrimination. However, it ruled that it was a necessary means of raising educational standards. In my report, written a year earlier, I predicted that in the future it would be pupils, not just teachers, who would lay claim to the right to conceal their faces. I didn't realise at the time that many girls were indeed already wearing the niqab to school with their head teachers' blessings. But in March 2007, the High Court upheld the right of a Buckinghamshire school to ban the niqab (the school had previously allowed the veil to be worn) on the grounds that it hampered pupil–teacher communication.

Not so long ago the veil was an unambiguous symbol of female oppression. As the human rights campaigner Ayaan Hirsi Ali once put it to me: 'The veil is to show that women are responsible for the sexual self-control of men.' This analysis unquestionably fits, for instance, with the outlook of the Mufti of Australia, Sheikh al-Hilali, who delivered a sermon in 2006 in which he argued that immodestly dressed women encouraged immoral behaviour in men. 'If you take out uncovered meat,' said al-Hilali, 'and place it outside on the street . . . and the cats come and eat it, whose fault is it, the cats or the uncovered meat? The uncovered meat is the problem.' But cultural feminists have, as they say, reappropriated the veil, arguing that it is in fact a show of female power and autonomy. In Saudi Arabia, where dress code is enforced by the religious police, women are not allowed to drive cars. In Britain women in veils that limit peripheral vision are often to be seen driving. As such the issue has been presented by veil supporters as one of rights. In a multicultural, diverse society, women should be allowed the right to dress in accordance with their beliefs and traditions. Chowdhury put the same, not unreasonable, argument to me herself. 'It's all about education,' she explained. I asked her if in the same spirit of cross-cultural exchange she would defend the right of naturists to walk around as God had made them, without clothes. 'No,' she admitted, 'as a Muslim I could not agree with that.' In other words, the right to dress how you please was to be vigorously defended on religious terms but not other grounds.

The more I looked at the issue of the veil, the more it seemed to symbolise the kind of Islam that saw Islamophobia everywhere. It was a loud public statement of privacy. If the purpose was communion with God, then the method was an active and visible withdrawal from the community. It placed the largely personal freedom of conscience conspicuously in the public domain. The veil offers nothing to the community other than a refusal to engage with it, while simultaneously demanding the respect of, and full rights available to, that community. A singularly uncompromising piece of social armoury that requires society to compromise, it insists upon a specific and separate identity – in so many words, 'I am first and last a Muslim.' But more than that the niqab helps create the conditions from which it supposedly offers sanctuary, it helps foster the very Islamophobia to which it is notionally a reaction. In her book *From My Sisters' Lips*, a celebration of Muslim womanhood, Na'ima B. Robert, a 'revert', complains that after she adopts the niqab: 'Many people no longer make eye contact, extend a friendly hello or start up casual conversation.'

What she means of course by 'people' is women because a niqab is meant to discourage casual conversation between the sexes and, indeed, even eye contact. But who can blame other women from not wishing to talk to someone who is not prepared to reveal her face to them?

Though the number is growing, there are still only a tiny minority of Muslim women who wear the niqab. Given the fact of this small percentage, it could be said that it is counterproductive to make it a divisive issue. Certainly that's what I think on the practical level of public usage. By which I mean, if a woman wants to enshroud herself, it's nobody's business but her own. Unless she wants to interact with other people. Then it becomes the business of others. Then it is a fit matter for public discussion.

In this sense, the veil is symbolic of a much wider problem that Islam and British and European society faces. For political Islam wants to take a more active and public role while simultaneously seeking to limit discussion of the nature and implication of that role by use of the Islamophobia accusation. All opinion polls suggest that the majority of Muslims simply wish to practise their faith within the legal and cultural framework of secular society, but those who presume to lead the Muslim community wish to adapt that framework without the scrutiny of secular society. After the High Court decision regarding the Buckinghamshire school, the schools minister stated that 'learning must take precedence'. He went on: 'If a pupil's face is obscured for any reason the teacher may not be able to judge their engagement with learning or secure their participation in discussions and practical activities.'

The chairman of the Islamic Human Rights Commission, Massoud Shadjareh, responded with dismay. 'Successive ministers dealing with education issues have failed to give proper guidance when requested by human rights campaigners about schools' obligations regarding religious dress, including the head scarf. To now proceed to issue guidance against Muslim communities is simply shocking.' The 'Human Rights' part of the commission's title is designed to sound irreproachable, but what of the human rights of the child who does not want to wear a niqab, and is forced to do so by her parents? And what of the human rights of her teachers, her fellow pupils and the community at large? These questions are conveniently sidestepped in the rush to defend an individual's expression of communal identity. Shadjareh once again framed the issue of an individual's rights as an assault on a community, or 'Muslim communities'. But why stop there? Allowing for Shadjareh's expansion of a particular problem into a general and indiscriminate prejudice, aren't Muslim communities part of a larger community. For if I am paying taxes to produce children with 'total Muslim personalities', I have earned the right to ask if that strengthens or weakens the social fabric. That question has nothing to do with abusing or demonising Muslims. It has everything to do with establishing what kind of society we, as a society, want to encourage or create. Islamophobia is a word that in most cases obscures legitimate and necessary debate. As such, it's a veil that needs to be lifted.

Conflicts

11

Baghdad Babylon

On the corner of the high street a few minutes from where I live there was for a number of years a piece of graffiti that read 'This way to Bagdad [*sic*]' with an arrow drawn beneath pointing west. As it happens, the capital of Iraq is 2,000 miles in the opposite direction of the arrowhead. It referred instead to a large, slightly forbidding building that is situated at the end of my street. From a distance, the sturdy structure looks like a somewhat functional Victorian church. But you only need to know that some days a couple of thousand people pass through its giant doors to realise that it is unlikely to be a Christian place of worship. Fifteen years ago it was a synagogue. But not for the first time in their history, the Jews moved on. Sitting on the roof, high above the entrance, are two incongruous green domes, like two giant meringues balanced on old red bricks. They are an original feature of the building but they suit its new role, or at least lend it an oriental flavour, so that they seem almost purpose-built. These copper hemispheres now decorate the al-Khoei mosque, arguably the most important Shia temple in Britain, and the cause of the traffic problems mentioned in the previous chapter. In a sense, the author of the illiterate graffiti was closer to the truth than perhaps he knew. Because the mosque is also a renowned meeting place for Iraqi émigrés, exiles and refugees from across the country. For many of them, both before and after the Iraq invasion, it was the closest to Baghdad they were going to get for a long time.

The mosque was set up by Abd al-Majid al-Khoei, the son of Ayatollah Al-Udhma Sayyid Abdul Qasim al-Khoei. The elder Khoei was born in Iran but later moved to Iraq, where he became a leading authority on religious jurisprudence in the holy city of Najaf. In 1971 he was recognised as the pre-eminent Grand Ayatollah. Spiritual head of the world's 200 million Shia Muslims is not quite a papal position but it nonetheless carries a global responsibility. Saddam Hussein was not unaware of Khoei's influence. Following the first Gulf War in 1991, the old man was placed under arrest. He died shortly afterwards at the advanced age of ninety-three. His eldest son, Sayyid Mohammed Taqi al-Khoei, died two years later in a car accident that many believe to have been the work of Saddam's secret police. But the younger son fled Iraq and came to live in London.

Majid was the same age as me, though with his beard and slight pudginess he looked older, or perhaps just more mature. The *Guardian* called him 'dignified beyond his years' and that seemed about right. I used to see him around the neighbourhood, mostly going in and out of the mosque. He always looked in a hurry, as if he was engaged in a constant and losing battle with time. But while he may have been preoccupied, he was not aloof. A friendly and open character, he came and personally apologised to local residents after kids from the mosque had been smashing milk bottles in the street.

He could have lived a comfortable life in north-west London, overseeing a charitable organisation with an international reputation. A forthright opponent of Saddam and his Baath dictatorship, he could have maintained his interest in Iraq from the safety of the London suburbs. Or he could, like many 'community leaders', have turned his critical attention to his adopted home. But he was not one of those exiles who was content to enjoy the fruits of asylum while attacking his hosts. Neither could he forget his homeland. He had high hopes for Iraq. And he was in no doubt that for the realisation of those hopes regime change was required.

If Majid was never quite a gung-ho cheerleader for the US-led invasion, he was certainly not opposed to it. One of the last times I saw him, he was angrily picking up anti-war leaflets distributed outside the mosque the day before the massive protest march in London. Some weeks later, on 3 April, Majid returned to Iraq. He had been warned of the dangers but he was convinced that he would be able to help create a peace between the potentially explosive factions that would vie for power in the post-Saddam era. Not long before he left, my street was filled with police officers. They were looking beneath cars, and I didn't think they were checking the upkeep of tyre treads. It turned out that Tony Blair was about to pay a visit to Majid. Blair later called him a 'religious leader who embodied hope and reconciliation and who was committed to building a better future for the people of Iraq'.

A week after he arrived back in Iraq, Majid visited the shrine of Imam Ali in his home town, Najaf. His visiting party was around fifty strong but, whether due to religious sensitivities or to show that he was no American puppet, Majid left his US protection team behind. 'These are my people,' he insisted. 'I have no reason to fear them.' Thousands of Iraqis had greeted Majid during the course of his visit and he went to and from the shrine a number of times. But on the last occasion there was a crowd of around two hundred armed and angry supporters of Moqtada al-Sadr, the hard-line Shia leader. Among Majid's group were Haidar Raifee Killidar, custodian of the Imam Ali mosque under Saddam, and Maad Fayad, a London-based Iraqi journalist who was also a close friend of Majid's. The mob began attacking Killidar and told Majid to leave. But Fayad told me that Majid refused to abandon Killidar. 'He had invited him along and so he would not leave him, even though it placed his own life in jeopardy,' explained Fayad. 'He was that kind of man.'

Most of the group, however, did leave and the remainder were bundled into the mosque. They were told by a man who identified himself as the manager of Moqtada's office that they were now 'hostages of Moqtada al-Sadr'. Their hands were bound, and Fayad, who had already been stabbed once in the back, was tied to Killidar, who was then stabbed to death in front of him. Fayad, the author of a book in Arabic about the murder called *A Very Hot Day*, believes that Majid was the real target all along and that Killidar, who lived unprotected in Najaf, could have been killed at any time.

'Moqtada wanted Majid dead because he was worried that he would unite the people, and because he was clever and was on good terms with the Americans and the British,' said Fayad. 'Majid did not care about religious differences – Shia, Sunni or any of that rubbish. I am a Sunni but we were best friends. In fact, we were only going to be in Iraq for ninety days, but Moqtada thought Majid was a threat that needed to be eliminated.'

Instructions were received (Fayad is certain they came from Moqtada) to kill all the hostages in the shrine. But some of the more religious present protested that it was *haram* (forbidden) to commit murder in a mosque. Majid and the others were then taken outside and marched along to the vicinity of al-Sadr's house. Fayad managed to escape into the crowd just as they began killing his friend. Majid was stabbed 120 times and shot in the head. Witnesses said that bloodstained American money that had been hidden in Majid's clothes began flying around. According to Fayad, al-Sadr's supporters had already stolen thousands of dollars from the group, which was earmarked to help the poor and destitute (Majid had spent part of the day handing out cash to the needy). Moqtada himself has always maintained that he sent his loyalists to defend the rival cleric. Fayad knows this to be a 'big lie'. He also believes that the Iranians, sponsors of Moqtada, had a hand in Majid's murder. 'He had told the Iranians many times to keep out of Iraq.' In any case my neighbour, who held such optimism for a new Iraq, was dead. He could stop young boys throwing bottles in Brondesbury but he was powerless against an extremist street mob in Najaf.

Majid's death was a terrible blow to Shia–Sunni relations in Iraq. Had the cleric lived, Fayad is convinced 'Iraq would be a very different place now.' He thinks that there would be much greater national unity and far less violence. The murder was perhaps the first of countless inter-confession tragedies that would lead, in February 2006, to the blowing up of the al-Askari mosque in Samarra, the point at which Shia–Sunni tensions hardened into a de facto civil war. In Britain, Majid's murder was news but not a lead item. He never gained the coverage that attended Ken Bigley, the ritually slaughtered British engineer, or the murder of Margaret Hassan, the Anglo-Irish aid worker and naturalised Iraqi. This was partly because, unlike them, he was not kidnapped. But it was also, no doubt, because he was an Iraqi, and therefore, in the time-honoured tradition of these things, less newsworthy. Before Iraq became impossibly dangerous for foreigners, and was merely very dangerous, I harboured an ambition to go to Najaf to try to find out what really happened to Majid. I had in mind that in Majid's death lay the story of Iraq in microcosm: the misguided optimism of Western exiles, the inability of American troops to impose order and security, and the lethal ruthlessness of the extremists, be they Baath, Sunni or Shia. But as the country descended further into murderous chaos, so the plan became increasingly notional, until one day I realised I was not going to go. It seemed inconceivable that I would manage to find out what really happened to Majid, and I didn't want to guest star in an Islamist snuff movie. Cynicism, and of course fear, had got the better of me. Perhaps Majid's death was meaningless, perhaps he was just a victim of anarchic circumstance. And perhaps that's how I would end up if I went in search of the 'truth'.

In the years since September 2001 the political map of the world has been radically redrawn. The loose post-war left-liberal consensus that survived the Cold War, the Vietnam War, the triumph of the free market and the fall of the Soviet Union appears irreparably damaged. People who have never read a word of Samuel Huntingdon now talk anxiously about a 'clash of civilisations'. A new cast of names and set of locations – Osama bin Laden, al-Qaeda, Najaf, Falluja – previously known only to experts in the field, and new taxonomies – 'neocon', 'Islamofascist', 'jihad' – have all entered common language. The same period has also witnessed an intellectual reckoning in which familiar political and philosophical bearings have shifted. Nowadays, for example, Enlightenment ideas of universal suffrage and equality before the law are increasingly seen by progressives as a zealous form of secular absolutism. At the same time the polarities of left and right have made some kind of magnetic reversal. To defend gay rights, freedom of speech and gender equality is now more likely to be seen as a 'right-wing' position, whereas 'left-wingers' give their support to religious fanatics, censorship and cultural separatism. In this disorienting new reality, in which left is right and right is left and liberals are 'fundamentalists' and religious reactionaries are 'radicals', the question of where I stand, where anyone stands, has been most testingly complicated by the lethal fog of the Iraq War.

At some point, and usually sooner rather than later, almost every debate comes back to Iraq. It is the issue that defines this generation. No one who is concerned about global politics, or indeed domestic politics, can ignore the chaos and mass murder unleashed by that war. In this respect, it is unlike the chaos and mass murder unleashed, for instance, by the war in Darfur, which almost everyone concerned about global politics, and in particular domestic politics, has been able to ignore.

The Iraq War and the events of 11 September 2001 do not enjoy a conventional causal relationship. No evidence exists, and none is ever likely to be uncovered, that links Saddam Hussein to the al-Qaeda attacks on New York and Washington. And yet without 9/11 it seems certain Iraq would not have been invaded, at the very least not in 2003. The destruction of the Twin Towers transformed not just lower Manhattan but global politics. It created a new paradigm – the rogue state as a facilitator of a previously unimagined scale of terrorism – and the rationale for 'dealing' with Iraq was in turn a function of that paradigm.

What has taken place in Iraq since 2003 is not easy to assess, in large part because key areas of the country are extremely dangerous for observers to visit – though that in itself tells us rather a lot. Opinion polls, while instructive, are also conflicting. As I write, one poll suggests just over half of Iraqis support insurgent attacks on coalition forces, but only one-third want the coalition forces to leave immediately. We do know for sure that tens of thousands of people have died in Iraq since the invasion and, leaving aside who was responsible for their deaths, we can assume that most of them would be alive today had the invasion not taken place.

In itself, mass killing in the Middle East is not something that in the past has much stirred Western protesters. Saddam Hussein sanctioned the brutal demise of at least 100,000 of his compatriots. Some estimates that take into account the Anfal campaign against Iraqi Kurds, the ethnic cleansing of the Marsh Arabs and the repression of the Shiite majority, place the death toll much higher, perhaps a quarter of a million. And many times that figure if you count the human cost of his war with Iran, not to mention the invasion of Kuwait. Yet barely a murmur of dissent was heard in the West, even though Western governments, including France and West Germany, joined the Soviet Union and China in actively arming Saddam, and the US offered intelligence support during the Iran–Iraq War. It was seen as a Middle Eastern story, an inevitable tale of dictatorship and death, the kind of thing they do all the time over there.

By convention, when it comes to Middle Eastern affairs, only a terrible abuse performed by the Israeli army tends to provoke Western liberals into organised condemnation. One such case was the 1982 massacre of up to eight hundred Palestinians in the refugee camps of Sabra and Shatila in southern Lebanon.

The murders were methodically carried out by a Lebanese Christian militia under the auspices of the Israelis, specifically an ambitious general by the name of Ariel Sharon, later to become the country's prime minister. Outrage at these killings spread almost instantly around the globe. I remember how disgusted I was by this war crime, all the more so because only months before I had travelled through Israel and the West Bank. At the time, a number of my friends had said that visiting Israel was just as bad as visiting South Africa, for it was simply another vicious apartheid regime (whereas travelling to countries in the Middle East from which Jews were forcibly ejected, or countries where a sexual apartheid operated or torture a standard practice, was a recommended means of broadening the mind).

Most Westerners with even the slightest interest in international affairs will instantly respond to the words 'Sabra' and 'Shatila'. The mental process will go something like this: the Lebanese militia was a proxy for Israel and Israel is a proxy for the West, ergo the West was responsible for those deaths. But most of the same people will show a blank face to any mention of 'Hama'. A few months before the atrocities in southern Lebanon, President Hafiz al-Assad of Syria put to death as many as 25,000 of his own citizens in the city of Hama. I myself did not learn of Hama until a few years after the massacre took place, and only then because I happened to study Middle Eastern politics at university. It was certainly not common knowledge among most people concerned with politics and current affairs. We can live quite comfortably, then, with large-scale death in the Middle East just as long as we feel it has nothing to do with us.

But the Iraq War did have something to do with us. 'Not in our name' read the banners on 15 February 2003, when hundreds of thousands of people marched through London – and over a million across Europe – in protest at the war. The British army's participation could be said to implicate all Britons. But that didn't explain why so many took to the streets in countries whose governments were opposed to the war and were not sending their troops. In Germany, for example, or Switzerland or France or Greece or Luxembourg. These people were not marching to distance themselves from their governments. As with all such large-scale demonstrations, people turned out for wildly differing reasons. There were hard-line Islamists marching alongside, figuratively at least, topless women carrying posters which read: 'Bare Breasts Not Arms' (and how one would like to eavesdrop on a conversation between those two comrades in protest). Some, we know, were pacifists who were against any and every war. But presumably, given their previous indifference to Iraqi deaths, most people were not marching out of a sense of universal humanitarianism. Therefore it's reasonable to assume that a majority of European demonstrators were demonstrating in protest at what they saw as reckless US militarism.

Of course there were opponents of the war whose enmity towards the allied forces ran much deeper than that. And many of them were to occupy influential positions in the Stop the War Coalition in Britain. Tony Benn, the sincere admirer of Chairman Mao, became president of the STWC. The communist and North Korea apologist Andrew Murray was chair. Lyndsey German, the Socialist Workers Party veteran anti-democrat, was its convenor, and George Galloway, the staunch defender of Saddam and ardent nostalgist for the Soviet Union, its key speaker. Another regular speaker for the STWC was Yvonne Ridley, the journalist and Islamic convert who would later sing the praises of the sado-terrorist Abu Musab al-Zarqawi. After one of Zarqawi's suicide teams blew up a wedding party in a series of hotel bomb attacks in Jordan in 2005 that killed sixty-one people and injured many more, Ridley wrote: 'While the killing of innocent people is to be condemned without question, there is something rather repugnant about those who rush to renounce acts of terrorism. They remind me of trembling slaves all scuttling forth for the approval of the boss class in the hope of receiving a few crumbs from the big man's table ... oh, if only they knew how pathetic they really are.' She was referring to those members of Zarqawi's family that renounced the leader of al-Qaeda in Mesopotamia. By Ridley's way of thinking, blowing up wedding guests is not so bad, after all, as she pointed out, 'the three hotels, Hyatt, Days Inn and Radisson, are all US-owned and are seen as dens of iniquity by Jordan's reserved Muslim community', but distancing yourself from this kind of indiscriminate slaughter, that's what's 'repugnant'.

These then were people who made maximum use of their own democratic freedoms but who in most other circumstances were seldom to be found on the side of democracy and freedom. Even so, there were plenty of people, almost certainly the great majority, who protested at the war in good faith, not because they were anti-Western or anti-democrats, but simply because they believed that it would cause more bloodshed than it would prevent and create more problems than it would solve.

Going over the rights and wrongs of the decision to invade is of course a vital democratic process, but it won't put the genie back in the bottle or the dictator back in power. Nevertheless I'll try to look back on what I, as a reasonably informed citizen with no special knowledge other than an interest in Middle Eastern politics, thought about the war and its aftermath, if only to draw attention to moral complexities that both neocon advocates and liberal protesters have preferred to overlook. I confess to conflicting feelings about the invasion. On balance I was against it. When asked – and for the first few months of 2003 there was no other topic of conversation – I would say that I was 40 per cent in favour of the war and 60 per cent against. I hoped that democracy, stability and civil liberty might be achieved, and I simultaneously feared that the whole region would go up in flames. The fear outweighed, but did not completely crush, the hope. Still, war is not a suck-it-and-see endeavour. It requires total commitment. Even if it goes well, a lot of innocent people are bound to lose their lives. If you say you're in favour of war, you need to be confident of what and whom you're fighting for, or rather what you expect others to fight for. You also need to be pretty sure that the war is winnable and have some idea how that victory will look. For the war's supporters those are basic moral requirements, for its prosecutors they are strategic necessities. That the Blair and Bush administrations wavered between homeland defence and Iraqi liberation as their reasons (seldom agreeing on the same one at the same time) was in itself a sign of the lack of coherence at the top. More troubling than any of these reservations, though, was the fact that nobody knew how the Iraqis would respond, including the Iraqis themselves and even, alas, well-informed Iraqis like Majid al-Khoei.

The American vision of a post-war Iraq as a beacon of freedom and democracy in the Middle East may have been unrealistic, but it was not, to my mind, unappealing. For Arab states, the second half of the twentieth century had been a tawdry tale of dictatorships, repression and corruption. That situation was and remains in urgent need of change. But as we all know, the Good Intentions paving company has long held the contract for laying the road to hell. If the invasion has led to a quagmire of communal murder, hatred and fear, a civil war fought by sectarian religious nihilists, then what does it matter what it said on the route map?

I'm sure I was not alone in finding the arguments on both sides confused and confusing. For example, one section of the anti-war movement had been calling for sanctions to end for a number of years. According to this argument, the inter-nationally enforced trade embargo with Iraq (which would turn out to be not that well enforced) had cost the lives of hundreds of thousands of children, the ill and the elderly, because the shortages had resulted in insufficient medical care, while leaving Saddam, his family and cronies in palatial luxury. Many supporters of the war agreed and counter-argued that, apart from anything else, overthrowing Saddam would bring an end to this suffering. At the same time, other anti-war protesters, again perhaps the majority, thought that the sanctions and indeed the whole status quo of no-fly zones and containment should be maintained indefinitely. The options on offer were essentially these: 1) allow Saddam to rebuild; 2) invade; 3) carry on as before. None of them made a great deal of sense. However, there was no fourth option, or none that made any impact in public debate.

The Iraq invasion came eighteen months after 9/11. There was a report of a Baathist agent meeting an al-Qaeda operative somewhere in Central Europe, though it was said to be false. Iraq housed a number of terrorists, among them al-Zarqawi, who would claim the local al-Qaeda franchise. But in terms of international terrorism nothing up to that point justified a full-scale invasion. The real question, in terms of a threat to the West, was what would happen in the future. Or could be prevented from happening. The World Trade Center attacks had demonstrated that Islamists were willing to kill on a grand scale. Their only limitation was firepower. If al-Qaeda could lay their hands on an improvised nuclear weapon, a so-called 'dirty bomb', there was little doubt they would use it. In the post-9/11 world, the threat posed by failed or rogue states like Iraq suddenly became far more grave and unpredictable. But grave and unpredictable enough to warrant invasion?

It is impossible to answer that question with certain knowledge because the efficacy of a pre-emptive war can only be established by not waging it. Had Saddam, for example, attained nuclear capability and passed on the technology to a terrorist group that went on to kill tens of thousands of people in London or New York, then no doubt there would have been widespread anger in Britain and America that he had not previously been disarmed and deposed. Still, this is pure speculation made idle, if not futile, by the absence of weapons of mass destruction in Iraq. What seems clear is that it is not viable, in the long term, to organise global relations on the basis of pre-emptive action.

However, once the invasion happened, being an opponent of or a proponent for the war became a subject of purely historical interest. The war had started, the Baathist regime fell, and thereafter the only question that mattered was what action would best help Iraq become a stable, peaceful and, ideally, democratic nation. Those aims were always going to be a tall order and the Bush administration fell unforgivably short. Thomas E. Ricks's *Fiasco: The American Military Adventure in Iraq* is just one of the many books that describe the disastrous mismanagement of the occupation. Each page reads like a litany of missed opportunities, poor decision-making and belligerence. Or there's Patrick Cockburn's *The Occupation*, a courageous and coolly observed account of unfolding catastrophe, or George Packer's *The Assassin's Gate*, a fine piece of extended journalism, haunted by disillusionment, that shows how America decided to stay in Iraq but withdraw from Iraqis. Reading these books, and following the news reports, it became all too apparent that there was no strategy worthy of the name for the day-to-day running of Iraq after the initial military battle was won. They are, in that sense, disheartening accounts, though not necessarily more depressing than Kanan Makiya's *Republic of Fear*, the meticulous exposé of the sadist police state that Saddam had inflicted upon Iraq. The fact remains, however, that if the removal of Saddam's regime ends in murderous anarchy, then the gains for Iraqis are rendered hopelessly theoretical. In the final analysis, that is probably the only meaningful judgement on the success or otherwise of the invasion, though when the final analysis is made is another question.

Yet the argument against intervention does not easily or automatically extend into an argument in favour of withdrawal. It may be that an immediate removal of allied soldiers from Iraq would, after much bloodshed, have led to some form of stability, whether a dictatorship or alliance of warlords. But troop withdrawal following the invasion was no more assured to be the best means of establishing peace than pulling a knife out of a stab victim is necessarily the best means of staunching a haemorrhage.

In among the conspiracy theories and paranoid fantasies that informed much of the most vocal anti-war sentiments, there were wise voices. They may not have been as loud as the Galloways but they rightly detected that the Bush administration had the determination to destroy Baathism without the ability, or even desire, to rebuild Iraq. For too many people in the West, however, the only relevant issue was getting out. Not because it offered the Iraqis a better chance of attaining freedom and stability, but because if we withdrew then it was no longer our problem.

Nearly 80 per cent of the electorate of Iraq would turn out for the Iraqi legislative election in 2005, many of them running a lethal risk for exercising their newly established right to a free vote. In Britain in the same year just over 60 per cent of the electorate took part in the general election. Though Labour won, its majority was dramatically cut, and the main reason cited for this diminution was the negative effect of the Iraq War. My local constituency of Brent East was a marginal seat with a large enough Muslim population to make an electoral difference. In June 2003 a by-election had been held following the death of the incumbent Labour MP, Paul Daisley. At the time it was a safe Labour seat. But a low turnout (just 36 per cent) and a massive swing away from Labour combined to hand the seat to Sarah Teather of the Liberal Democrats. It was widely seen as a protest vote in opposition to the Iraq War. So in 2005 my local Labour Party put forward an anti-war candidate, Yasmin Qureshi, who was opposed to the Labour leadership. More than that she was a Muslim. I know this because it was the first thing she told me when she came to canvas for my vote. At the time I thought it was a bizarre opening gambit, rather as if I had introduced myself by telling her I was an atheist. But what she meant was this: 'I'm a Muslim and therefore I'm against the war in Iraq.'

So the candidate for the most progressive party – the Labour

Party – was selected for the job because she defined herself primarily in terms of a religion. Perhaps she highlighted her Muslim faith to underline her status as an oppressed person, in the way that some politicians like to insist they are working class. But my own impression was that she used Muslim as shorthand for 'opposed to the war'. She accepted, when I put it to her, that the Muslims at the mosque in my street, the Muslims from Iraq, were, at least at the outset, either in favour of the war or not against it. But what did they know? How could an Iraqi's knowledge of Iraq possibly begin to compare with the grievance of a Muslim from rural Pakistan or Somalia? People like Majid, with his lifelong dedication to liberating Shia Iraqis from the religious repression imposed on them by a ruling Sunni clique, and his dream of interfaith harmony, how could his experience of persecution in Iraq measure up to the pain of Islamophobia felt by Muslims in north-west London who were free to worship however and wherever they so chose? Qureshi had no answer to these questions. How could she? Her identity as a Muslim offered her no more insight into the rights and wrongs of the Iraq War than a Paraguayan's Catholicism would provide special understanding of the Croatian conflict. Despite the best efforts of Tony Benn and Ken Livingstone, who came to Brent to support her, Qureshi failed to win back the seat for Labour. Instead the 'troops out' Liberal candidate held on.

The Qureshi campaign was just one small instance of how Iraq was employed by opponents of the war as the main stage in the global drama of Muslim injury. Or to reverse the emphasis, how Muslims, regardless of their contacts with the country, were encouraged to lay special claim to Iraq's pain. In fact the war was recruited to a series of far-ranging debates and arguments. Prominent among these was the anti-liberal democracy cause, and closely related to it, the attack on Enlightenment and humanist principles upon which liberal democracy rested. Many, if not all, of those who supported the war in Iraq invoked the spread of liberal democracy as justification for the invasion. Thus many of those who were against the war identified liberal democracy as the culprit. Some did so because they felt guilty about the war, guilty about being Western, and guilty about being a liberal, and some, like the hierarchy of the Stop the War Coalition, because they were opposed to liberal democracy itself. In particular, the notion that there were universal human rights came in for some sustained opposition, often from the same people who protested at the abuse of human rights in occupied Iraq and at home. So, for example, those who were loudest in their condemnation of the abuse of prisoners at Abu Ghraib, and staunch in their support of terrorist suspects held, in lieu of deportation, at Belmarsh prison, were often silent about Saddam's incomparably greater abuse of human rights. They also turned a blind eye to the endemic violation of human rights in countries like Iran, reasoning, as one commentator explained to me, that to bring attention to Iranian abuses would only encourage Americans looking to bomb the country. In this respect, the response of the Iranian Nobel Peace laureate Shirin Ebadi to an anti-war protester in the States demands quotation. The protester asked Ebadi to desist from talking about human rights abuses in Iran so as not to play into neoconservative hands. Her reply was to the point: 'Any anti-war movement that advocates silence in the face of tyranny can count me out.'

Others began to question whether the whole project of the Enlightenment was not in fact a giant hoax, a spurious piece of history that was nothing but an excuse for Western hegemony. One correspondent suggested, after I'd written a column defending Enlightenment principles, that my real intention was support of the Iraq War. To be an advocate of universal human rights, it seemed, had become a neoconservative position. It was as if all intellectual roads led to and from Baghdad.

In the atmosphere of guilt and recrimination that thickened as the news from Iraq got worse, concepts like rationalism, empiricism and scientific enquiry became implicated in the military folly. In a piece that reverberated around the blogo-sphere, the *Guardian* columnist Madeleine Bunting suggested that the Enlightenment, if it ever existed, was really an anti-Muslim movement, and wondered why it was 'invoked by the self-styled "hard liberals" as if it amounts to their tablets of stone'. Bunting was only voicing the increasing sense that there was nothing much to choose between empirical ration-alism and religious fundamentalism. They were two dogmas that both set out to justify violence.

This kind of moral equivalence is not new. Nor is the desire to question the morality of humanist values. Even before the Enlightenment reached its intellectual climax, Jean-Jacques Rousseau had argued that reason was no safeguard against violence and injustice. In fact, perhaps one of the defining characteristics of the Enlightenment, which actually laid the ground for a provisional rather than absolute understanding of truth, is that it contains the seeds of its own destruction. From the Frankfurt School through to Foucault, much of twen-tieth-century philosophy was concerned with the irrationality of reason. Not content with that task, many of the critics of the Enlightenment also sought reason in irrationality. In Foucault's case, it was provided by the Iranian revolution in 1979, which he described approvingly in terms of 'a political spirituality'.

Foucault was not the first, and won't be the last, intellec-tual to pin his colours to an illiberal utopia. Entranced by the revolutionary moment, he was myopically enthusiastic about a gang of theocratic tyrants. The misery that awaited the long-suffering Iranians was something that Foucault was unable or unwilling to see. Yet it's fair to say that very few people in the world were prepared for what took place in Iran in 1979. It was the first example of Islamic fundamentalists seizing power of a state in the modern period. I remember reading radical left-wing rags that insisted the revolution required our unbending support. Being an 'American stooge', the Shah of Iran was reviled by the Western liberal-left, far

223

more than, say, Saddam, who came to power in 1979 and was a much more ruthless killer than the Shah – but was not seen as pro-American. In that same year of 1979, fundamentalists also tightened their grip on Saudi Arabia, a theocratic monarchy that was already firmly medieval in its attitudes and practices.

Twenty-five years later, it made solid sense to argue, as many did, that fundamentalism would spread in reaction to America's involvement in Iraq. But it was no longer possible to be blind to the true nature of fundamentalism. Or to believe that left to its own devices, it would evolve into a progressive movement. An Endarkenment was underway in many parts of the Islamic world that involved the suffocating stranglehold of divine revelation, the promotion of superstitious belief and the suppression of intellectual enquiry, and it came with the added power of modern totalitarian means and methods. I could see on what moral and strategic basis one could oppose the Iraq War, not least because that had been my own position. There was no getting away from the fact that the liberal democracies of America and Britain had made reasoned arguments for a war that was to lead to the deaths of tens of thousands of people and effectively destroyed (an albeit corrupted and severely reduced) civil society. But that was not sufficient reason to look into the poisoned heart of the approaching Endarkenment and conclude that the real problem was the Enlightenment. After all, the vast majority of indiscriminate murders in Iraq were the work of anti-Enlightenment groups, be they Shia or Sunni extremists.

The coalition of left-wingers and religious reactionaries that joined forces to attack Enlightenment values was, in political terms, a rerun of the Iranian revolution debacle. Not a marriage of convenience so much as a spousal homicide waiting to happen. George Galloway, the MP for Bethnal Green for the Respect Party – an unlikely alliance between the Stalinist Galloway, the Trotskyist Socialist Workers Party, and the Islamist Muslim Association of Britain (MAB) – has said that 'socialism and Islam are very close'. But Yusuf al-Qaradawi strongly disagrees. Qaradawi is something of a spiritual leader to the Muslim Brotherhood, the global Islamist movement of which the MAB is the British arm. He has drawn the support of a number of nominal progressives, including Ken Livingstone and Madeleine Bunting. In his book *Priorities of the Islamic Movement*, Qaradawi insists that Marxism and Islam are incompatible. 'Marxism is a dominating totalitarianist philosophy,' he writes, 'that, by its very nature, does not leave room for Islam or any other religion, except, under conditions of leniency and necessity, when such religion is allowed to take the place of the tail, not the head, and act as a follower, not a leader.'

Perhaps Qaradawi and Galloway are both right: Marxism and Islamism are indeed close – both totalitarian – and therefore incompatible. In any case, the idea that Iraqi Islamists are left-wing revolutionaries who just haven't realised it yet is ludicrous. But it's one that a number of seemingly intelligent people appear to hold on to. In an infamous 2004 piece for *The Nation*, Naomi Klein sang the praises of the bloodthirsty Moqtada al-Sadr, and called on readers 'to bring Najaf to New York'. Again the same reverse principle applied: if the forces of democracy had created anarchy in Iraq, let's import anarchy to democracy.

I gained an up-close view of this outlook in New York the following year at a debate held between Christopher Hitchens, arguably the most consistently outspoken voice in favour of the invasion, and Galloway, among the most unswerving supporters of the insurgents and religious terrorists. Hitchens and Galloway loathed one another. The two men shared a history on the 'left', albeit at a distance. Hitchens, the extravagantly gifted essayist, was accused of having defected to the neocons, while Galloway had thrown his lot in with Middle Eastern dictators like Saddam and the Syrian despot Bashar al-Assad. In the run-up to the debate Galloway had accused Hitchens of being a 'drink-soaked ex-Trotskyist popinjay' and

Hitchens had in return identified the Scotsman as 'not just a pimp but a prostitute' for dictators. Originally I had planned to visit the two rivals in their separate camps: Hitchens in the politico-literary milieu of his Washington DC home, and Galloway at his Portuguese dacha, where he worked on his 'Gorgeous George' permatan. Unfortunately Galloway pulled out after reading a comment I had written about his contradictory views on religion. Specifically, I brought attention to his warning, voiced to a panel that included Salman Rushdie, that TV executives had to be 'very sensitive about people's religion . . . or deal with the consequences'. And I wondered how he reconciled this position with his support for the Soviet Union, a country in which, according to Solzhenitsyn, people were sent to slave labour camps for twenty-five years for the crime of praying. I thought I had been rather circumspect, for Galloway's hypocrisy was far more flagrant than I had suggested. After all, the self-styled defender of Muslims, proselytiser for Islamist insurgents in Iraq, was a supporter of the Soviet Union's war on Afghanistan in which an estimated 1.5 million Muslims were killed. Though I didn't make mention of that inconvenient fact, the Portuguese dacha invitation was still revoked.

The audience in a college hall in Manhattan was made up mostly of Galloway supporters. By and large, they knew little about the man, and cared even less. All that mattered was that he was against an American presence in Iraq. By contrast, they knew Hitchens and hated him with that special passion reserved for defectors. It was an ugly atmosphere. Outside the hall, one of those queuing to get in told me that America was 'the most evil empire the world has ever known', and it was far from a minority opinion. Inside, Galloway resorted to his speciality of base insults, and the crowd yelped and cheered. But he had nothing perceptive to say about Iraq. His most telling comment had been made a couple of months before in Syria, where he had paid tribute to the '145 military operations a day' launched by the jihadists and Baathists that formed the Iraqi 'resistance'. 'These poor Iraqis – ragged people with their sandals and their Kalashnikovs, are writing the names of their cities and towns in the stars.'

The morning of the debate 160 poor Iraqis, ragged people without Kalashnikovs, were blown up as they were queuing for jobs. When Hitchens asked for a minute's silence to remember the slain, he was booed by the audience and abused by the MP for Bethnal Green. These were deaths over which nobody wanted to vent their outrage, nor share their condolences.

The very last thing that Galloway, the poet of child bombers and torturers, wanted was the victory of Iraqi democrats because that would have meant a victory for the United States. And the same went for most of the audience. And the possibility remains that in a very limited sense they were right, albeit for the wrong reasons. Perhaps Iraq would be a more tolerable (though less tolerant) place to live if the Americans and British abandon the country and the jihadis and Baathists gained power. It's a possibility, however remote. But on this Galloway and his friends had no doubts. The kind of people who approvingly quote Mao's deputy Zhou Enlai's comment on the historical effect of the French Revolution – 'It's too early to say' – knew for certain right from day one that Iraq was better off with the old regime and its new jihadi allies.

In their radical fervour, the liberal-left audience in Manhattan seemed to believe that they had, as Klein advised, brought Iraq to New York. Yet Iraq seemed ever such a long way away. Hitchens had said something to me the night before the debate that stayed in my head. 'It's not really an argument about the facts of the matter,' he said. 'It's an argument about the mentality.'

I knew what he meant. It seemed to me that there were perfectly serious arguments right across the spectrum about what should have been and should be done in Iraq, from principled anti-imperialism through to principled internationalism. But there was a cynical attitude which had nothing to do with principles, and though he was just a small-time politician with a big-time ego, Galloway appealed to this cynicism. It was the attitude I saw in that hall in Manhattan and in the local election in Brent. I saw it when I interviewed the American actor Tim Robbins and the director of *Fahrenheit 9/11*, Michael Moore. And I saw it among many friends and people I knew in Britain and Europe and America. It is the attitude that not only sees American policy as incurably evil, but also views Iraq as little more than a cipher for that evil. It's an understanding that is interested only in those aspects of reality in Iraq that add to that country's power as a symbolic victim of American imperialism. And because it can only countenance defeat, it is an attitude that did nothing to challenge the Bush administration's tactical and strategic errors in Iraq. This way to Baghdad, it says, the American way, the way that leads to hell. It's an attitude that turns away from people like Majid al-Khoei and the Iraqi democrats who oppose the bombers and torturers.

The Bush administration can be said to have betrayed Iraqi democracy. The same charge cannot be laid at the door of the leaders of the anti-war movement. For they never supported the democrats in the first place.

12

Wake up and smell the cordite

The London Underground system was not built for emergencies. On many of the lines, the trains run along single-track tunnels, as tight as a bullet in a gun barrel. The tunnels are not only narrow but deep, up to a hundred feet beneath the ground. It would be hard to think of a more claustrophobic setting for something to go wrong. Perhaps that's why passengers tend to sink into themselves on the tube, in an effort to forget where they are. They read newspapers and paperback novels, listen to their iPods, daydream or do whatever it takes to escape, mentally, the cramped cylinder in which they find themselves temporarily entombed. Some never find the comfort of distraction. They're too aware of their confinement. These are the people you see frozen with fear whenever a train stops in the middle of a tunnel. They close their eyes and mutter to themselves, desperate for the train to move again. When the carriage finally shunts off, you can almost feel their jolt of relief.

From the middle of the train, the only way out between stations is to walk through the adjoining doors of each carriage to the end carriage. Even if a train were fairly empty, this would prove a difficult task because some doors are locked and the release mechanism is protected by a glass cover that needs to be broken. That's a challenging job for someone in a rush or a panic. If a train were full, then getting out would be a nightmare, even if everything else was normal. In the event of death and destruction, of blood and fire, it would

become a man-made inferno, a realisation of our most prim-
itive fears. The London Underground, in short, is the last
place you would want to find yourself in close proximity to
an exploded bomb.

At 8.50 a.m. on the morning of 7 July 2005 there were tens
of thousands of Londoners travelling to work. They were made
up of all ethnicities, religions and heritages. Men, women,
teenagers, atheists, Muslims, Christians, Jews, Hindus,
Buddhists, representatives from every continent and very close
to every nation. A more diverse group of people it would have
been difficult to find anywhere on earth. And by the law of
averages, a fair percentage of them would have taken part in
protests against the war in Iraq.

That morning I was travelling on an overground train to
east London, to the proposed site of the 2012 Olympic Games
that had been awarded to London the previous day. I was
researching a piece in which I planned to extol the virtues of
my home town, Britain's capital, and so I wanted to talk to
east Londoners in Stratford, where the Olympic village was
to be built. Though it was a grey morning, I felt enthusiastic
and optimistic – not necessarily common emotions in journalism – about the Olympic committee decision. I had been
surprised at how moved I was by the sight of thousands of
Londoners celebrating in Trafalgar Square. Conscious of an
unusually upbeat and yet characteristically mellow mood in
the air, I was also pleased that it was my last week of work
before my summer holiday.

Just after 9 a.m. I got a call from my wife. There had been
a 'power surge', she said, and she had to get off the tube,
just west of Paddington station. As we would later find out,
there was no power surge. In fact a thirty-year old primary
school 'learning mentor' by the name of Mohammed Siddique
Khan had let a bomb off on a tube train travelling between
Edgware Road and Paddington stations. It killed seven people
including Khan himself. Seconds either side of the Edgware
Road bomb, a train travelling to Aldgate station in east London

exploded and a southbound Piccadilly Line train also blew up just outside King's Cross station. This last train was deep beneath the ground, trapped in an inescapably narrow passage. Had these been the only bombs then there would have been no public image of the horrific events on that day. We would have had to rely on our imaginations to conjure up the sub-terranean hell of body parts and black smoke and screams and fearful, breathless panic. But just under an hour later, a red double-decker bus, the defining symbol of tourist London known around the world, was blasted apart in Tavistock Square, the famed literary environ of Bloomsbury, outside the offices of the British Medical Association. The top deck of the number 30 bus was ripped clear off. A picture postcard from a war zone.

Not including themselves, the four bombers killed fifty-two people and injured a further seven hundred. It was the worst attack on London since a German V2 rocket landed in Stepney in March 1945, killing 131. Why had this happened on this jubilant hangover of a day? Who was to blame for this dreadful assault on innocent lives? The first answer came from a statement, claiming to be from the 'The Secret Organisation Group of Al-Qaeda of Jihad Organisation in Europe', that was posted on an Islamist website a few hours after the attack.

'In the name of God, the merciful, the compassionate,' it began, 'may peace be upon the cheerful one and undaunted fighter, Prophet Muhammad, Allah's peace be upon him.'

Without wishing to become bogged down in theological pedantry, I feel a rational urge to make a couple of observa-tions about this typically florid introduction. First, one wonders what kind of operations an unmerciful God, lacking compassion, might sanction in his name. And second, how strange, how superstitious, that the prophet, supposedly God's messenger, requires the blessings of every two-bit loser who utters his name. Is he not in credit with Allah yet?

'Nations of Islam and Arab nations,' it continued. 'Rejoice, for it is time to take revenge against the British Zionist crusader government in retaliation for the massacres Britain is committing in Iraq and Afghanistan. The heroic Mujahideen have carried out a blessed raid in London. Britain is now burning with fear, terror and panic in its northern, southern, eastern, and western quarters.'

What massacres had British troops committed in Iraq and Afghanistan? Whether or not they should have been in Iraq, the British were essentially involved in policing the Shia-dominated area of Basra. Had they not been there, the Americans would have been, which may well have further inflamed ill-feeling. There were massacres taking place, of course, sectarian murders by Shia death squads. But the most indiscriminate and bloody massacres were those perpetrated by the Sunni jihadists with whom the authors of the statement were in sympathy. At the time in Afghanistan the story was much the same, with British forces largely restricted to a protective role, namely, for example, trying to prevent Sunni jihadists from murdering teachers who blasphemed by teaching girls.

A more detailed answer as to the identity of the killers came within a week from the police, after they raided properties in Leeds and Luton. The bombers, along with Khan, were twenty-two-year-old Shehzad Tanweer, twenty-year-old Germaine Lindsay and eighteen-year-old Hasib Hussain. It was they who had put to death, burned and blown the limbs off men and women from amazingly diverse backgrounds, all for their merciful, compassionate God.

A week later another culprit was named. The front cover of the *New Statesman* attributed the atrocity to 'Blair's bombs'. Not Islam's, or fundamentalism's, or religion's. Not four misguided young men's. No, the bombs, which were made in a bomb factory in Leeds by Islamic nihilists, belonged apparently to Tony Blair, the British prime minister. He owned responsibility for the murders. He made the young Muslim men do it. What choice, after all, did they have? The accompanying piece was written by John Pilger, who has never been slow to point the finger of blame away from the perpetrators, if the perpetrators are not sufficiently Western.

'In all the coverage of the bombing of London,' he wrote, 'a truth has struggled to be heard. With honourable exceptions, it has been said guardedly, apologetically. Occasionally, a member of the public has broken the silence, as an east Londoner did when he walked in front of a CNN camera crew and reporter in mid-platitude. "Iraq!" he said. "We invaded Iraq and what did we expect? Go on, say it." With the exception of Galloway, not one so-called anti-war MP spoke out in clear, unequivocal English . . . The bombs of 7 July were Blair's bombs.'

Pilger also went on to dismiss those who pointed out that 9/11 occurred prior to the invasions of Afghanistan and Iraq: 'Anyone with an understanding of the painful history of the Middle East would not have been surprised by 11 September or by the bombings of Madrid and London, only that they had not happened earlier. I have reported the region for 35 years, and if I could describe in a word how millions of Arab and Muslim people felt, I would say "humiliated". When Egypt looked like winning back its captured territory in the 1973 war with Israel, I walked through jubilant crowds in Cairo: it felt as if the weight of history's humiliation had lifted. In a very Egyptian flourish, one man said to me, "We once chased cricket balls at the British Club. Now we are free."'

Unfortunately, he continued, the Americans resupplied the Israelis and the Egyptians 'were not free'. Did this mean that they would still have to chase cricket balls? He didn't mention that the Egyptians lost because they were fighting for desert, while their tiny enemy, Israel, was fighting, against hugely superior numbers, for its existence. Nor did he mention that Israel signed a peace deal with Egypt two decades ago that handed back all captured Egyptian land to Egypt. It followed, therefore, that he also omitted to note that since that peace deal, Islamists in Egypt had murdered countless Egyptians, terrified secularists and atheists into silence, and slaughtered scores of tourists. Humiliation comes in many forms, and sometimes its most debilitating version is self-inflicted. The number of books translated into Arabic across the entire Arab world in the period between the end of Second World War and 2002 was less than had been translated into Spanish in Spain in a single year. The humiliation contained in that sobering statistic is not easily dramatised – there's no rolling cricket ball to grab on to, no Great Satan to finger. Rather it's a humiliation created and concealed by ignorance, a self-willed ignorance. The Israelis and Americans have not been killing Arab translators (they can leave that particular job to the jihadists). The translation of books is not contingent on the return of the Golan Heights. Multinational companies do not have a monopoly on printing presses. Authors are not preventing their books from being sold. Instead, it's symptomatic of the lack of intellectual curiosity and freedom of expression in the region. As a result the Arab world, despite its vast natural resources and stunning wealth, has had to import all of its technology and know-how. The people who blew up commuting Londoners on a benign summer's day represented an ideology that believes the answer to underdevelopment in the Arab and Muslim worlds is to crush the free exchange of ideas and to institute the fixed code of God's manual, the Koran. You can call these people many names but you cannot, in any meaningful or accurate use of language, call them freedom fighters. But that's exactly what I've heard intelligent liberal well-meaning friends do.

Four years after 9/11, my familiarity with the brand of fanatical masochism that Pilger took such solemn delight in articulating had indeed bred contempt. Had it just been Pilger, or a few far-left desperadoes, then this propensity to glorify nihilism could have been put down to a matter of eccentric taste, like self-flagellation or end-of-the-world prophecy. But the truth was that Pilger's piece represented a conspiratorial view of the world – the Americans, the British and the Israelis (or, as they were increasingly referred to, the Jews) were the cause of everything that was wrong – that was held far more widely than among just the *New Statesman* readership. To that extent Pilger was right. The guy who walked in front of the CNN camera and shouted 'What did we expect?' was not some lone random voice in the wilderness. There were a great many people who, one way or another, felt the same thing. Most would take their time expressing it, at least in print, but the murmurings started before 7/7 and only grew louder afterwards.

For this constituency, the release of a video 'martyrdom' tape of Mohammed Siddique Khan, broadcast on al-Jazeera on 1 September 2005, served only to endorse their view that Tony Blair was responsible for Khan's psychopathic actions.

'I'm going to keep this short and to the point because it's all been said before by far more eloquent people than me,' Khan began, almost as if he was paying testament, from beyond the grave, to the tireless work of Pilger. 'Therefore I'm going to talk to you in a language that you understand. Our words are dead until we give them life with our blood . . . Your democratically elected governments continuously perpetuate atrocities against my people all over the world. And your support of them makes you directly responsible, just as I am directly responsible for protecting and avenging my Muslim brothers and sisters. Until we feel security you will be our targets and until you stop the bombing, gassing, imprisonment and torture of my people we will not stop this fight. We are at war and I am a soldier. Now you too will taste the reality of this situation.' He then went on to profess his love for Osama bin Laden, Ayman al-Zawahri and Abu Musab al-Zarqawi, before asking that he and his cohorts be accepted 'into the gardens of paradise'.

Khan, it was said, liked cricket. As a teenager and in his early twenties, he was not particularly religious or attracted to an Islamic identity. Many of his friends were white and non-religious. They called him Sid. Although he became more observant as he grew older, he also became a more active participant in community life. After he left Leeds Metropolitan University, he worked at Hillside primary school and was involved with the Hamara Healthy Living Centre in Beeston. He was married to Hasina Patel, a 'community enrichment officer', and they had a daughter, Maryam. Colleagues said nice things about him. How could this man possibly become a mass killer? The answer for people like Pilger we already know. It was Iraq. And more specifically, Tony Blair. Blair created Khan, transformed him from a normal cricket-loving lad and conscientious dad into a determined and indiscriminate killer. Others believed that the answer was that Khan did not do it. That he was framed by the security service. This was the position of Dr Mohammed Naseem, the chairman of the Birmingham Mosque Trust, who claimed that the tape of Khan was doctored. 'We are in the twenty-first century,' said Dr Naseem. 'The cows can be made to look as [if] dancing, the horses can speak like humans, so these things can be doctored or can be produced.' Dr Naseem was also a major donator to George Galloway's Respect Party, as well as head of the Islamic Party of Britain, a group that believes Mossad orchestrated the 9/11 attacks. It would be tempting to dismiss Dr Naseem as a crank, but in fact he is well respected in Birmingham, where he is seen as a vital community leader by the West Midlands police. He has often been described as a 'moderate', not least for banning the Islamist group al-Muhajiroun from the mosque grounds and preventing Hizb ut-Tahrir, the pro-Caliphate group, from organising at the mosque. Both of these were deemed as bold attempts to combat extremists.

Instead, Dr Naseem's comments can be seen as symptomatic of the deep level of denial that exists within the Muslim religious community, in much the same way that selective finger-pointing afflicts the liberal-left. Together Naseem and Pilger mirror the Noam Chomsky (and Edward S. Herman) line on the Cambodian genocide back in the 1970s, which is to say that the genocide had not happened, and if it did happen, then America was to blame for creating the circumstances in which genocidal hatred could flourish. In other words, it's just two different ways, describing two completely different realities, that amount to the same thing: America is the culprit. Similarly in the case of Pilger and Naseem, they both reached the same conclusion – that Britain was the villain (it went without saying that America was the greater villain) – from two entirely different scenarios. In one the British security services conducted the 7/7 bombings, in the other they were an inevitable response to Britain's presence in Iraq. Either way it was Britain's fault.

What neither Pilger nor Naseem wanted to confront was the specific agency of ideological Islamism in the 7/7 bombings. We know that Khan had become a jihadist no later than 1999, when he tried to recruit Muslims to train in terror in Afghanistan. For Naseem, it was just too close to home. For Pilger, Islamism could only be a symptom, never a cause. To study the evolution of Islamism, especially in its twentieth and twenty-first-century guise, is to encounter an ideology of totalitarian ambition and nihilistic appeal. It is also to witness irrationality on a grand scale, an anachronism that the liberal mind struggles to take seriously. Surely, says the sophisticated observer, no one really believes that stuff about seventy-two virgins. And all that talk about regaining al-Andaluz, the reformed Caliphate, sharia law, that's just the frustration of the oppressed finding expression in an ancient form. If it wasn't for Islamophobia and Western neo-imperialism then these earnest young men would not have felt so alienated as to have blown themselves and others apart.

It was certainly easier to think like this than to wade through Sayyid Qutb's *Milestones* or *In the Shade of the Koran* or *Islam and Social Justice*. And, anyway, books like those, which inspired bin Laden and modern-day jihadists, were surely themselves merely expressions of resistance to Western imperialism, and ought to be understood in that context rather than as manuals of religious totalitarianism. If you believe that humans are essentially decent beings who, given the chance, treat one another with care and respect, then it's more comforting to think that men like Khan did not have a chance, that they were drawn to an extreme not by its attractions but forced there out of desperation. For who in their right mind would want to kill themselves, let alone complete strangers?

Even if Shehzad Tanweer, the Aldgate bomber, claimed in another taped message – released by al-Qaeda on the eve of the anniversary of 7/7 – that 'We love death the way you love life', he couldn't possibly mean that. For did he not also say that 'Your government has openly supported the genocide of more than 150,000 innocent Muslims in Falluja'? OK, so he had an inflationary way with numbers, and he didn't understand the meaning of the word 'genocide', but wasn't the point that he didn't love death? Was he not in fact saying that he hated death so much that he was driven to kill? These were the assumptions to which many guilty liberals were sentimentally disposed to jump.

After all, Khan, as the *Guardian* reported, 'spent his working life with young, vulnerable children'. One of his pupils was quoted in the same report: 'He [Khan] seemed a really kind man, he taught the really bad kids and everyone seemed to like him.' The co-author of that news story was a young man named Dilpazier Aslam. It appeared in the *Guardian* on 14 July 2005, one week after the bombings. The day before Aslam had written another piece, entitled 'We rock the boat'. This time it was published in the comment pages rather than the news section. 'I think,' Aslam wrote, 'what happened in London was a sad day and not the way to express your political anger.' He said this, he admitted, as 'an out-clause to being labelled a terrorist lover', before going on to all but justify what had happened. Aslam asked that we 'do ourselves a favour and not act shocked'. Shocked, he said, implied that we were unaware of the danger, when in fact we had been warned many times by the police. Shocked, he went on, would suggest that we had forgotten the dead of Falluja. 'Shocked would also be to suggest that the bombings happened through no responsibility of our own.' Muslims were angry about Iraq, he continued, and the freedoms of liberal democracy could not contain their anger. 'Second- and third-generation Muslims are without the don't-rock-the-boat attitude that restricted our forefathers. We're much sassier with our opinions, not caring if the boat rocks or not.'

One day – in fact just six days after the atrocity – Aslam was explaining away the indiscriminate murder: 'the same cry – why punish us? – is often heard from Iraqi mothers as the "collateral damage" increases daily'. The very next he was reporting on the man who organised and committed that murder. Leaving aside whether this arrangement undermined notions of objective or impartial news coverage, the first thing to say is that freedom of speech necessarily entails having to deal with opinions that you may dislike or find offensive. And sometimes a newspaper's duty is to publish material that some might find offensive because it represents a minority or neglected opinion and because it generates debate. So whatever I thought about Aslam's argument, such as it was, I could never say that it should not be published, although there's a time and a place, and, for me at least, they were not six days after the murders and in the *Guardian*. Still, that's just my opinion as a *Guardian* reader, and I don't doubt that other *Guardian* readers would disagree. But I thought I would exercise my own freedom of speech and, in the cause of expanding the debate, write to Aslam.

I'll confess that I was offended by the tone and language of his piece. It seemed to me that words like 'sad' and 'sassy' did not really reflect what took place in the asphyxiating darkness beneath London's streets. Of course I wasn't offended as gravely as a religious person might be by a blasphemy, for how could my feelings of sympathy for my fellow Londoners – dead, injured and bereaved – possibly compare to the hurt felt by someone at an insult to a fictional being? As a liberal journalist friend explained to me, religious feelings are different, 'they're about someone's identity'. As an atheist, I'm prepared to admit that I don't possess a soul, but I like to think that I still have a right to an identity. And part of my identity, the liberal part I thought, is paying due respect to innocent victims. Earlier that week there had been a particularly vicious Islamist bomb attack in Iraq on a school that had killed many children. Aslam made no mention of this act – to do so, of course, would have been to really 'rock the boat' – so I decided to write to him. It was not a rude letter. I began by commending Aslam for the forthright manner in which he had expressed himself. And I finished by suggesting that we meet up, as colleagues, to discuss the matter further. In between I asked him why it was that 'angry' Muslims such as himself never made mention of the genocide taking place in Sudan, or the fear in which secularist intellectuals live across the Muslim world, or the Christians terrorised in Pakistan, or the hundreds of thousands of Bangladeshis killed by Pakistan in 1971, while they frequently speak of Pakistan's claim on Kashmir. Were Sudanese deaths not worthy of anger, I wondered, because, like the children blown up in Iraq earlier that week, they were killed by Islamists? And why was it that ten years on from Srebrenica, when eight thousand Muslim men were massacred, that apologists for terrorism never acknowledged that it was American intervention that finally came to the rescue of Bosnian Muslims? In closing my email to him, I also felt compelled to make a lexical point. 'I think you should take the time to consider the difference between the words "shock" and "surprise". It may not have been a surprise that Muslim extremists planted bombs in the London Underground but of course it's a shock when innocent workers going about their daily business are blown apart. Just as it's a shock when it happens to young children in Iraq. When it ceases to be a shock is the point at which we lose our humanity – the point at which the bombers operate. No, shocked does not imply that we were unaware of the imminent danger. It means that we are capable of feeling, not just hating.'

He never replied.

Later it emerged that Aslam was a member of Hizb ut-Tahrir, an unsavoury fundamentalist group that, like the BNP, has been careful in recent years to conceal its anti-Semitism (though it is established and on the record). The group or party is international and long-standing but it first came to notice in Britain in 1986, when Omar Bakri Muhammad assumed the leadership. The sinister-comical Syrian would later flee Britain, after having praised the 7/7 bombers. While leader of Hizb, Bakri also ran al-Muhajiroun, a group he set up in Saudi Arabia in 1983. In 1996 he left Hizb and devoted himself to al-Muhajiroun. Among Bakri's disciples were the shoe-bomber, Richard Reid; Haroon Rasheed Aswad, who was arrested in 2005 and accused of attempting to set up a training camp for British jihadists in Oregon; Asif Hanif, the suicide terrorist who in 2003 blew up the backpackers' hangout, Mike's Bar in Tel Aviv; and Omar Khyam, a young Anglo-Pakistani who in 2007 was found guilty with four other men of conspiring to commit terrorist atrocities. One of their intended targets was the Ministry of Sound nightclub in London, which was identified by the group as worthy of attack on the grounds that it contained 'slags dancing around'. Khyam was also connected to Mohammed Siddique Khan. They were photographed together by MI5, though at that time the intelligence services were ignorant of Khan's identity, and the pair are thought to have attended the same terrorist training camp in Pakistan.

It also transpired that the *Guardian* knew that Aslam belonged to Hizb ut-Tahrir. Though not as overtly jihadist as al-Muhajiroun, Hizb believes in replacing democracy with a global Islamic Caliphate. It stresses that it wishes the transition to be peaceful, though it believes a clash of civilisations is inevitable and, indeed, desirable. Ed Husain, a former member of Hizb, writes in his revelatory memoir *The Islamist*: 'More than any other group, Hizb ut-Tahrir introduced the notion of jihad to the streets of Britain . . . Home-grown British

suicide bombers are a direct result of Hizb ut-Tahrir disseminating ideas of jihad, martyrdom, confrontation, and
anti-Americanism, and nurturing a sense of separation among
Britain's Muslims.'

Husain used to hand out Hizb leaflets. A not untypical
example read: 'The only meeting place between a Muslim and
a Jew is the battlefield.' In 2004 the *Guardian* had quoted one
imam who criticised Hizb ut-Tahrir for its 'racist ideas'. In
August 2003, a prominent Muslim leader, disguised to maintain anonymity, told the BBC's *Newsnight* that 'if Hizb ut-Tahrir
are not stopped at this stage, and we continue to let them
politicise and pollute the youngsters' minds and other gullible
people's minds, then what will happen in effect is that these
terrorism acts and these suicide bombings that we hear going
on around in foreign countries ... will actually start ...
happening outside our doorsteps'.

In the same year leaflets from Hizb ut-Tahrir were found
in the home of Omar Sharif, the British suicide bomber who,
along with Asif Hanif, killed three and injured sixty others
in Mike's Bar. Sharif and Hanif, it later turned out, worked
together with another jihadi to recruit young Muslims to the
Islamist cause. The name of the other man was Mohammed
Siddique Khan.

So after the attacks on the World Trade Center and the
Pentagon, after the bombing in Madrid, the exposure of
the networks of Islamic fundamentalists operating in Europe
and, in particular, in Britain, here was Britain's most respected
liberal newspaper employing an avowed anti-democrat and
Muslim fundamentalist to report on the avowed anti-
democrat and Muslim fundamentalist, Mohammed Siddique
Khan, who had slaughtered his fellow nationals in the name
of God.

To some liberals, including friends of mine at the *Guardian*,
this was a good thing. It demonstrated tolerance, inclusive-
ness and a diversity of views. 'We're always saying we want
to be more representative,' said one, 'and then when we are,

we start demanding what other people should think.' Aslam had not incited violence in his work at the *Guardian*, they pointed out, and Hizb was not an illegal organisation. And as they reminded me, there were plenty of reporters with political affiliations who reported on subjects about which they were not disinterested observers. As long as they drew a distinction between news and comment, what was the problem? For these supporters of Aslam the problem lay with the 'American right-wing bloggers' who brought attention to his Hizb membership. It was these 'raving obsessives' who were the troublemakers.

There was a time when the words 'American' and 'right wing' put together would have been, for me, almost enough to settle the argument. It was a handy short cut for the busy, confused or the lazy. Rather than considering the merits of the argument itself, you just needed to find out who the right-wingers were, and take the opposing view. Especially if those right-wingers were American. There was a time when I would have tried to accept the comparison of other reporters with political affiliations. But I now recognised it to be all so much evasion, unprincipled, blinkered, desperate evasion. No liberal would have defended, much less employed, Dilpazier Aslam had he been called Bill Ashman and was a member of the BNP. And please try to imagine *any* newspaper, let alone a liberal newspaper, publishing a piece by a BNP member following David Copeland's bombing spree, a piece in which readers were told not to pretend to be shocked because white heterosexual nationalists had been warning for years that black immigration and gay liberation had left them feeling humiliated and angry. Imagine the outrage, in the days following the nail bombing of the Admiral Duncan pub in Soho, if a BNP member wrote about the 'sassy' attitude of his generation who were now prepared to 'rock the boat'.

At this point, there will be those who will say that the two situations are not comparable. And they will base this assertion on this simple fact: Dilpazier Aslam is an Asian Muslim, and therefore part of an oppressed minority, whereas the hypothetical BNP member would be a white heterosexual, and therefore part of the oppressing majority. They may also take the argument further and point out that David Copeland was expressing a violent hatred of black and gay people, that black and gay people had done no harm to him, and that there was no deeper political statement in his actions than nihilistic hatred of difference. Whereas Mohammed Siddique Khan was motivated by the oppression of 'his people' both in Britain (where Muslims were more likely to be undereducated and unemployed or low-paid) and, more particularly, in Afghanistan and Iraq. Therefore, while his actions may have been regrettable, they were born of a genuine grievance and a sincere political commitment.

Now if you possess an ounce of white liberal guilt in your body, you may conceivably feel a pang of sympathy for such arguments. For that's what these arguments are: white liberal guilt. But that's all they are. They don't stand up to inspection in any other moral or political terms. First of all, Khan and his cohorts were not victims of oppression. Khan had every opportunity to flourish in British society – he went to university, he had a job and a family – but, for his own reasons, he did not want to develop those opportunities. Second, members of the white working class, the group from which Copeland emerged, perform almost as poorly in education and job prospects. By any objective criteria, there is not much to choose between the two, except that immigrant groups tend to be upwardly mobile. Typically, ethnic minorities in this country, who often come from peasant cultures, start off slowly on the academic and employment graph and then race ahead after a couple of generations. If anything, the 7/7 bombers were part of this success. Similarly, their victims were not representative of the 'majority', whoever that might constitute, but, as has already been stated, a random group of amazingly diverse people. The 7/7 attacks were just like Copeland's bomb: indiscriminate. Andrea Dykes was four months pregnant when she and her unborn child were killed in Copeland's attack on the Admiral Duncan. Her husband was seriously injured but survived. Would Copeland's crime have been any less malevolent had he only targeted these heterosexuals?

Before me I have a list of the surnames of the dead on the number 30 bus: Ly, Gordon, Russell, Parathasangary, Hyman, Wise, Islam, Fatayi-Williams, Wundowa, Rosenberg, Jain, Hart, Hartley. That doesn't include the killer, Hussein. Each of them in their own way has an extraordinary story. Anat Rosenberg, for example, was a charity worker who was born in Israel and completed her national service there (so the Islamists would have been pleased with that hit) before moving to London to study ballet. Giles Hart was a humanist who was born in Sudan and was an active supporter of the Polish Solidarity Campaign during the eighties. He didn't ignore the human rights of his fellow Europeans in the East but instead laboured long and hard to help in the cause of Polish freedom. He was also chairman of the H.G. Wells Society and a supporter of the Anti-Slavery Society. A man who treasured freedom was killed by those who abhorred it. I spoke to his daughter a few months after her father was murdered. She and the family were still devastated by their loss. But rather than stray into emotional territory, let's stick with the more acceptable matter of identity. Shaharah Islam was a devout Muslim. Neetu Jain was a Hindu. Her boyfriend Gous Ali, a Muslim. This is what he said of the Islamist beliefs of the killers. 'It's all brainwashing by some wacko scholar who believes his own version of the Koran and has made it his own battle. There is no holy war. They [the Islamists] have so much coverage, it's damaging, yet the voices of the innocent victims are not being heard.'

The liberal argument that has grown more popular as the Iraq War has become less popular is that, when it comes down to it, the commuters murdered on that summer morning were not innocent victims. Obviously no one but the most demented Islamists condones the 7/7 bombs but the Pilger school of thought maintains that Britain took part in the Iraq invasion, lots of people lost their lives in Iraq, therefore it stands to reason that people will lose their lives in Britain. And in this Pilger, and his fellow Islamist apologists, are undoubtedly correct. People *have* died in Britain and their killers *have* said that it was revenge for Afghanistan and Iraq. So let's assume the position of the Islamist themselves and, like them, not dwell on the fact that the most indiscriminate killers in Iraq and Afghanistan are their fellow Islamists. And let's accept that Khan and his young acolytes acted in good faith.

Whatever else the bombs did, they offered a challenge. They forced us to consider what Iraq had to do with Britain. Why should we risk our civilian lives with our presence there? But it only seems polite, not to say logical, to throw the question back: What does Iraq have to do with Khan and his chums? None of them was from Iraq and, as far as is known, none of them had been there. The same goes, by the way, for the failed bombers who attacked London Undergound a fortnight after the 7/7 bombers. None of them, as far as is known, ever organised against Saddam's repression, supposedly secular in nature. I've yet to meet an Iraqi who thinks that the 7/7 bombers were acting for them. My local mosque, which is overwhelmingly patronised by Iraqis, organised a memorial service for the 7/7 victims. It's true that the bombers are thought to have visited Pakistan a few times. But Pakistan has scarcely any cultural links with Iraq. Iraq is an Arab country, Pakistan, of course, is not. Iraq is majority Shia, Pakistan is majority Sunni. They are separated by the vast land mass of Iran and historically that separation has been more than just geographical. Pakistan and Iraq are both 'Muslim' countries but only insofar as Russia and Italy are both 'Christian' countries. But none of these differences concerned Khan and company. Khan spoke of 'my people' and Shehzad Tanweer said: 'And ask yourselves: why would thousands of men be ready to give their lives for the cause of Muslims?'

The answer, of course, is ideology. Khan and Tanweer

believed in the totalitarian ideology of Islamism. And Islamism was not a function of the Iraq War, though it unquestionably added recruits to the cause. The cause of Islamism is much larger than the Iraq War. As Tanweer also said: 'You will never experience peace until our children in Palestine, our mothers and sisters in Kashmir, and our brothers in Afghanistan and Iraq feel peace.' Naturally, Tanweer, like Aslam, said nothing about peace in Sudan, where Islamists inflicted upon millions of mothers, sisters and brothers only the feeling of war. But Tanweer's concern was not just for Afghanistan and Iraq, where Islamists were also working day and night to make sure that no one felt peace. It was also for Palestine and Kashmir, situations that the British were essentially power-less to influence. In addition Tanweer demanded the release of 'all Muslim prisoners from Belmarsh and your other concen-tration camps'. By this he meant people such as Abu Qatada, the man who has been called 'Osama bin Laden's ambassador to Europe' and 'mentor' to the shoe-bomber Richard Reid, and who had been found guilty *in absentia* in Jordan of terrorist offences. Tanweer saw himself as a soldier, and part of his battle was to ensure that Qatada and other foreign Islamists suspected of organising or encouraging terrorism were main-tained by the British state in the style to which they had become accustomed – given asylum, housing benefits, and free to agitate for the destruction of their generous hosts. For Britain had allowed itself to become a safe haven for Islamists, like Abu Qatada, during the eighties and nineties. The deal had effectively been that as long as they caused no domestic trouble then they would be left alone. And the unstated other side of that deal was that as long as they were left alone they would cause no domestic trouble. Of course, the contract was broken, as it were, by the liberation/occupation of Afghanistan and Iraq, because then the Islamists more openly began inciting violence against the British at home and abroad.

The appeasement argument has it that Afghanistan and Iraq radicalised the Islamists and the only way to deradicalise them is to pull out of these campaigns. But you only have to listen to what the Islamists have been writing and saying for many years to see that they were already radicalised, only we hadn't paid any attention. No amount of appeasement is likely to alter their beliefs, and their beliefs determine their actions. Once Britain had complied with all Islamist demands, even if it could, would the Underground trains be safe from murder and maiming? Would it all stop there? Would radical Islam return to the more arcane matters like when it was appropriate to stone women to death? Or would there be some other issue somewhere in the world that would trigger a whole new threat?

The 'root-cause' fraternity, of which Pilger was high priest, dismissed these concerns. Because, by their way of thinking, Islamic fundamentalism was simply a new vanguard, a means of resistance against global capitalism. If you removed what the Islamists were resisting then the attractiveness of Islamism would diminish, or even disappear. This root-cause analysis, however, only focused on those causes that suited its proponents' world view – namely the malign influence of the West, in particular the United States and Britain. Of the enormous investment by Saudis in the exportation of the Wahhabi or Salaafist version of Islam, with its literalist and fundamentalist interpretations, the root causers had little to say, other than that Saudi Arabia was an American ally. The pernicious effect of the fundamentalism produced by the corrupt disaster of Iran, genocidal Sudan, and the psychopathic militias that disfigured Algeria and Somalia, these too were passed over. Indeed, the evangelical war ethic that forms a core message of the Koran was also deemed to be practically incidental to Islamism. For Islamism was first and foremost a manifestation of anti-imperialism, what Pilger called, in his best bin Laden prose, 'the latest stage in a long struggle against the empires of the west, their rapacious crusades and domination'. That the Islamists demand an Islamic empire is, of course, neither here nor there.

Still, as I say, in the first few days and weeks after 7/7 the opinion of people like Pilger, Aslam and Galloway was not widely expressed on the liberal-left, at least not in public forums. At the same time, nor did the liberal-left organise to oppose Islamist terrorism. Even though Islamism is an explicit attack on everything the liberal-left holds dear, it's not, in truth, a cause that sets the liberal blood pumping. In fact, it must be said that with the exception of fascism and racism (or rather fascist racism), there are very few non-state issues that really perturb liberals. And I think this is an existential problem for contemporary liberalism. Rather like the British guns at Singapore that faced out to sea in preparation for a naval attack, and were as a consequence useless against the Japanese land assault, so too has liberalism grown used to aiming its defences in an increasingly irrelevant direction. Liberals are hawk-eyed to the threat to liberty presented by the state. The problem is that, despite scare stories, the state has grown progressively more liberal in the last fifty years, whereas a number of non-state groups have become progressively less liberal. In this circumstance some kind of re-evaluation of liberalism is required, in particular in regard to what liberalism means in a liberal state challenged by illiberal citizens. And how best to defend liberalism in those conditions.

It was noticeable that many of the voices that did not know what to say after 7/7, suddenly found their eloquence after the tragic shooting of Jean Charles de Menezes in a misinformed and botched counterterrorism operation. A Metropolitan Police surveillance team wrongly identified the Brazilian electrician as Hussain Osman, one of the suspects in the failed bombing attempts of 21 July. The police were instructed not to allow him to enter London Undergound, but, owing to operational confusion, that's exactly what they did, and disastrously tried to rectify this mistake by shooting him seven times in the head. Here, at last, was a foe that liberals understood and knew how to attack: the police and, by extension, the government. Here was an opportunity to feel shame and guilt. The relief was palpable. Suddenly there was a Justice4Jean campaign, human rights lawyers mobilised, columnists condemned, vigils were held, Stop the War Coalition organised a protest, the anti-racist activist Asad Rehman, formerly of Amnesty International and latterly a member of George Galloway's campaign team, became the de Menezes family spokesman, and de Menezes was posthumously recruited to the anti-imperialist cause. As Craig Murray, the former British Ambassador to Uzbekistan, put it: 'The real blame lies with those who sanctioned the "shoot to kill" policy defended in such macho fashion by Jack Straw and Charles Clarke [home secretary]. They must now resign. British liberty will not recover until Charles Clarke and Ian Blair [Metropolitan Police Commissioner] stand in the dock for their part in this murder.'

There was no precedent for the events that took place that July. There had never before been a known active suicide bombing squad operating in Britain. In the week before I went on holiday, the city was in a state of near phobic paralysis. Londoners were suspicious, if not terrified, of the person sitting next to them on the tube and the bus, especially if that person happened to look like a Middle Eastern, Asian or North African Muslim. The pressure on the police to apprehend the culprits was enormous. And it grew in the week that I was away. I followed the news reports from abroad and friends at home testified to the the tense atmosphere of panic and uncertainty. The police hunting the team would also have been aware of what happened to one of the policemen who raided the Leganés safe house of the bombers of Madrid: he was killed when the bombers blew themselves up.

No one felt that the tube passengers should have grabbed the failed bombers as they fled. To do so would have meant risking their lives. And in our society individuals are discouraged from intervening to protect the community. It was universally agreed that risking your life in defence of your community, your city, your nation, was a job for the police. None of that makes the actions of the police right. But the de Menezes murder was a grotesque error. It had nothing to do with Iraq, or imperialism or any of the other issues hung on de Menezes. Instead, rather like a pedestrian mown down by a speeding police car, he was in the wrong place at the wrong time.

I did not think what happened to de Menezes was a 'sad' day, or 'not the way to express your political anger'. I think that it was unequivocally a terrible tragedy. The police had choices and they made the wrong one. But they were not easy choices, they were the kinds of snap assessments and pressured decisions that only a handful of people will ever face in life. By contrast, the bombers of the 7 July and 21 July and the many would-be bombers and conspirators who have followed in their wake had limitless options. They chose to attempt mass murder because that's what they believed was the most effective way of undermining and demoralising secular, democratic, liberal society. And in this assessment of British and Western European society they may yet prove to be correct.

Two of the 21 July bombers were eventually arrested a few minutes' drive from my home, in a block opposite where my wife used to live. The bombers used to meet at a café I frequented in west London, where they planned to kill as many citizens as possible of the nation that gave them asylum, housing and all the social benefits they could claim. To me these people are no different to David Copeland. They have no claim to be Third World freedom fighters. To accord them that unwarranted status – which is what Pilger did – is a shameful betrayal of those like Nelson Mandela and Steve Biko who earned the title. At best, they are misguided misfits, manipulated by cunning ideologues. These people boast that they love death, which is really just another way of saying that they are terrified of life: freedom, choice, responsibility, modernity, reality. Death brings an end to all of these challenges. It is the annihilating equaliser. It takes a certain demented courage to kill yourself, the kind of courage that comes from intoxication, be it chemical or spiritual. But it takes a far more profound courage to live, to struggle, to achieve. Islamism, in its call to moral submission and sacrifice of the intellect, not only provides a means for those who lack that determination, it positively encourages the abandonment of the will to find it. To this end it has located sympathetic accommodation in the West. Liberal societies, guilt-laden and complacent, ask little of the Ramzi Mohammeds or Yasin Omars of this world, and, unsurprisingly, they give little. Afghanistan and Iraq, whatever the respective merits of the military campaigns therein, are no more than excuses, pseudo-grievances, to conceal the moral void of a death cult. There is no reason to avoid stating this point with emphatic clarity, even if you want the troops to withdraw from Afghanistan and Iraq tomorrow and leave the democrats to their bloody fate.

And yet that is not what has happened. For while it's true that only a small minority was as determined as Pilger to absolve the bombers of any culpability in the carnage they wrought, the opinion that Blair, or British foreign policy, caused the 7/7 bombs soon became voiced right across the liberal spectrum from the far-left usual suspects through to Kenneth Clarke in the Conservative Party. And as each new bomb plot was thwarted and came to light, so the conviction grew that if only we abandoned Afghanistan and Iraq then everything would return to normal at home. We could relax and forget about these strange people with their strange loathing for the Western way of life.

In August of 2006 a conspiracy to blow up a number of transatlantic planes was uncovered, and the country was placed on high alert. By this stage, the sense of anger towards the government was widespread and open. Even commentators in the London *Evening Standard*, hardly a radical publication, began whining about the privations to which the government had subjected the nation.

'Why us?' asked one. 'What have we done to deserve this hatred? Why are we bearing the brunt when other countries escape relatively lightly? Why can't we be left alone to get on with our lives?' The answer, he went on to say, was because Britain was too closely tied to America, especially in Iraq. If we pulled out the troops, his argument ran, then we could fly once more without fear.

I could see why people might think that the American and British presence in Iraq was in fact creating the social chaos in that country it was supposed to stop. But at the very least it was worth considering that the opposite might be true, that victorious Islamists would increase the attacks as they set about dismantling the fledgling democracy. The daily diet of massive car bombs and suicide attacks in Baghdad was, after all, aimed at Iraqis not British or American soldiers. Yet troop withdrawal as a means of improving the situation in Iraq was a morally legitimate argument. To call for troop withdrawal so that Sunni extremists would not target British train commuters and airline passengers was not just a cop-out but total capitulation. Worse than immoral, it was amoral.

Still, it had the advantage, however meagre, of at least entertaining reality. Which could not be said of the opinion that dismissed every exposed bomb plot and terrorist conspiracy as another example of Islamophobic policing. Azzam Tamimi, the Hamas-supporting director of the Institute of Islamic Political Thought, wrote a piece after the planes conspiracy was revealed headlined 'I BET YOU IT WILL TURN OUT TO BE A HOAX'. His reasoning was that a) the conspirators were arrested by the British police, who had a track record of targeting innocent Muslims, and b) the government-backed 'hoax' was a means of diverting attention from Israel's war with Hizbollah in Lebanon. His suspicion was that the police had arrested the men 'to smear the image of Islam and the Muslims at the time when the entire world can see that they are the victims of a most unjust world order dominated by the USA and UK, who both support and sponsor Israeli terrorism against Muslims in Palestine and Lebanon and who both oppress Muslim peoples of Afghanistan and Iraq through direct occupation'.

And so it goes on, the refusal to look at what Islamism entails, and the blind hope that terrorism is simply the protest of the voiceless and the frustrated. As I write, the Islamist terrorism in Iraq has reached a new level of homicidal violence, a video of a twelve-year-old Taliban recruit beheading an 'informer' has been posted on the Internet, there are over a hundred people awaiting trial in Britain for terrorist offences, and the head of Scotland Yard's counterterrorism command has issued a warning that further attacks on Britain are highly likely. And many liberals are still unsure of who the enemy is.

13

The liberal heretic

Perhaps it's the mark of true freedom not to live in constant appreciation of its existence. The beauty, if not the value, in saying rude things about our political leaders or taking 'the Lord's name in vain' is that we are able to do both every day without giving the liberty to do so a second thought. For it would not be very liberating if one was obliged to dwell on all those who suffered and died in the cause of securing the right to blaspheme or to say 'Tony Blair should be imprisoned for war crimes'. However, there is a problem with this complacency. The more we take freedom for granted, the less able we are to recognise when it is under threat. As a result there are occasions, particularly in the rush to suck up to anti-Western forces, when we seem to treat our hard-won freedoms as if they were an embarrassing inconvenience.

Unfortunately, it is in the nature of freedom that it is difficult to attain but easy to lose. In the immortal lyric of Joni Mitchell: 'Don't it always seem to go / That you don't know what you've got / Till it's gone.' In fact, a great deal of a certain kind of freedom has gone from daily life since I was a child, but we have adapted to its departure with fatalistic resignation. Freedom of movement has been markedly altered by the proliferation of violence. The area I grew up in, for instance, is now a no-go zone after dark and worryingly dangerous during the day. The fact is there are large areas of our towns and cities into which old people, women, children and anyone carrying anything of worth are discouraged from venturing. For decades the decline in street safety was seen by liberal society as too sensitive an issue to focus upon. The policy, by and large, was either to pretend it wasn't happening, to downplay its significance, or to blame the uneven distribution of wealth and the reactionary nature of the police. It is only very recently, as the situation has got completely out of hand in parts of London and Manchester, that liberals have shown some willingness to talk about these criminally imposed limits on freedom, although seldom with much conviction.

I got thinking about this readiness to accept a curtailment of our freedom, after I was invited to dinner by a friend. It was January 2006 and my friend was playing host to a distinguished guest, a brave and extraordinary woman who, it had to be said, certainly did not take freedom for granted. For in making use of it she had been threatened with death, her co-film-maker slaughtered, and she was forced to live surrounded by a police guard. I was wondering what that must feel like, to be conscious of strangers wanting to kill you, when I set out for my friend's flat, which was less than a fifteen-minute walk from my house. Even though it was a mild night for January, I didn't walk. It was not laziness but a sort of unconscious fear that led me to my car. On the whole, I'm not a particularly risk-averse character. But the fact is it was one of those nights when I didn't feel in urban survival mode, all beady eyed and prepared for the unexpected. And these days there are more and more of those nights. As I drove the short journey I chastised myself for what I preferred to think of as my indolence but was in fact a form of cowardice, especially when I made sure to park right outside the flat. It was, after all, a well-lit Victorian avenue, not some nightmare sink estate. The woman I was about to meet lived under constant threat of death and yet she made sure to present a fearless face to the world. The same, it seemed, could not be said for me.

That evening at the dinner there was conversation about street crime. Horror stories were exchanged. Someone who lived in New York said he felt London was a far more dangerous place now. I recalled the first time I went to New York in 1980, when people were so terrified of street crime that no one would stop to give me the time of day. New Yorkers, America's most liberal population, seemed perversely proud of the murders and muggings that made them scared to use the subway, or linger in Central Park after sunset or walk certain streets day or night. It was as if they thought their fear was a sign of their freedom, rather than the lack of it. Back then, any attempt to deal with violence was seen as an incursion of liberty, as though street crime were some sort of expression of urban creativity. Whereas in fact violence was the chief factor inhibiting the freedoms of New Yorkers. Eventually, the mayor, Rudolph Giuliani, and his police commissioner, William Bratton, instituted policies that drastically reduced crime and New Yorkers discovered that the freedom to walk home in safety enhanced their quality of opportunities more than the freedom to be mugged. Still, in spite of the giveaway use of my car that evening, I didn't want to believe that London had become the new pre-Giuliani New York.

A couple of days later I learned that a young lawyer named Tom ap Rhys Pryce was stabbed to death the day after the dinner party, just along the same street that my friend lived in, at about the same time of evening. He was killed by two teenage serial muggers who stole his mobile phone and a tube pass. That was it. His life was ended for a phone and a week's free travel on the Underground. He was going to get married. His fiancée was waiting at home. Their adult lives were just flowering. And the lives of the two boys, his killers, they too were placed on the indefinite hold of decades of imprisonment. Rhys Pryce meant nothing to them. It could have been anyone who happened to walk along that street at that hour. They were products of a culture of unbridled violence, a culture from which most people, well-meaning or not, prefer to look away. As most of the murders this culture generates are deemed to be community-specific – so-called 'black-on-black' crimes – it is, alas, not that difficult for society at large, especially our communally separated society, to ignore them.

The strangers who want to kill Ayaan Hirsi Ali – the guest that evening – are motivated not by money but God. She looked so slight and delicate at my friend's house, like some exotic figurine, that it was hard to believe anyone could ever be so scared of her as to commission her murder. But this slender Somali woman is one of the most hated figures in political Islam. In November 2004 a Dutch Moroccan called Mohammed Bouyeri sent a death threat to Hirsi Ali. Along with the destruction of Holland and Europe, Bouyeri called for the murder of the woman he termed the 'fundamentalist unbeliever'. His method of delivery was to impale the note with a knife in the chest of Hirsi Ali's collaborator in film, Theo van Gogh, having already shot him eight times and cut his throat to the spine. Bouyeri enacted that entire bloody scene one morning in broad daylight on a busy high street in Amsterdam.

I had learned about Hirsi Ali a few months before van Gogh's murder during a conversation with a Dutch artist. She, the artist, was in many respects the typical European liberal – tolerant, interested in other cultures, an advocate of immigration and state subsidies. But she spoke hesitatingly about Hirsi Ali, uncertain how to voice her approval, as if she were afraid I might take offence. She was worried that I would confuse or conflate Hirsi Ali's views with those of Pim Fortuyn. The arrival of a flamboyant gay maverick on the Dutch political scene, which by convention had been a testament to the blandness of consensus, had muddied the ideological waters. A former Marxist, Fortuyn had been portrayed, inaccurately, in Britain and other parts of Europe as a far-right politician. He earned this epithet because he had called for an end to immigration in tiny, overcrowded Holland. The country was 'full', he announced. What prompted this proclamation was the yawning chasm that had opened up between mainstream liberal society and a growing strain of Islamic fundamentalism, which was virulently anti-gay and, as far as Fortuyn was concerned, misogynistic. Fortuyn argued that Holland's renowned tolerance was placed in jeopardy. He was, he said, 'in favour of a cold war with Islam'. In 2002 Fortuyn was shot dead by an animal rights activist in what was said to be Holland's first political assassination since the lynching of the De Witt brothers in 1672.

The artist's concern was not misplaced because in the forthcoming months and years I would regularly see Hirsi Ali described in the British liberal press as a member of a 'far-right' political party and even, on one occasion, a member of Fortuyn's party. What had she done to deserve this designation? Essentially this: she had renounced her religion, the religion of Islam.

In particular, she renounced the sexism, homophobia, racism and cult of violence that she found to be thriving and unchallenged in the core of Islamic doctrine. Which is to say, she set herself against some classically 'far-right' attitudes. But she chose the wrong far-right target. Had she selected an obscure grouplet of neo-Nazis in Holland who had never achieved anything beyond their bedroom fantasies, then she would no doubt have been hailed as a fearless campaigner for progress and truth. But as a woman who had lived in the Islamic societies of Somalia and Saudi Arabia, and as someone who had witnessed close up the violence suffered by Muslim women in Holland, she chose instead to aim her considerable intellectual powers at the limiting and far-reaching effects of dogmatic Islam. And in so doing she made herself an enemy not only of fundamentalist Islam but also its liberal apologists. Hence my Dutch friend's careful deliberation in explaining Hirsi Ali's opinions. She didn't want me, as a liberal, to think that she was some kind of fascist.

I started reading up on Hirsi Ali after that conversation and I also began to take a greater interest in Holland itself. Long seen as a sort of laboratory for liberal ideas, the

Netherlands provided a fascinating window into contemporary Europe. I paid a couple of visits to Amsterdam and The Hague and I became acquainted with the Dutch political set-up, some of the main politicians and intellectuals. Consequently I heard about the television screening of *Submission Part One*, the short film Hirsi Ali had made with van Gogh. As a child in Africa, Hirsi Ali had been subjected to female genital mutilation – not in itself an Islamic ritual but one often encouraged by clerics and the religious-minded in Islamic countries. She was also severely beaten by her Islamic teacher, so badly that she required an operation to relieve swelling on her brain. And she was given by her father to a cousin to marry. In working as a translator for the Dutch social services, Hirsi Ali also saw a great deal of female suffering among Muslim communities. These experiences and her own reading of the Koran she channelled into *Submission Part One*, which focused on physical abuse and restriction of Muslim women. It was her contention that the mistreatment of Muslim women was specifically encouraged by statements in the Koran, and to underline this point she and van Gogh depicted women in diaphanous veils with the relevant Koranic texts superimposed on their near naked bodies. All these developments I followed with growing curiosity. Intrigued, I requested an interview with Hirsi Ali.

But before that meeting could be arranged, van Gogh was murdered. I was astounded when I learned of the brutal and public nature of the killing. 'Can't we talk about this?' was van Gogh's futile appeal as he lay shot and bleeding in Linnaeusstraat, a bustling high street in east Amsterdam. Bouyeri didn't want to talk. Talking was what he was against. Talking was what the inveterate provocateur and polemicist van Gogh did. It was Bouyeri's mission to stop the talking by cutting van Gogh's throat right down to the spinal column. And that's what he did, coolly, deliberately, without a flicker of doubt or mercy. One witness said it was like watching a butcher slaughter an animal.

There is arguably no more shocking image in peacetime Europe than van Gogh's murder. For in a way it is more traumatising than the Srebrenica concentration camp or even the Madrid and London bombs. Something about the indiscriminate terror, the sheer scale of carnage of those atrocities, serves to render them incomprehensible. They are just too big, too spectacular, too immediate and too bloody to process. Our imaginations are not up to the job. Instead, we tend to think of them like acts of war or even acts of God (of course the perpetrators thought the two were the same thing), a terrible demonstration of fate's caprices. But the specificity of van Gogh's murder and its gruesome public performance was something the imagination could really get to work on. Here was a writer, a film director, an artist cycling to work, when in plain view of hundreds of bystanders he was ritually slaughtered as he begged for his life and – the most haunting detail – the right of debate.

Yet once again, and still not for the last time, I was dismayed by the manner in which the liberal media absorbed the shock and moved swiftly on. In news reports in the *Guardian*, Hirsi Ali and van Gogh were admonished for behaving 'with magnificent disregard for the feelings they might be offending'. Gary Younge, a columnist in the same newspaper, claimed that the killer was 'a lone Muslim extremist', contrary to the available evidence. Younge condemned the secular left for its refusal to engage with religious communities, and criticised the Dutch for their spiralling 'Islamophobia' – 'the Dutch government is considering the closure of mosques that spread "non-Dutch values"', he wrote. 'Would these be the values of the people who sheltered Anne Frank or those who shopped her?'

In fact, the Dutch government was considering withdrawing public funds from mosques that were set against the Dutch state itself, not just its values of sexual, religious and racial tolerance. In Younge's view the very idea of even thinking about not subsidising reactionary organisations that called for the destruction of the state that was subsidising them was akin to being a Nazi collaborator. If that were not enough, an editorial in *Index on Censorship*, a liberal organisation dedicated to freedom of expression, entitled 'Free speech fundamentalist on a martyrdom operation' accused van Vogh of 'roaring his Muslim critics into silence with obscenities. An abuse of his right to free speech, it added injury to insult by effectively censoring their moderate views as well.' The author of this piece, Rohan Jayasekera, suggested that van Gogh had built 'an exploitative working relationship with Somali-born Dutch MP Ayaan Hirsi Ali, whose terrible personal experience of abuse has driven her to a traumatizing loss of her Muslim faith' and concluded by inviting readers to 'applaud Theo van Gogh's death as the marvellous piece of theatre it was'.

Jayasekera spoke of van Gogh 'censoring' moderate views, though it was not clear how the outspoken writer and film-maker achieved this feat. Perhaps he meant that moderates were afraid of appearing to go easy on van Gogh, so they said nothing or made their comments less moderate. If so, that would show a remarkable lack of intellectual resolve. For what does it say about a 'moderate' if he is afraid of appearing 'moderate' because it might look weak to extremists? Contrast the position in which van Gogh supposedly placed notional moderates with that in which Bouyeri placed critics of Islam. In the first case, there was the danger of being seen to be insufficiently opposed to van Gogh's invective, in the second there was the danger of death. Which, does any sane person suppose, is the more effective at censoring opinion? Yet just as many liberals, even today, are loath to admit street violence limits freedom of movement, so did they prove unwilling to acknowledge that Islamist violence restricted freedom of speech.

Jayasekera's piece also demonstrated the multiculturalist double bind, in which the outsider is always an intruder and the insider a misguided sell-out. Thus van Gogh was characterised as the cunning white exploiter of the naive black innocent Hirsi Ali, who was tricked into betraying her religious or racial group. The prevailing wisdom seems to be that if a member of a minority offends his or her own community, they should be left to sort it out among themselves in an offstage administration of tribal justice. And if someone from outside the community dares to comment they must, by definition, be racist. With these constraints in place, you wonder how a debate is supposed to be had or disagreement registered. It's the perfect means of preventing dissent. You're either a racist or an Uncle Tom. In fact, it was Hirsi Ali who recruited van Gogh, and it was Hirsi Ali who determined the style and content of *Submission Part One*. Van Gogh did little more than point the camera. After much criticism, Jayasekera withdrew his comment about Hirsi Ali. But there were plenty of others who were content to see van Gogh and Hirsi Ali as architects of their own misfortune.

Another sentiment that was expressed in the liberal press and on various blogs was that van Gogh had it coming to him because he had a history of saying offensive things about Muslims. Indeed, he did have a history of saying offensive things about everyone, Catholic, Protestant, Jew, communist, fascist, liberal, you name it. In particular he said some unforgivable, and very nearly unspeakable, things about Jews. Saying the unsayable was an integral aspect of his style, a style which could often be wearisome as well as offensive. He referred to Muslims as goat fuckers, a reference to a ruling apparently made by Ayatollah Khomeini on when and in what circumstances it was acceptable to have sex with a goat and under what conditions the goat meat could then be eaten. This phrase 'goat fucker' was often cited by van Gogh's critics as an incitement to the violence that did for him. Alas, while it made for a neat excuse for all those who like to shout racism first and ask questions later, its only failing was that it did not correspond to actual events.

At his trial, as Ian Buruma records in his book *Murder in Amsterdam*, Bouyeri told the court: 'So the story that I felt insulted as a Moroccan, or because he called me a goat fucker, that is all nonsense. I acted out of faith. And I made it clear that if it had been my own father, or my little brother, I would have done the same thing.' Buruma goes on to note that Bouyeri also explained to the court that 'he was obligated to "cut off the heads of all those who insult Allah and his prophet" by the same divine law that didn't allow him to "live in this country, or in any country where free speech is allowed"'.

That's not quite the statement of a helpless victim of racism. But then little about Bouyeri conforms to the preconceived liberal-left line on society and its discontents. In the British model, for example, poor social housing, lack of youth centres, institutional indifference of a heartless society are all seen as the classic contributory factors in creating the alienated individual who is prepared to commit a rash or violent act. But none of those problems existed in Bouyeri's case. I went to Amsterdam to see Bouyeri's neighbourhood. It was the sort of pleasant, well-ordered housing of which we used to dream on my council estate. Residents in Bouyeri's family's apartment block were consulted by the local authority on redesign and refurbishment. Bouyeri himself took part in the consultations but walked out when he was informed that the council were not prepared to construct a passageway that would enable women to go from kitchen to sitting room without being seen by men. He was an active member of a youth club and a community centre. Every household in the Bouyeri apartment block was assigned its own social worker, though Bouyeri dismissed his. It is nigh on impossible to turn Bouyeri into the abandoned outcast, living in a ruthless and uncaring capitalist state, that would satisfy well-meaning prejudices. Though, of course, that has not stopped some from trying.

Nor was Bouyeri a lone extremist. He was part of what became known as the Hofstad cell, a group of young Islamists who were implicated in, among other things, plots to bomb Schiphol airport and a nuclear reactor. Several were arrested after a siege in which two policemen were attacked and injured by a thrown hand grenade. Links to other Islamist cells and groups across Europe were made and it was revealed that the mosque Bouyeri attended was used as a meeting place by the 9/11 pilots Mohammed Atta and Marwa al-Shehhi and planner Ramzi Binalshib during a 1999 conference on Islamic Puritanism. It was just about possible to look at the terror links and shared contacts and conclude that they were all coincidence and circumstantial, but it would require an ideological need to believe in Bouyeri's solitary status to sustain that judgement. And that ideological need would be to distance Bouyeri from any wider Islamist cause.

The difficulty here was not only that there was evidence linking Bouyeri and the Hofstad cell to other Islamist terrorist suspects, but Bouyeri himself had clearly stated his motive. It was there in the Koran, he insisted. His faith demanded that he kill van Gogh 'In the name of the Allah, the merciful bringer of mercy'.

The irony was that this was Hirsi Ali's whole point, and the further irony was that both Bouyeri and Hirsi Ali's liberal critics could not see the irony. She maintained that the Koran did indeed instruct Muslims to kill those who insulted Allah and his prophet, just as she said that it instructed husbands that they had the right to beat their wives if they failed to fulfil their wifely duties. As it says in my copy of the Koran 4:34: 'If you fear high-handedness from your wives, remind them [of the teachings of God], then ignore them when you go to bed, then hit them.' That's not in the least outrageous in the setting of the seventh century, either in Arabia, Europe or anywhere else. In fact, the recommendation of violence only comes after two stages of warnings. You could say that such measures, in the context of the time, were positively enlightened. And there are passages elsewhere in the Koran that are relatively progressive regarding the role of women. It's that kind of book: there's something for everyone. But if the book is read as the literal word of God, then its statement advising men to hit their wives is also the word of God, which, as a moral directive for the twenty-first century, is problematic. And it has been problematic for some time.

Hirsi Ali wanted to draw attention to this problem in a forthright manner because she felt that vagueness and evasiveness had done little to challenge the sexist attitudes that it reinforces. And this essentially was why she was forced to live under round-the-clock police protection.

In Holland, a short while after van Gogh's murder, I found little sympathy for Hirsi Ali among the Muslims I spoke to. Many expressed regret and sadness at van Gogh's murder, but few extended those sentiments to Hirsi Ali's plight. A typical response came from a taxi driver, originally from Morocco, who paid tribute to van Gogh's talents as an interviewer and artist. 'In a way,' the taxi driver said, '[van Gogh] was a victim.' Not, you understand, in the way that he was shot, virtually decapitated and then stabbed through the heart. But in this way: 'It wasn't him but Ayaan Hirsi Ali. This woman is the cause of all the problems, telling lies about Islam. If she hadn't sucked him into this, he'd still be alive today.'

One of the 'lies' she told about Islam was the suggestion that insulters of the prophet should be killed. That's why van Gogh was dead, according to the taxi driver, not because he was an opponent of Islam, but because Hirsi Ali had said that the Koran said opponents of Islam should be killed. Therefore van Gogh was killed. Within eighteen months there would be placards in London that called for the beheading and blowing up of anyone who described Islam as violent. After such displays, it is customary for someone – usually but not always a Muslim cleric – to quote these lines from the Koran 5:32: 'If anyone kills a person it is as if he kills all mankind.' What is without exception omitted is the parenthesis in that injunction that comes between 'person' and 'it' – 'unless in retribution for murder or spreading corruption in the land'. The 'spreading corruption' is a broad and encompassing category, but the punishment is quite specific: 'Those who wage war against God and His Messenger and strive to spread corruption in the land should be punished by death, crucifixion, the amputation of an alternate hand and foot . . . unless they repent before you overpower them.'

Like millions of Muslims, Hirsi Ali had grown up memorising these lines, steeped in the legacy of Koranic thought. Having fled a brutalised upbringing and an arranged marriage, she gradually abandoned her religion for the freedom and rationalism she discovered in Holland. She managed to get a place at Leiden University, one of the birthplaces of the Enlightenment, where she studied political science and came to appreciate not just eighteenth-century philosophers but also her great liberal hero, John Stuart Mill. Like Mill, Hirsi Ali has an extraordinary and bracing gift for clarity of thought. And like Mill, she confronts a formidable and resilient enemy in the forces of anti-reason. 'So long as an opinion is strongly rooted in the feelings,' wrote Mill, 'it gains rather than loses in stability by having a preponderating weight of argument against it.' That observation comes at the opening of his extended essay *The Subjugation of Women*, very likely the most powerful feminist tract ever written by a man, and one of the most eloquent written by anyone. It was published almost 140 years ago in 1869. At the time, the very idea that women were equal to men, and therefore that they should enjoy the same opportunities, was deemed not only ludicrous but offensive. It struck at the emotional foundations of society, at family, religion and the underlying power structure which feminists used to call patriarchy. We don't hear that word much today. It sounds po-faced and old-fashioned, and much of the reason it makes us wince is because of the success of feminism in challenging patriarchy – in the West, that is. Of course the condition of men and women is still far from equal but there is a much more even distribution of opportunity than Mill could possibly have dreamt. When Hirsi Ali read Mill, however, she did not find a historical work but a living vision that was unrealised in the worlds in which she grew up and saw around her in the ghettos of Dutch cities. She looked at Islamic-influenced society and saw women treated as second-class citizens, passed from father to husband, imprisoned in the home. And she came to the conclusion that it was the precepts of Islam, the traditions either stemming from the Koran or unchallenged by it, that stood in the way of female emancipation. In other words, she wanted to make the argument, with reference to her own culture and society, that Western feminists had long ago won. Or to make it even clearer, she wanted for Muslim women the same liberties and rights that Western women now took for granted.

If she expected support and encouragement from the movement that inspired her she could not have been more mistaken. In its postmodern phase feminism had fallen prey to cultural relativism. 'What sticks in the throats of many of her readers,' wrote Natasha Walter, author of *The New Feminism*, about Hirsi Ali, 'is not her feminism, but her anti-Islamism. It is not patriarchy as a whole that she is battling with, but a specific patriarchy sanctioned by a specific religion.' And it did not do to focus on the patriarchy that was responsible for stoning to death adulteresses, forced marriages, and domestic imprisonment, if it meant ignoring the patriarchy that resulted in a shortage of nursery places and inequality in earnings among male and female millionaires in the City.

For much the same reason, Muslim feminists were even less forgiving. In the *New Statesman* Fareena Alam, editor of the Muslim magazine *Q-News*, tore into Hirsi Ali for her straightforward way with words. Alam acknowledged that 'forced marriage, genital mutilation, sexual violence, lack of education, economic underachievement and the obsession with static gender roles' were 'genuine challenges' facing Muslim women, but rejected the idea that they were in any sense Islamic in their nature. Alam also compared Hirsi Ali unfavourably with Muslim women who want to 'maintain a strong, spiritual connection with their faith, a choice Hirsi

Ali seeks to deny them. These brave women sadly do not have the luxuries of monetary resources, bodyguards, spin-doctors and PR agencies that she takes for granted.' Alam did not explain how Hirsi Ali sought to deny women from maintaining a spiritual connection with their faith, much less how such a private matter of conscience could ever be denied, or indeed why it is 'brave' to maintain religious faith. But she certainly skipped over the fact that there are Islamists seeking to deny Hirsi Ali from maintaining a physical connection with her windpipe. Under such a threat are bodyguards really a 'luxury'? Or would a reasonable person call them a 'necessity'? It is with people like Fareena Alam that Hirsi Ali is constantly rebuked for not seeking to form alliances.

Perhaps the most revealing aspect of her denunciation of Hirsi Ali, though, was Alam's defence of Yusuf al-Qaradawi, the Qatar-based cleric, as a supporter of women. She pointed out that she had met al-Qaradawi's wife at a conference and she 'defied every stereotype, sitting at the head table with her husband and other leading scholars'.

Lucky Mrs al-Qaradawi. Here is Mr al-Qaradawi on the subject of female masturbation, in a lecture he gave on Qatar TV on 28 October 2006.

Female masturbation is more risky than male masturbation. Male masturbation is not as risky. Sometimes women insert a finger, and some women insert objects that may be risky, especially since the hymen is very sensitive, and any playing with it may tear it. This might expose the woman to accusations. She may tell them this or that, but they will not believe her. They will think she must have had forbidden relations with some guys. This way, a person exposes himself to accusations of fornication, a woman might be accused of fornication. She will bring disgrace upon herself and her family. This will be a disaster, and some relatives might kill her. Some people do not stop at the boundaries of religious law.

Driven by jealousy and rage, they might commit a crime and kill the girl. Obviously, killing her is forbidden and is a grave sin. Even if she did fornicate, she does not deserve to be killed. At most, she should be flogged, if she confesses four times, or if there were witnesses. Therefore, I do not advise the girls ever to resort to this.

One must particularly appreciate al-Qaradawi's concern for the hymen, coming as it does from a man who is on record as a proponent of female circumcision.

Such are the attitudes that Hirsi Ali seeks to confront and expose. There is no shortage of people lining up to embrace the al-Qaradawis of this world, to understand where they're coming from, to give them platforms in the name of cultural diversity, but a voice like Hirsi Ali's is striking for its undaunted readiness to say: 'No, this is nonsense.' The criticism most often heard of Hirsi Ali, at least among her more rational critics, is that she fails to bring Muslim women along with her. But such is the fate of all radical reformers. It will take a generation, she believes, before Muslim women feel confident enough to assert themselves. At the moment, as Mill observed, the emotions that Hirsi Ali provokes may well strengthen the beliefs she's opposing even as she wins the intellectual argument. Is that a good reason not to make the case? It was almost half a century before the suffragettes began to demand what Mill had articulated in *The Subjugation of Women*, and over a century after Mary Wollstonecraft had published *A Vindication of the Rights of Women*. Most British women, let alone men, in 1869 would have thought that Mill was wrong and, what's more, insultingly wrong. The same goes of Wollstonecraft in 1792, only more so. Does that mean they should have remained silent?

Perhaps the silliest thing that is said about Hirsi Ali, and too often by the cleverest of people, is that she is herself an extremist, a mirror image of the fanatics against whom she argues. Rageh Omaar, the former BBC foreign correspondent, who cannot be accused of exceptional cleverness, compared Hirsi Ali to Yasin Hassan Omar, one of the failed suicide bombers of the 21 July attacks. Both were driven by 'bigotry and hate', claimed Omaar in his autobiography, but Hirsi Ali was protected by the 'liberal fascism' of the West. 'It's ironic,' wrote Lorraine Ali in *Newsweek*, 'that this would-be "infidel" often sounds as single-minded and reactionary as the zealots she's worked so hard to oppose.' The Oxford historian Timothy Garton Ash expressed much the same sentiment when he called Hirsi Ali 'a slightly simplistic Enlightenment funda-mentalist' in a *New York Review of Books* essay. What does it mean to be an Enlightenment fundamentalist? That you believe in the freedom of speech not just as a principle but also a practice? That you consider liberal, secular, democratic society to offer the most freedom and security and rights for all people, including the religious, and are not afraid to say so? That you consider female masturbation to be completely healthy and unworthy of punishment? If Hirsi Ali occupies an extreme, it is this: she believes that people should be able to say and do what they please as long as it does not harm anyone else, and that what we say and think should be open to free debate and criticism without fear of violent intimida-tion. The religious fundamentalist believes that we should be free only to do what they say, and if we don't do it we should be punished or killed. If it is proposed that these are polar extremes, with the implication that 'moderation' lies some-where in the middle, then they are the polar extremes of good and bad. Many liberals appear to labour under the impres-sion that their duty is to find a position equidistant between the two. But like the clown who thinks he's a wit, they are only half right.

Though Hirsi Ali's subject is the illiberal nature of Islamic doctrine, her concern is the defence of liberalism. In this respect, it is liberals that most urgently need to listen to her arguments. There may well be cultural-tribal-emotional reasons why religious Muslims want to reject what Hirsi Ali has to say, but what excuse do liberals have? I've lost count of the times liberal friends, even feminist liberal friends, have responded to Hirsi Ali's arguments against misogyny and sexism by pointing out that she belonged to a 'right-wing' party in Holland, or that she had joined a 'neocon' think tank in the States, as if these political categories, regardless of their accuracy, rendered her stance invalid. In fact, it's worth looking at Hirsi Ali's political alignments because she started out on the left but found it a difficult place to express liberal values, as the left was more concerned to support religious reactionaries. She worked for a Dutch Labour think tank, but her research, for example, into honour killings was frequently stifled by well-meaning politicians and bureaucrats whose priority was to avoid stigmatising any minorities. When the same thing happened to other areas of research, including funding for fundamentalist mosques and extremist faith schools, she decided that her liberal instincts were being smothered by communalist politics. Moreover, the Dutch Labour Party would only countenance socio-economic explanations for the poor performance of Muslim children in schools and Muslim youths and women in the workplace, refusing to acknowledge the possible influence of cultural factors. Feeling restricted, if not quite censored, Hirsi Ali accepted the Dutch Liberal Party's offer to became an MP. At the time of the move she was already beginning to receive death threats and it probably struck her that if she was going to put her head on the block she might as well do it in a party which was prepared to give her a proper platform, even if she did not share all of its political views.

In the end, Hirsi Ali's four years in the Liberal Party came to a disastrous conclusion. She had her citizenship revoked by the hard-line interior minister, ostensibly for lying on her original asylum application. Fleeing an arranged marriage was not cause for asylum, so she said she was a refugee from war in Somalia – which she was, but she did not mention that she had been living in Kenya. Hirsi Ali had for many years been quite open about her lie, not least with the Liberal Party themselves, and in countless interviews. But if losing her status in her adopted homeland was bad enough, she also lost her home. Neighbours in her apartment block had success-fully managed, under terms of the Human Rights Act, to have Hirsi Ali evicted as a potential threat to their safety and well-being. Like the girl I saw who was stabbed by a gang as numerous bystanders looked on, she had nothing to do with them.

This, I think, was symptomatic of a malaise in European liberalism, an attitude of social indifference and political evasion. The idea being that if Hirsi Ali would just shut up and go away then everything would return to normal. If the troops were pulled out of Iraq then everything would improve. And if we stay in our homes and avoid certain streets we can forget about the social breakdown taking place elsewhere.

Hirsi Ali was not allowed to stay in her home in The Hague because she dared to bring attention to malign social forces beyond. She is a quietly spoken woman, charming and gently amusing, not at all the kind of person that you would single out as a 'contrarian' or 'troublemaker', and you be would be right, because she is neither. She has been spoken of in terms of a modern-day Spinoza and Voltaire, both of whom took refuge in Holland. The difference, of course, is that those giants of reason lived in a time when religious tyranny and arbitrary justice were the norm. They laid the intellectual groundwork for the secular humanism that was instrumental in shaping liberal democracy in Europe today. Whereas Hirsi Ali was simply saying that the price of neglecting those foun-dations would be the collapse of the tolerant society liberals are supposed to hold dear. As such, wrote Ian Buruma, 'Hirsi Ali is no Voltaire. For Voltaire had flung his insults at the Catholic Church, one of the two most powerful institutions of eighteenth-century France, while Ayaan risked offending only a minority that was already feeling vulnerable in the heart of Europe.'

Which begs the question, would Hirsi Ali's principles be more admirable if she was under death-threat from a more powerful institution than the disparate European groups inspired by Saudi-sponsored Wahaabism? It's likely that ideological Islam could only ever constrain, and not defeat, secular humanism, but there is also a significant chance that it could gain a crushing grip on European Muslims. Hirsi Ali's error was to speak plainly about this issue at a time when the liberal vogue was for obfuscation.

Effectively turfed out of her home and adopted homeland, loathed by guilty liberals – one commentator suggested his antipathy was such that the very idea of writing about Hirsi Ali caused 'serious damage' to his blood pressure – and living under a death sentence and armed protection, Hirsi Ali moved to America and a job with the American Enterprise think tank. For her detractors, who celebrated her departure, this was proof that she was 'right wing' and a 'neocon' all along. Presumably she should have sought employment with one of the European liberal think tanks that didn't want her. And she could have been housed on a military base or an aircraft carrier, somewhere that her presence would not have offended our delicate and tolerant sensibilities.

Europe's loss is America's gain. Hirsi Ali may well be wrong on any number of questions, but on the critical matter of the need to defend secular humanism and freedom of speech against not just fundamentalist Islam but any totalitarian ideology she will undoubtedly be proved right. But then, don't it always seem to go that you don't know what you've got till it's gone?

14

The loud american

When I was eighteen I considered moving, like Ayaan Hirsi Ali and countless millions, to America. In my imagination it was much like its legend, a place to restart, to be socially reborn. Back then Britain seemed to be a rigid, inflexible society, so limiting that half the time you weren't even aware of the things that you didn't dare do. Having managed to save £500 and purchased a Freddie Laker cheap flight, I flew to New York. Arriving in Manhattan remains perhaps the greatest cinematic experience to be had in real life, a blockbuster of visual and sensory excitement. Yet not very far beneath the pulsating surface was a harsh, uncompromising city, impatient, lurid and aggressive. Suddenly London appeared almost genteel by comparison. If I could make it anywhere, it wasn't going to be New York. I travelled round the country on Greyhound buses, hitching lifts here and there, and I became aware of a feeling that I'd never had before, a powerful sense of inverted vertigo. Outside a strip of stores somewhere on a highway in Colorado, I felt a mad urge to cling to the ground, because there was nothing else to hold on to, and it seemed momentarily as if I might fall off the planet. The shop facades looked like temporary film sets with no foundation and no background. They could have been knocked down the next day and no one would have noticed or cared. Or so it seemed to me. I had a deep and surprising hankering for the age-old certainties of Europe, the solid stone of history, and I knew in my bones that America, for all its infinite incarnations, was not somewhere that I would be able to call home. Within a couple of months I was back home working as a porter in Harrods' sub-basement, buried in – or by – history.

Since then I've enjoyed a love-hate relationship with America, one that is probably too familiar to detail. It's enough to say that I'm as attracted to as I am repelled by what Philip Roth called the American Berserk, its creative and destructive energy, and in this ambivalence I am no different, it seems, to the great mass of humanity. The life I've lived in a Western European liberal democracy, with all its unprecedented freedom and security, I owe in large part to the existence and support of the United States of America. It's an inescapable fact that without America's intervention, the First World War would not have been won and the Second World War would have been lost. Or won by the Soviet Union, which would have been a different – but not *that* different – kind of nightmare.

These monumental events in history are now so banal that their recapitulation embarrasses sophisticated people. If we're honest, we resent the idea that America was our saviour. Just as no good deed goes unpunished, so it is that we hate to think of ourselves as requiring the aid of another, especially one so rich and powerful and cocksure. The French, who enjoy an even more complicated relationship with the United States, have never really forgiven the Americans for liberating them from the Nazis. And the same can be said to a greater or lesser extent for most of the rest of Europe. Deep in the European soul we maintain a complex about America which dates back to its creation as first a refuge and then a republic. And what a complex complex it is, marrying inferiority and superiority, indifference and obsession. We dismiss America as crass and uncivilised, yet are in awe of its novelists, artists, film-makers and musicians. We think of Americans as naive and inward-looking, yet our cultural debate and social policy is dominated by ideas and initiatives from across the Atlantic. We deride their earnestness and absence of humour, and yet strangely all the great comedy and comedians of the modern era appear to have been American. We laugh at the showbiz shallowness of American politics, then treat American celebrities with the seriousness previously reserved for philosophers and elder statesmen. We don't know whether to sneer or fawn, bow or look down, and so, like a character from the Ministry of Silly Walks, we jerkily adopt all positions simultaneously.

Perhaps confusion is the only sensible way to deal with a country as vast and multitude-containing as America. There is simply too much of it, and too many of them, to come to any definitive understanding about the place and the people. But it's always reassuring to reach a conclusion and the one that so many Europeans come to is that America, on the whole, is a land of malevolent simplicity or simple malevolence. I've thought and written as much myself and, of course, there are plenty of examples of American behaviour – political, economic, cultural, military – that illustrate the point. Only the Americans could come up with Guantánamo Bay's (now defunct) Camp X-Ray. Those orange jump suits: so vivid! Those masks and blindfolds: so creepy! And, naturally, only the Americans would photograph unconvicted – indeed, uncharged – prisoners in that gear on their knees with their arms bound together, and then send images of the whole grizzly scene around the world. What demented innocence, what catastrophic self-righteousness. Similarly Abu Ghraib. Such a needless horror show. Although it was not in the same league of sadism as that practised in Iraqi prisons, and Abu Ghraib itself, under Saddam – when brandings and amputation were standard practices – it was sickening enough. Why do they shoot themselves in the foot with such unfailing accuracy, the Americans? Why is it that a nation which turned sales into a science and invented public relations is so bad at selling itself?

One answer is that this is what imperialists always do, and Americans are imperialists with a de facto empire. Certainly that's the default position of the liberal-left. Another, not unrelated reading, is that there is something in America's view of itself as a standard-bearer of all that is good and proper which allows the Americans to issue themselves a licence to do wrong in the name of good. This is the version that Graham Greene portrays in *The Quiet American*, in which Pyle, the upstanding American secret agent in Vietnam, with the 'fanatic gleam' and 'indefatigable young brain', embodies the clumsy idealism of the land of the brave and home of the free. It also informs the outlook of celebrated figures like the Nobel laureate Dario Fo, who sent out a circular email shortly after 9/11, when the death toll was thought to be much higher, in which he wrote: 'Big speculators joyfully splash about in an economy that lets millions of people die every year in misery. What are 20,000 dead in New York by comparison? . . . Regardless of who carried out the massacre, this violence is the legitimate daughter of the culture of violence, hunger and inhumane exploitation.' And the third, and arguably now the most popular, belief among European liberals and conservatives alike is that Americans are just stupid: they don't understand or care about other cultures, they're untravelled, illiterate, fat, bigoted, ignorant and brash; they get their world view from Hollywood blockbusters and politics from radio shockjocks and Fox News. This is the line repeated by every third-rate alternative comedian, lazy journalist and dinner-party bore with an opinion to spare. Various documentary-makers have built entire careers on peddling these stereotypes. Naturally, few of us know any Americans like that ourselves but that doesn't undermine our confidence that they exist in large numbers. In certain superior moods I've reached for the same reassuring caricatures, even though all my American friends are well-informed internationalists in everything but football. Nonetheless, what well-meaning European, willing to see the best in everyone, has not stood behind a loud American, with his fast-food impatience and expansive sense of entitlement, and thought:

'You think you own world, you dumb redneck'? It's the prejudice of choice for all those who pride themselves on their lack of prejudice.

This conception of Americans isn't restricted to Europeans, of course; it's also shared by large parts of the rest of the world. But perhaps the most influential disseminators of this view are Americans themselves and among them the lead propagandist is a loud, extravagantly entitled fat man. Author of a number of bestselling books that tell us the worst about America, as well as a series of high-earning cinematic documentaries on the same theme, his name is Michael Moore.

I first laid eyes on Moore back in the 1980s at the London Film Festival. Twenty years ago he wore a baseball cap and oversized glasses as a kind of blue-collar buffoon costume. He was slimmer, if not slim, back then and his trademark duck waddle was not quite up and walking. If success led to weight gain, it can't be said that it spoiled him because his prickly character was in evidence early in his career. He was in England to promote his first documentary film, *Roger and Me*. It showed the damage wrought by General Motors on Moore's home town of Flint, Michigan, when the company closed its car plants and moved production to Mexico, where the labour costs were much cheaper. It was fun, quirky, and it made some serious points about the price of globalisation. I liked the film and it garnered favourable reviews. But there was something about Moore himself that I didn't entirely trust. In the audience conversation that followed the screening of the film, he was asked if he wasn't being a little disingenuous with his presentation of the story. 'I don't know what that word means,' replied Moore with a scowl. 'I'm from the working class.'

At the time, I put it down to the defensiveness of the artist. But it turned out to be a far more revealing comment than I then realised. Critics would soon discover that quite a lot of chronological manipulation was used in *Roger and Me* to give the impression that Flint's suffering was directly due to GM's departure, when in fact much of it predated the move. Moore, who did indeed know the meaning of the word, had been disingenuous twice over. The working-class label, too, would become a defence to which Moore would repeatedly resort, though it would emerge that Moore grew up in an affluent suburb and benefited from a private education. Much later I learned that he gained the money to make *Roger and Me* by suing the alternative San Francisco-based magazine *Mother Jones*, which he briefly edited, for wrongful dismissal. As editor, Moore refused to run a piece on Sandinista human rights abuses written by Paul Berman, later to become known as the author of *Terror and Liberalism*. Berman, as I mentioned earlier, had spent a long time in Nicaragua, and he wrote perceptively about some of the more authoritarian aspects of the Sandinistas – a tendency which would later cause most of the top Sandinistas to leave the party in protest. Moore, who knew little of the reality on the ground in Nicaragua, pulled the piece all the same. Following a series of disputes, he lost the confidence of his staff. Moore saw the disagreement in class terms, casting himself, predictably, in the role of working-class hero.

The next time I saw him was over fifteen years later when I interviewed him in Cannes. By then he was a star, an Oscar winner and a seasoned tantrum thrower, who stayed in the best hotels, travelled in a limousine and was surrounded by a team of bodyguards. Moore had berated those killed on planes in the 9/11 attacks for not fighting back, suggesting that they were spoilt whites who were used to having others look after them. '[T]he kind of people who fly in airplanes want someone else to clean up their mess; that's why they let hijackers take the plane,' Moore told his audience at the London Roundhouse, presumably after having rowed across the Atlantic. 'If the passengers had included black men, those killers, with their puny bodies and unimpressive small knives, would have been crushed by the dudes, who as we all know take no disrespect from *anybody* . . . The passengers on the planes on 11 September were scaredy-cats, because they were mostly white.' During the same residency at the Roundhouse Moore made such a fuss about the lack of security that the auditorium's staff threatened to boycott the show.

At Cannes, as at all his public events, he was accompanied by his team of private security guards, and his limousine was afforded police protection. He was the toast of Croisette for his film *Fahrenheit 9/11*, a manipulative and cleverly edited attack on the Bush regime and its 'war against terror' that, on closer inspection, was shamelessly contradictory. The film critic Richard Schickel once called Moore 'the very definition of the unreliable narrator' and the narrative of *Fahrenheit 9/11* was reliable only in its desire to have it both ways at the same time. In the film Moore finessed the manoeuvre practised by a lot of people who had been opposed to the war in Afghanistan, which was to blame the war in Iraq for diverting troop resources and military attention from the war in Afghanistan. There were numerous other inconsistencies, misrepresentations (Saddam's Iraq was portrayed as a peaceful idyll) and evasions, but they were all thrown together with such brass-neck sentiment, kinetic verve and cheap-shot humour that you barely noticed. Even the promotion of the film Moore turned into a giant fabulation, casting himself as the victim of a conspiracy between Hollywood and the White House to prevent the film from getting a release. The French went mad for the film, which registered a record standing ovation at the Palais and won the Palme d'Or.

And the French were not alone. Many international critics loved the film. John Berger called it 'astounding'. He praised Moore as an 'artist' and said, '*Fahrenheit 9/11* reminds the spectator that when courage is shared one can fight against the odds.' The film was a huge box-office hit in America and Europe. But then Moore was already a one-man multimedia phenomenon. His book *Stupid White Men*, a sort of folksy Noam Chomsky screed for the attention deficient, was the bestselling non-fiction book in the US in 2002. There were

4 million copies in print worldwide and 600,000 of those were in the UK. At one point the book and its follow-up, *Dude, Where's My Country*, stood at numbers one and two in the German bestseller list. Here's a typical piece of political analysis from *Stupid White Men*: 'You name the problem, the disease, the human suffering, or the abject misery visited upon millions, and I'll bet you ten bucks I can put a white face on it faster than you can name the members of 'N Sync.' In fact, that rather underplays Moore's ability because the book doesn't just attribute all wrongdoing to white men, but to white American men in particular. Was that the secret of its appeal? A critic on BBC2's *Newsnight Review* described *Stupid White Men* as a 'fantastic book'. 'It starts off by attacking George Bush's ascendance to the presidency, then goes on to completely pull America apart . . . It's full of facts that you want to tell your friends, like Laura Bush having killed one of her seventeen-year-old friends in a car crash when she was younger . . . It's really nice to have a P. J. O'Rourke on the other side.'

These comments came in a studio discussion and were probably not the result of long deliberation but they reveal an attitude so commonplace that it usually passes without comment. To earn praise in liberal media circles, a book need only say that George Bush is bad and America is crass. America is somewhere that very many people, including people who spend a lot of time in America and who are enthralled by American culture, enjoy seeing pulled apart. And then there is the widely expressed idea that it doesn't matter what Moore's failings are, he's on 'our' side, the anti-American side. He's the liberal answer to P. J. O'Rourke.

In reality, Moore tends to enlist liberal causes as and when it suits his own ends. He was an enthusiastic campaigner for the independent Ralph Nader in the 2000 presidential elections, claiming there was no difference between Al Gore and George Bush. Many observers felt that the votes Nader took from Gore were instrumental in delivering Bush's disputed electoral victory. When I asked him whether he had any regrets about his role in that electioin, Moore claimed that he didn't campaign in swing states. In fact, he did campaign in swing states and, according to Harry Levine, writing in the *Village Voice*, Moore was vehemently against calling for Nader voters to back Gore in 'battleground states like Florida'. When Levine suggested the idea, Moore 'puffed up like one of those fish that expand when threatened, leaned into me, poked his finger into my face, and yelled: "you can't say that! You can't say that! You can't say that!"' Fahrenheit 9/11, claimed Moore, is the temperature at which truth burns. And it does appear that he would know.

Like that other man-of-the-people manqué, Bertolt Brecht, who thundered against capitalism and capitalists while screwing every last cent out of business deals (and screwing his partner Kurt Weill out of his performing rights at the same time), Moore has always known how to play the market. Back in 2002 a TV reporter turned the tables on Moore and asked him why he organised his book promotion tour through corporate chains rather than independent bookstores. Moore did not like the taste of his own treatment and launched a tirade against independent shop owners, based on his experience of small business in Flint. 'They were the people that supported all the right-wing groups,' he said, reaching for his favourite off-the-shelf insult. 'They were the Republicans in town, they were in Kiwanis, the Chamber of Commerce – people that kept the town all white. The small hardware salesman, the small clothing stores salespersons, Jesse the Barber who signed his name three different times on three different petitions to recall me from the school board. Fuck all these small businesses – fuck 'em all. Bring in the chains.'

I've never yet visited an independent bookstore in America that isn't owned and staffed by quintessential soft liberals, the kind of people, alas, who forgive Moore his absurd self-justifications. There are endless examples of this kind of behaviour but for me the defining Moore moment came the day after 9/11 when Moore wrote his response to the attacks on his website. 'If someone did this to get back at Bush, then they did so by killing thousands of people who DID NOT VOTE for him. Boston, New York, D.C., and the planes' destination of California – these were the places that voted AGAINST Bush.' Had the terrorists hit Dallas, Oklahoma City and Salt Lake City, Moore seemed to imply, then their actions would have been defensible. This is the big-hearted, compassionate little guy, apparently willing to see several thousand of his countrymen and women slaughtered and incinerated if they happen to live in Republican-majority cities.

And I suspect that much of Moore's popularity exists not in spite but because of this sort of outlook. The kind of anti-American sentiment that is extensive and largely indiscriminate in Europe either endorses or flirts with the notion that America is the main architect of wrongdoing in the world. Such a view is not restricted to the fruitcake fringe, the types, for example, like the Communist Party of Britain, the Islamic Party of Britain and Hizb ut-Tahrir, whose representatives argued at the Oxford Union in 2006 that the founding of the United States of America had been a disaster for the rest of the world. The intellectual advantage that such extremists have over the fashionable reflex liberal stance is that they follow through on the logic of their anti-Americanism. They don't want America to exist, and they certainly don't want the world's superpower to be America.

It's fine and good fun to adopt an anti-American bias but what liberals are then obliged to ask themselves is what the world would look like with a different superpower. If we look at the real world alternatives the twentieth century threw up – the British and French Empires, Nazi Germany and the Soviet Union – then the United States begins to look quite benign. And the options don't appear a whole lot more attractive in the twenty-first century. Would the lot of humanity improve were China to become the most powerful nation on earth, as some on the left seem fervently to wish? Or what about a neo-Caliphate with nuclear weapons? And while we are at it, perhaps we should try to envisage a world in which the energy supply was held to ransom by religious fundamentalists.

Ultimately, these are not just hypothetical scenarios but situations that, given the right circumstances, and a lack of Western will, could well develop. As I say, if you were a member of the Communist Party of Britain or the Islamic Party of Britain then such outcomes would be cause for celebration. But if you are a liberal who values human rights and political freedoms, not to mention electricity, then, no matter how much one might disagree with Republican policy on climate change or intervention in Iraq, dislike McDonald's and American corporate might, feel uncomfortable about Bible Belt reactionaries, resent the hassle of getting through American customs or find Los Angeles dispiriting and American patriotism all rather embarrassing, it's necessary to recognise the advantages of having a functioning democracy in the position of lead power. Or to put it another way, to imagine the disadvantages of a dictatorship gaining primacy. That's not to say that America is in any way exempt from criticism, or that the rest of the world should not seek to limit American power. It's simply to acknowledge a bottom line of shared interests and values. Perhaps the best formulation of this refusal to cast America as the ideological omniculprit is the French philosopher Bernard-Henri Lévy's 'anti-anti-American'. Levy is a severe critic of many aspects of America, not least its penal system, yet he appreciates the extraordinary energy, diversity and optimism of a young and precocious nation whose creation, as Martin Kettle wrote in the *Guardian*, 'has proved to be the single greatest collective human achievement of the past four centuries'.

When I read those words, I wondered if they could possibly be true. After all, as Kettle acknowledged, slavery played a shamefully long and leading role in the establishment of America, and segregational racism lasted almost as long after that. And yet the mark of America, for all its inequalities and racial division, is that at the very core of its identity is the sustaining belief that life can be improved and freedom extended for everyone. When Thomas Jefferson wrote in the Declaration of Independence, 'We hold these truths to be self-evident, that all men are created equal, that they are endowed by their Creator with certain unalienable Rights, that among these are Life, Liberty and the Pursuit of Happiness,' he gave voice to an essential truth against which all social injustice and hypocrisies, including his own, would have to be judged. Jefferson, of course, was himself a slave owner, despite being opposed to slavery. America was both the product of and the challenge to racism. The issue is far from resolved but America unquestionably offers more opportunity to people of more races than any other nation on earth. It may not be the picture of harmonious diversity but, as things stand, it's the best picture we've got. Add on top of that the phenomenal scientific, economic and social developments for which America is responsible – from polio vaccination to the invention of fibre optics, from the moon landings through to *The Sopranos* television epic. In the sciences, medicine, the arts, political theory, America remains at the cutting edge of innovation and adaptation. And, of course, though it has abused its power like all previous leading powers, it has been the most steadfast bulwark against global totalitarianism. For all America's faults and foibles, there's not a field of intellectual endeavour which it has failed to influence or reshape and most often improve. Taking all this into account, I think Kettle is perhaps on to something.

However, while allowing for its global reach, America is its own distinct entity, with its own particular history. It may be the place where the future is most relentlessly road-tested but it need not be the example that the rest of world slavishly follows. Yet the fact remains that it's easier to follow than come up with one's own ideas, solutions and initiatives, and it's even easier to follow while resenting the pacesetter. That's the position of Europe at the moment, metaphorically (and often literally) sitting in a Starbucks, sipping coffee, reading a newspaper and moaning about the spread of American culture. This is the lazy anti-Americanism on which Moore so profitably trades, what Levy calls 'the absurdity of a discourse that turns the United States into a figure of speech, a cliché, as well as a scapegoat for the mistakes, insufficiencies and inconsistencies of other countries'.

So it's obvious why Moore is popular with Europeans who want to point the finger of blame – historically aimed at themselves – somewhere else. But why is he successful in America, too? Could it be due to the self-loathing of American white liberal guilt?

Interestingly, Moore absolves himself from this guilt on the novel basis, for a multimillionaire, that he is working class. Thus he is able to berate Americans for maintaining social divisions while, with a clear conscience, sending his daughter to an exclusive Manhattan private school. 'We'll continue our fight to see to it that our society is such that you don't have to have a metal detector at the entrance to schools,' he told me in Cannes. 'But our daughter is not the one to be sacrificed to make things better.' This seemed a little rich coming from someone who in *Fahrenheit 9/11* made a big moral stunt of going up to Congressmen who voted for the war in Iraq and trying to get them to sign their children up for the army. But Moore went on. 'Whatever I can afford, I'm going to get my kid the best education I can get.'

How was this any different from the Republican philosophy of each man for himself and his family that Moore affected to despise?

'I'm not a liberal,' he responded. 'When you come from the working class and you do well enough whereby you can provide a little bit better for your family, get a decent roof over their head and send them to a good school, that's considered a good thing. *If* you're from the working class. What's bad about it is if you get to do that and then shut the door behind you so nobody else can do that.' Which can only mean that everyone should be able to send their children to exclusive private schools in upper Manhattan. If, of course, they're from the working class.

Most of our conversation was taken up with Moore's increasingly self-serving and self-excepting justifications. He struck me as a mountebank, a theatrical charlatan who would say anything to elicit a desired response or emotion. In the chapter 'Kill Whitey' in *Stupid White Men*, Moore calls on white people to 'Hire only black people'. 'I'm done hiring white people,' he says. Three years after he wrote those words I met a couple of his more recent employees. They were white. I didn't see any black employees. Obviously it's silly, this kind of 'black and white' analysis, and certainly no grounds on which to judge a writer, a director, or an artist, just as it makes no difference where he sends his daughter to school. But by making such a noise about his own good conduct, by setting standards he has no intention of matching, Moore brings into question the veracity of his method and the nature – good or bad – of his faith.

Is he not then like Jefferson, the slave owner who proclaimed all men free and equal? Surely it's more important to laud the sentiment than judge the man? Well, perhaps it would be if Moore's sentiments made any collective sense. But they are contradictory and deliberately so because they are not intended to make us think, they're meant to make us feel, to feel superior to Americans or feel guilty about being Americans. And to fall for that trick it really does help if you are a stupid white man.

At the same time, let's admit that America has much to be criticised for, and in a culture that is sometimes overpoweringly patriotic, Moore dares to be an outspoken critic. His defenders are therefore prepared to forgive his idiosyncratic relationship with the truth. It should also be said that among the cadre of American graduates trained in postmodern humanities, truth is in any case a discredited concept, and thus Moore cannot be faulted for negating a non-existent value. As he said in his Oscar acceptance speech for the manipulative and misleading *Bowling for Columbine*, a speech he said was unplanned, and the speech he also warned fellow competitors he was going to make, 'we live in fictitious times'. The greatest fiction currently doing the rounds among populists and intellectuals alike is that America is the source of all that is wrong in the world, and the most successful exploiter of that lie, at least from a financial perspective, from his calculated maximisation of the market he affects to despise, is Michael Moore.

I had an emotional reaction to America when I first went abroad at eighteen. I felt very strongly that it was not a place in which I wanted to live. But America, its 300 million inhabitants, its enormous and far-reaching media, its intellectuals and artists, its dense network of political institutions and local democracy, cannot be reduced to visceral feelings however tempting the urge to do so might be. Hatred of America, which is very possibly the animating emotion of European liberals, is like the rebellious adolescent's hatred of his bourgeois parents, a childish indulgence that requires and feeds off the comfort and safety the parents supply.

If democracies, as has often been observed, get the politicians they deserve, then perhaps ideologies also get the proponents they deserve. Loud, unprincipled, inconsistent and an unabashed beneficiary of American capitalism, Michael Moore, the overgrown adolescent par excellence, is the perfect spokesman for the intellectually and morally bankrupt ideology of anti-Americanism.

15

A cartoon world

'I sketched a comedy about harem life; being a Spanish writer, I assumed I could be irreverent towards Mohammed without any scruples: but at once an Envoy from somewhere complained that my verses offended the Sublime Porte, Persia, a part of India, all Egypt, the kingdoms of Barca, Tripoli, Tunis, Algiers and Morocco; and there was my comedy burned, to please some Mohammedan princes not one of whom I suppose knows how to read, and who keep cursing away at us all as "Christian dogs" – not being able to degrade the human spirit, they take revenge by abusing it.'

This is an excerpt from the celebrated speech made by Figaro, the valet to whom his master is certainly no hero, in the fifth act of *The Marriage of Figaro*. Written by Pierre Augustin Caron de Beaumarchais in 1778 as a sequel to *The Barber of Seville*, the play was a comedy that satirised the absurdity of hereditary privilege. Accordingly, it was banned for a number of years, but on finally being performed it became a key theatrical text of Europe's Enlightenment. Beaumarchais himself was a supporter of the French and American revolutions, and instrumental in saving the dispersed works of Voltaire. His main preoccupation was the injustice of the aristocracy, though that did not prevent him from buying himself into the French nobility. Figaro's observation about his disastrous harem play is little more than an aside, but it nonetheless suggests an image of Islamic hypersensitivity. This could be dismissed as an atavistic form of Iberian Islamophobia – the memory of Spain's Muslim past, what has been aptly termed the Andalusian Enlightenment, was still very much alive in southern Spain (and remains so to this day). Or it could have reflected a general European unease about a presumed threat from the East. After all, as the sort of anti-imperialist guilt addicts who feel compelled to apologise for the Crusades conveniently forget, Vienna almost fell to the Ottoman Empire in 1683. Or it might just be that Beaumarchais, ridiculer of contemporary European mores, found no reason why Islamic customs should be exempt from his satirical remit.

Over 225 years later, it's possible in Europe to write a play about the aristocracy, even royal families, without threat of censorship or punishment. It took a long time – the Lord Chamberlain was still able to censor plays in Britain right up until 1968 – but one of the many enduring achievements of Enlightenment thought is that nowadays we take it for granted that a play can be written about anything. Or almost anything. The exception is religion. Not Christian religion. You can say pretty much what you like about Christians and their idols. For example, Terrence McNally's play *Corpus Christi* depicted Jesus and his acolytes as homosexual. There are protests every now and then, as was the case with *Jerry Springer: The Opera*, in which Jesus was deemed to have been portrayed in an unflattering manner. But in the best dramaturgical tradition, the show still goes on. Unless the subject is a non-Christian religion. In December 2004, *Behzti* (Dishonour), a play written by a British Sikh named Gurpreet Kaur Bhatti, was stopped and then cancelled, following protests from Sikhs in and outside the Birmingham Rep theatre. Censorship was effectively instituted not by some anachronistic arm of the state, like the Lord Chamberlain of years past, but by a minority of religious extremists. Still, at least *Behzti* made it to the stage, before falling victim to victim mentality, and at least liberal arts figures signed a petition of protest at the play being pulled. That would simply not have happened had the play taken a critical or satirical look at Islam. For if any such play were written, it most certainly would not be performed. Two centuries on from Figaro's jibe, his fictional comedy could not hope to find a theatre willing to stage it. And no playwright in his right mind would even try. Certainly not after the Danish cartoon crisis of early 2006.

There is a school of thought that looks at the 'Muslim question' and sees a problematic clash of cultures that cannot be resolved. They argue that God's law will always come before secular law for Muslims, that within Islam women and gays and infidels will always be seen as, at best, second-class citizens, and that Europe is under threat from 'within' by a Muslim population that is destined, by increasing weight of numbers, to turn the Continent into 'Eurabia'. This seems to me to be hyperventilated rubbish, but there are occasions when it seems less hyperventilated than it should, and chief among those was the orchestrated international furore surrounding the publication of a few cartoons in a hitherto obscure Danish newspaper (obscure, that is, outside Denmark).

For me it was a watershed, the moment at which I decided to write this book. I saw fear masquerading as tolerance and censorship dressed up as restraint, and I realised that liberalism had reached a critical point at which it would far sooner accommodate the illiberal, the intolerant, the violently superstitious, than support defining liberal principles like the freedom of expression and the rule of law. Once again the same tactics of blaming the victims and sympathising with the perpetrators were employed. The Danish nation as a whole was traduced by alleged liberals, desperate to ally themselves with the most reactionary sections of Islam; *Jyllands-Posten*, the Danish newspaper, was routinely denounced as 'racist' and 'right wing'; and no thought was spared for the plight of the cartoonists themselves who were sent into hiding under threat of death. In short, it was a shameful episode for European and, in particular, British liberals, and one from which Britain, if it really does want to be tolerant and liberal, urgently needs to learn.

The origin, and indeed nature, of the cartoon illustrations have since become buried beneath myth, hearsay and misinformation. The standard line put about by apologists for Islamist provocateurs was that cartoons depicting Muhammad had been commissioned by anti-immigrationists at *Jyllands-Posten* with the express purpose of offending Muslims. Even if that story were true, of course, *Jyllands-Posten* could have in theory been prosecuted under blasphemy and discrimination laws. For in Denmark, like many other countries, religious groups have greater protection from insult than do, say, Marxists or fascists or liberals. It should go without saying that no one, including Muslims, was obliged to buy the newspaper, much less look at the cartoons. And indeed in the ensuing debate it did go unsaid.

The story, however, was not true. There was a context: intellectual, historical and current. Perhaps the first thing to say is that Denmark has the oldest and strongest tradition of free speech in Europe, enshrined in the constitution since 1849 and only suspended during the Nazi occupation. Reporters Without Borders placed Denmark top of its Worldwide Press Freedom Index in 2005. In other words freedom of speech was not suddenly invented in Denmark in 2006 as a means of offending Muslims. What actually started the cartoons ball rolling was the difficulty the children's writer Käre Bluitgen experienced in finding an illustrator for a book entitled *The Koran and the Life of the Prophet Muhammed*. One illustrator he approached cited the murder of Theo van Gogh as the reason for turning down the commission, while another mentioned a lecturer who was assaulted by a gang at Carsten Niebuhr Institute in Copenhagen for reading the Koran to non-Muslims. Another Danish newspaper, *Politken*, ran a piece about Bluitgen's search for an illustrator (he found one eventually who agreed to do the job anonymously) in mid-September 2005. A couple of weeks later *Jyllands-Posten* responded by publishing twelve cartoons under the title of 'The Face of Muhammed'. As many as five of the cartoons did not depict Muhammed and at least two were critical of *Jyllands-Posten*.

Flemming Rose, the cultural editor of the newspaper, wrote an accompanying text which warned of a 'slippery slope' of 'self-censorship' and argued that putting up with insults and mockery was a necessary part of living in a free society, though 'it does not mean that religious feelings should be made fun of at any price'. Two weeks later a delegation of eleven ambassadors from Muslim countries petitioned the Danish government 'to take all those responsible to task under the law of the land in the interest of interfaith harmony, better integration and Denmark's overall relationship with the Muslim world'.

The Danish government pointed out that it was not the place of a government in a liberal democracy to interfere with the freedom of the press. And an investigation by the public prosecutor found no evidence to build a criminal case against *Jyllands-Posten*. Dissatisfied with this response, a group of Danish imams put together a dossier and toured the Middle East to raise awareness of the 'pain and torment' caused by *Jyllands-Posten* and the Danish government's refusal to act. The dossier contained not just the cartoons but other more extreme images that had nothing to do with the newspaper (for example, a photo of a Frenchman dressed up as a pig with a caption identifying him as Muhammad), as well as other spoof images that another Danish newspaper had used to make fun of *Jyllands-Posten*'s perceived pomposity. It also featured statements such as this: 'Even though the Danes belong to the Christian faith, secularisation has overcome them, and if you say that they are all infidels, then you are not wrong.'

The spokesman for the Danish imams was Ahmed Akkari, a leading figure in the European Committee for Prophet Honouring, and originally an asylum seeker from Lebanon. As a teenager, Akkari became a cause célèbre when he lost his refugee status after his family returned temporarily to Lebanon once the civil war ended. With the help of the Danish press that would later be internationally vilified, Akkari gained humanitarian residency. He explained that he would rather leave his family than return to Lebanon. 'I am Danish,' he announced. In 2001, the twenty-three-year old Akkari was imprisoned for severely beating up an eleven-year-old boy who, apparently in a schoolyard game, pulled off Akkari's sister's headscarf.

Akkari and his fellow imams proved successful at generating disaffection on their tour. The Egyptian minister of foreign affairs, Aboul Gheit, had already written in protest to the Danish prime minister, Anders Fogh Rasmussen. Significantly, some of the cartoons had already been reprinted in the Egyptian newspaper *El Fagr* without public incident or, indeed, protest from the Egyptian government. But by the time Akkari, the refugee who pronounced himself Danish, and his other Danish cohorts were finished, a consumer boycott of Danish goods was organised across the Middle East. Exports to the region went down by over 15 per cent, which cost about €134 million to the Danish economy. In America, Christopher Hitchens called on supporters of free speech to buy Danish goods. Later, the *Guardian* attributed the increase in Danish imports in the States to 'fervent rightwing Americans', as though showing solidarity with a small embattled liberal European nation, suffering a campaign of organised intimidation by religious fundamentalists, was ipso facto a reactionary attitude.

On 4 February 2006 the Danish Embassy was set alight in Syria, and for good measure, the Norwegian Embassy too. In Lebanon, the Danish Embassy was burned down and a protester died. It's estimated that in demonstrations from Nigeria to Pakistan 139 protesters perished. A reward of over $1 million was offered by Haji Yaqoob Qureishi, a minister in the Indian state of Uttar Pradesh, to anyone who beheaded one of the Danish cartoonists. Later, Amer Cheema, a Pakistani student, was apprehended with a knife in the *Die Welt* newspaper offices in Berlin. He admitted that he intended to kill the paper's editor, Roger Koppel, for reprinting the cartoons. And two undetonated bombs were discovered on German trains, planted by Lebanese suspects who, according to German federal police, claimed to have been acting in response to the 'assault by the West on Islam' that the Danish cartoons represented. Reports in Germany stated that one of the suspects was heading to Denmark, and in his pocket the police found the telephone number of Abu Bashar, the main imam responsible for putting together the dossier and organising the boycott-promoting trip to the Middle East. Though Bashar denied knowing the suspect, he suggested it was only a matter of time before Osama bin Laden made good his threat to punish those countries, like Denmark, with troops in Iraq.

All of this because of a dozen comic line drawings.

The fate of Figaro's comedy was to be burned. Two centuries later and it was not just a newspaper that was burned, but embassies. Whose fault was this step backwards in enlightened attitude? As I read the British newspapers, particularly the liberal press, I learned that the blame lay with the Danish people as a whole, the Danish government in particular, and most specifically the 'arrogant', 'right-wing' Danish newspaper, *Jyllands-Posten*. It was accepted that the mobs in Damascus and Beirut could not help themselves, such was their sensitivity to presumed insults made in a far-off country of which they knew little. There were countless examples of this stock response, so it is unfair to pick out just one, but sometimes one must live with injustice. It was again published in the *Guardian*. It may seem that I have been over-reliant on the *Guardian* for attribution but that is for two simple reasons: one, it is *my* daily paper, and two, it is *the* liberal paper. I happen to think that it is not only the most significant liberal paper but also the best, so its over-representation in these pages is a forehanded, rather than backhanded, compliment. Writing on 17 February 2006, Martin Jacques dismissed the idea that there was a principle of free speech at stake. 'The decision of *Jyllands-Posten* to publish the cartoons . . . lay not so much in the tradition of free speech but in European contempt for other cultures and religions: it was a deliberate, calculated insult to the beliefs of others, in this case Muslims. This kind of mentality – combining Eurocentrism, old colonial attitudes of supremacism, racism, provincialism and sheer ignorance – will serve our continent ill in the future.' Jacques argued that minorities in Europe were now rightly taking revenge, what he called 'feedback loops', for the crimes of European empires. 'The subject of these feedback loops, or consequences, will concern not just present but also past behaviour,' he warned.

In other words the Danes had it coming to them for imperial misdeeds, and it didn't matter what they did now or in the future, or what steps they had taken in the recent decades, they were going to feel the consequences of their past actions as a colonial aggressor. Now let's just check the map again to look at the old Danish Empire. Well, there was Iceland, Greenland, the Faroe Islands, Orkney and Shetland. None of whom, it has to be said, had joined in the cartoons protests. It's true that the Danes built a trading fort in Tharangambadi, in the Indian state of Tamil Nadu in 1620. Which is to say, sixty-three years before the Islamic Ottoman Empire was at the gates of Vienna. But no matter. It was payback time for the Danes. The feedback loops were on the way. Let's not get pedantic about geography and history, Jacques seemed to say, the Danes are European, so they had it coming to them. The Danes, who stood up with tremendous courage to the Nazis, refusing to hand over Jews to the occupying forces, these were the vile racists that needed to be taught a lesson.

The sheer ignorance displayed by Jacques and other commentators was astounding to witness. And as British liberals raced to point the finger of blame at Denmark, Islamists took to the streets of London in protest at the cartoons that had never been published in this country. Standing outside the Danish Embassy, they held up placards with such legends as 'Butcher those who mock Islam', 'Behead the one who insults the Prophet' and 'Britain you will pay, 7/7 is on its way'. Despite the incitement to violence and murder, no arrests were made at the demonstration. 'Those gathered were well natured and in the main compliant with police requests,' said a Metropolitan Police statement. A few weeks later I would watch as a group of six or seven senior police officers agreed on the urgent need to arrest a solitary man holding up an image of one of the cartoons at a demonstration in favour of freedom of expression. The man, an Iranian refugee from religious tyranny, was in good spirits and completely unthreatening but he was swiftly hauled off by several policemen.

In arguably the most competitive print media market in the world, every single British newspaper decided not to publish the cartoons. Although they had become the subject of a global dispute, and featured as the main news story for over a week, each newspaper concluded that the potential offence to some readers outweighed the responsibility to inform all readers what exactly the fuss was all about. Yet despite this uncharacteristic show of caution by the British press, a number of Muslim bodies, including the Muslim Council of Britain, decided that the best means of calming tempers and exercising restraint was by organising a massive demonstration against Islamophobia in central London.

Only a couple of weeks before, the government had failed by a single vote to pass legislation, long campaigned for by the Muslim Council of Britain, that created a crime of religious insult, punishable by seven years' imprisonment. In this crime factual truth and the intent of the accused were no defence. It was one of the most draconian laws put before a British parliament in living memory, and yet the liberal establishment, cowed by the insistent claims of Islamophobia, barely made a squeak of protest. It was left to comedians like Rowan Atkinson to mount a campaign to defend the right of humorists to make religious jokes. And on the eve of the bill's presentation, the government was forced to admit that, under terms of the proposed law, it would be a crime to publish the Danish cartoons. On the subject of the serious, free and robust debate of religious beliefs, however, there was an echoing silence.

Even those who supported the right of *Jyllands-Posten* to publish the cartoons felt obliged to preface their support with an acknowledgement of the unpleasant and offensive nature of the cartoons. Writing about the most notorious cartoon, which depicted Muhammad wearing a turban shaped like a bomb, the critic Philip Hensher noted: 'The cartoonist can't be accused of ignorance or lack of research – he has scrupulously transcribed a verse from the Qur'an on the turban – and there's no doubt that this is seriously offensive, and not just to Muslims but anyone who values truthful debate. It just isn't true to say that, from its founding, Islam would inevitably lead to suicide bombing, or even that its founder's teachings bear responsibility for this particular brand of atrocity.'

Was the cartoon seriously offensive to anyone who valued truthful debate? Had the cartoonist actually suggested that Islamic teaching would inevitably lead to suicide bombing? And was there nothing in the Koran that could be construed as encouraging atrocity? Clearly, members of al-Qaeda and other Islamist groups believed that there was such an endorsement for their actions, and certainly there are passages in the eighth sura that are, at the very least, open to interpretation. In one sense it's ridiculous to parse a seventh-century book for literal meaning, but then the kind of thinking that maintained that the book was the literal word of God also insisted that it was unacceptable to depict the prophet in any manner whatsoever. From a dispassionate perspective, it seemed bizarrely selective to address one issue without involving the other. Hensher went on to argue that the aim of many of the anti-Danish protesters was 'to limit free speech on religious matters'. And let's be honest, in this, as Hensher himself inadvertently demonstrated, they were successful. In terms of artistic, satirical and, indeed, intellectual critique, Islam was to all intents and purposes now beyond examination in Europe. A few months later the French philosopher Robert Redeker went into hiding after he wrote a piece accusing Muhammad of being a 'merciless warlord, looter, a mass murderer of Jews and a polygamist'. That mistake was unlikely to be repeated. As Gary Younge put it, again in the *Guardian*: 'If you are bold enough to knowingly offend a community then you should be bold enough to withstand the consequences,' adding, as one must, 'so long as the community expresses displeasure within the law.' Alas, the problem was expressing displeasure outside the law, the kind of displeasure of which Theo van Gogh had been on the receiving end.

The other received wisdom on the cartoons was that they were badly drawn. It was repeated again and again as if comic illustrations were supposed to be works of transcendent art, and as if British newspapers would have published them had a better artist – perhaps Leonardo da Vinci back from the dead – put pen to paper. What never seemed to be mentioned was that there were Muslims who were not offended by the cartoons, or were offended but felt that *Jyllands-Posten* still had a right to publish them, and who believed other newspapers had a duty to do so when the cartoons became an international story. Instead, much to the satisfaction of the fundamentalist lobby, 1.3 billion Muslims were portrayed as uniformly outraged and steadfastly in favour of censorship.

Of course, I couldn't speak for Muslims other than the ones I knew, and I didn't want to, but I did feel the need to voice the opinion of a rational being living in the twenty-first century, a voice that, like that of the non-outraged Muslim, had been notable for its absence in what passed for the cartoons debate. I wrote a piece for the *Observer* about some of the issues that had been overlooked in all the recrimination and foaming. Such was the climate that, in spite of the essay's delicate tone, the *Observer* slapped a health warning on it in the shape of the introductory epithet 'provocative'.

One of the points I wanted to emphasise was the remark made by Jihad Momani, the editor of the Jordanian weekly *al-Shihan*, who was sacked and charged with insulting religion for publishing the cartoons. What is the greater defamation of the prophet, asked Momani, an unflattering cartoon or blowing up innocent commuters in his name? And I wondered why it was that MCB and other Muslim groups could organise demonstrations against one blasphemy but not the other.

I asked its spokesperson, Inayat Bunglawala, why the MCB had not seen fit to protest against the 7/7 bombing. But he flatly refused to accept that the 7/7 bombing was a defamation of the Prophet Muhammad or the Islamic religion. 'We reject the very assumption that it was done in the name of Islam,' he told me. Come now, let's stop for a moment as serious adults and examine this statement. The blowing up of scores of innocent people by a group who claim to be not only inspired by, but dedicated to, Islam, in an action that a significant minority of British Muslims consider to be justified, is *not* worthy of religious protest. It has nothing to do with the religion and can be left to others to mark. But a dozen cartoons published months previously in another country in a newspaper of which none of their members would have heard, for that grievous body blow to Islam the MCB can get the crowds out marching.

The author Kenan Malik, himself from a Muslim background, suggested that the reason that groups like the MCB protested about cartoons but not bombs was that the demonstrations were not primarily concerned with religion. 'What they are mostly about is a sense of victimhood,' said Malik. '"We're being victimised by Western secular society." You can articulate that sense of victimhood in relation to the cartoons but you can't articulate it in relation to the use or abuse of Islam by certain groups.'

Bunglawala, who was a propagandist for Osama bin Laden prior to 9/11, claimed that his main concern was to protect the faithful rather than the faith. 'What we're interested in is protection for the followers of the faith, not the belief itself,' he explained. 'By all means criticise the faith, ridicule the faith, lampoon it, but do not go after the followers.'

This was, as it turned out, a fairly meaningless distinction, because to ideological Muslims, not least Bunglawala himself, to ridicule the belief was to ridicule the believers. That is, there was freedom to ridicule the faith just so long as that freedom was not exercised. For the exercise of the freedom, in the MCB view of things, was necessarily an unacceptable insult to Muslims. As Bunglawala went on to tell me. 'You can say that Christians are subjected to this day in and day out and they take it. But the fact is Muslims are not taking it and they don't take it. Insulting the Prophet goes to the core of Muslim belief. It's very powerful and it's sometimes difficult to convey to secular Europe.'

I pointed out that secular Europe was where we were all living, and Bunglawala snapped back: 'Yeah, it's something *you* need to understand. That's the reaction it provokes and *you* need to deal with it.'

And he was right. 'We', as in secular Europe, do need to deal with that attitude. We need to assert that the freedoms that may sometimes cause unpleasantness are a necessary and vital constituent of liberal democracy. And the very advances and achievements that have made Europe a destination for so many hundreds of thousands of refugees, like the young Akkari in Denmark, are founded on freedom of expression and freedom from religious law. That doesn't mean that abuse of religion should be the Trojan Horse for covert racists. But by the same token arguments and art that offend Muslims, or some particularly sensitive Muslims, should not be ringfenced as racist. No one in their right mind believes that Salman Rushdie wrote *The Satanic Verses* for racist reasons. As anyone who has read the book will know, it is not a text designed to rally anyone against Muslims, much less Muslims of any particular race or nationality. And it was also fiction. Yet despite Bunglawala's claims that he accepted the right to lampoon religion, he was proud of the campaign of vilification and intimidation that formed the background of the fatwa against the novelist and his retreat into police protection. It was the means, he claimed, through which British Muslims discovered their 'Muslim identity'.

One of the aims of ideological Muslims is to gain legal racial parity with Jews: that is, to be afforded the same protection that Jews and Sikhs enjoy under race laws. In fact Muslims already have that protection as members of constituent races and nationalities: Pakistani, Sudanese, Somalian, etc. But because Jews form a distinct racial category and share a common religion (even if they are non-practising), racial attacks could be construed as religious attacks and vice versa. That's the theory. In practice anti-Semitism rarely takes on a religious form in Europe. No one much cares if the Torah (supposedly revealed to Moses by God) is mocked. The concern is Jews being libelled or insulted not for what they believe but who they are: Jews. As it happens, that's a common occurrence in the large parts of the Muslim world, where anti-Semitic cartoons, complete with the most distasteful characterisations run regularly in Arab newspapers. Yet once more the suggestion was frequently made during the cartoon crisis that Muslims were the new Jews in Europe, suffering the same kind of discrimination and hatred that Jews endured in the 1930s in Germany and elsewhere.

By coincidence, at the same time as the Danish cartoon drama, another freedom-of-expression issue was aired in Austria. The revisionist historian David Irving was imprisoned for three years for the crime of Holocaust denial, stemming from speeches he made in Austria in 1989. Again, a lot was made of double standards: a law existed to imprison anti-Semites who deny genocide of Jews, why not the same punishment for Islamophobes who print cartoons of the prophet? While I think the two are self-evidently not analogous, I still believe that Holocaust denial, though offensive and potentially dangerous, should not be deemed a criminal act. Irving's argument did not and does not withstand public scrutiny, as Deborah Lipstadt, author of *Denying the Holocaust*, proved when Irving unsuccessfully tried to sue her for libel. In a free society the limits on freedom ought to be as few as possible. Therefore it's one thing to say the Holocaust never happened – overwhelming empirical evidence proves otherwise – but quite another to call for Jews to be attacked. The two positions are invariably anti-Semitic and often made by the same people, as is the case with the Iranian president Ahmed Amadinijad, but one is an incitement to ignorance, the other an incitement to violence.

An opinion about history, however wrong, should not be criminalised. In Turkey it is illegal to express the opinion that genocide was committed against Armenians, though again documentation, reports and testaments suggest that around 1 million Christian Armenians were systematically murdered or starved to death between 1913 and 1915 by Muslim Turks under the direction of the secular regime of the Young Turks. In France there have been recent attempts in the lower house to criminalise the denial of the Armenian genocide. All of this heavy-handed lawmaking cannot hope to do what it sets out to achieve. As the conspiracy theorists who maintain that 9/11 was a US plot only too plainly show, people will believe what they want to believe and suppressing those beliefs by law will not make them go away. In the end, the solution to prejudice and ignorance is not legislation but education. But education is not just a matter of facts, it is also grounded in a set of principles and attitudes. Which is why the study and discussion of the Holocaust, the Soviet Gulags, the Armenian genocide, the slave trade, the Bengal famine, the suppression of the Mau Mau uprising, the subjugation of women, though absolutely vital, needs to be placed within a consistent moral framework. And at the moment there is considerable uncertainty among liberals about how that framework should look.

In its 2007 report *Teaching Emotive and Controversial History*, the Historical Association noted: 'A history department in a northern city recently avoided selecting the Holocaust as a topic for GCSE coursework for fear of confronting anti-Semitic sentiment and Holocaust denial among some Muslim pupils.' It went on: 'In another history department, the Holocaust was taught despite anti-Semitic sentiment among some pupils, but the same department deliberately avoided teaching the Crusades at Key Stage 3 because their balanced treatment of the topic would have directly challenged what was taught in some local mosques.'

Here are the advance signs of the culturally tailored study that multiculturalists aim to see instituted, whereby historical truth is subservient to group prejudice. And as with the Danish cartoons, you start out with the intention of avoiding offence and very soon you manage to circumvent inconvenient truths and skip over historical reality. Liberal education is meant to challenge, not accommodate, prejudice. And to challenge prejudice, sometimes you need to risk offending.

As Malik argued: 'The interesting thing about the multicultural argument is that it fails to understand what is good about diversity. Diversity isn't good in and of itself; diversity is good because it allows us to think beyond the tight box we often find ourselves in. It allows us to ask: should we change our way of life? Should they change their way? What's better? And therefore to create a political dialogue which, paradoxically, can help us form a more universal sense of citizenship.'

The Danish cartoons crisis illustrated in the most graphic and telling fashion this unwillingness to engage in political dialogue. Not only was the image of a historical religious figure pronounced off-limits but more significantly, the reasons why it was off-limits, and the means used to maintain that embargo were also deemed to be unfit for frank public debate. And if you want to know what frank public debate looks like, here is a relevant example. The year after the cartoon crisis, the *Guardian* ran a disturbing photograph of the execution of Saddam Hussein. Many readers wrote in to complain and the editor of the newspaper, Alan Rusbridger, replied with a temperate and well-argued explanation of why he thought, on balance, that he was right to publish the image. 'I cannot agree with those who argued that the picture should not have been used at all,' he wrote. 'A newspaper which retreats from reporting the crueller realities of the world is, in an important sense, retreating from its duty of bearing witness.'

In Britain every newspaper, and nearly all other media outlets, retreated from that duty in early 2006, when the cartoons crisis was the biggest story across the world. Indeed, not only did they not reproduce a single cartoon, they failed to describe them in proper detail. I discovered that many people had no idea what the most explosive images in cartoon history looked like. So emphatic was the consensus that the illustrations were deeply offensive that few reports found it necessary to go into unpleasant particulars. The single image that was vividly described was the turban bomb. Given the number of bombs let off in the name of Islam in New York, London, Madrid, Baghdad, Bali, Istanbul, Casablanca, Dar es Salaam and Nairobi, to name but a few, this was a cartoon that was not without relevant context. Like the cartoon itself, this context did not appear in British or American newspapers. But what of the other eleven cartoons? Was a line drawing of a man in a turban walking along with a mule more offensive than a real-life image of a hanged man? Or what about the image of a boy pointing at a blackboard with the words, written in Arabic, *'Jyllands-Posten*'s journalists are a bunch of reactionary provocateurs'? Was this really beyond publication?

Who can seriously doubt that there was only one reason why newspapers failed to publish such tame material: terror. They feared, perhaps correctly, that they would make themselves, their staff and anyone who stocked the newspapers potential targets for terrorists. As if to underline the point, and the implicit threat, an incident that was largely overlooked formed a stinging coda to the cartoons saga. A French-Algerian journalist named Mohammed Sifaoui secretly filmed Ahmed Akkari, the spokesman for the Danish imams, in conversation with another member of the imam delegation, Sheikh Raed Hlayhel. They were talking about Naser Khader, a Danish politician, originally from Syria, who for his advocacy of peaceful coexistence between democracy and Islam was under police protection from Islamist extremists. 'If Khader becomes minister of integration,' said Akkari, 'shouldn't someone dispatch two guys to blow up him and his ministry?' (Incidentally, at around about the same time yet another member of the delegation, Ahmad Abu Laban, was caught on camera talking enthusiastically about a recruit who wanted 'to wreak absolute havoc . . . join the fray and turn it into a martyr operation'.)

When confronted with his remarks, Akkari initially denied that he made them. However, on being presented with the evidence, he admitted what he had said but claimed that it was a 'joke'. Here was the madness of the whole drama contained in one word. A joke about a long-dead religious prophet had been turned into an international crisis costing many lives and tens of millions of dollars. But a threat, made by a man instrumental in creating that crisis, to kill a democratic European politician dedicated, in his own words, to 'stand up for his opponent if he or she is subjected to spiteful treatment' was passed off as a joke.

The essay I wrote for the *Observer* drew a large response. The newspaper received scores of letters and emails from readers who expressed relief that a different opinion had been published. Nearly all of them described themselves as rational liberals who felt frustrated by the narrow parameters of debate. And most of them expressed the wish that, should their letters be published, their names and addresses be withheld, out of fear of retribution. The fear may well have been misplaced but the fact that so many correspondents admitted to it was in itself all too telling.

Shortly afterwards I entered into an exchange with a lecturer in politics who suggested that by publishing the cartoons, *Jyllands-Posten* had acted like a Belfast Loyalist running into a Republican pub and shouting out Unionist propaganda. I'd heard some silly comments but this was probably the most revealing. If the sectarian analogy meant anything, my correspondent saw Denmark as an Islamic stronghold. That seemed to me a depressing analysis but it turned out in a later reply that my correspondent saw things in terms of a hostage crisis, in which all of us in Europe were hostages and we should say nothing that might provoke our hostage holders in the Islamic world. Now this was clearly a bonkers line of thinking but an apparently intelligent, liberal-minded politics lecturer believed it to be true. 'Surely we have to accept that other people think differently to us and respect that,' he wrote, 'in the hope that they will eventually grow to respect us.'

It was just one man's opinion but it was an all too familiar one. Here was the soft underbelly of Western liberalism exposed in all its unsightly slackness. Appease the men of violence and intimidation and they will respect us. Apart from anything else, this wishful attitude shows a contempt for those who are supposedly appeased. The violent wing of Islamism, which was the wing to which the self-censors anxiously listened, has no intention of compromising its beliefs or position. It wants nothing less than everything. As things stand, Islamism has close to no chance of achieving its aims, though its prospects improve every time liberals acquiesce to the illiberal. And it does not need to succeed for liberalism to fail.

Liberalism's failure is far more likely to be self-inflicted, born of a crisis of confidence and a loss of conviction. It's happened before in Europe, this self-destructive urge to entertain extremism and to exalt irrationality, and with catastrophic results. But it won't happen again the same way. What's certain is that the threat in the first instance is not political but intellectual. And owing to an accumulation of flabby attitudes and misguided assumptions, born of guilt and complacency, liberalism is in poor fighting shape to meet any ideological challenge. Indeed, the most energetic wing of liberalism, the postmodernist, relativist school of thought, has devoted itself to exposing liberalism as just another self-serving cultural construct, a white, Western justification for neo-imperialism. The beauty of that argument is that it can't be disproved, at least not by a product of white, Western culture. And perhaps it's a waste of time to try. I happen to believe that there are a number of universal values – freedom of expression, protection from tyranny and arbitrary power – that are best served by secular, humanistic, democratic liberalism, and if it turns out that this belief is a cultural mirage then surely it's still my prerogative to defend the culture that produced it and me. It's nowhere near perfect but, in terms of the opportunities and rights and freedoms it offers, it is immeasurably less imperfect than the alternatives.

Liberalism, especially left-leaning liberalism, is a social philosophy and in recent years liberals have been guilty (there is more than one kind of guilty liberal) of focusing on government and communal groups and neglecting the common bonds that hold society together. Society doesn't work because of laws or even law enforcement, as vital as they are. It works because of shared, or at least complementary, attitudes and aspirations. Liberalism needs to reconnect with the public imagination and foster a greater sense of social responsibility and participation. It *does* have something to do with us.

Two hundred and thirty years after Beaumarchais wrote those opening words to this chapter, European liberalism is again confronted with the threat of religious censorship and, more-over, violence. Sometimes it seems as if the struggle for Enlightenment will have to be fought all over again, but that's only because too many liberals appear too cowed or constrained by the diktats of post-colonial discourse (translation: guilt) to assert the importance of reason and robust intellectual debate. To stress this point is not to take up an anti-Muslim stance, and nor is the message of this book intended as anti-Muslim.

But in its defence of liberal society it is explicitly an argument against appeasing Islamism. It may demonstrate several novel characteristics, but Islamism works on an old principle: the threat and use of terror delivers results. Thus it is absolutely crucial that liberals, be they secular, Christian, Muslim or any other kind, do not allow the people of violence to impose the limits of freedom. And, however you dress it up, that is precisely what the people of violence did during the cartoons saga. 'So what?' it might be said. A dozen Danish cartoons, what did or does it matter? You can, if so minded, represent such an attitude as tolerance, but that would only be a comforting cartoon of what actually took place. A more appropriate word for the liberal response to the intimidation is submission. And it will not have gone unnoticed by the intimidators.

Liberalism is by definition a broad church but its adherents now face a defining choice. We have to decide if the things we take for granted – the freedoms of expression, movement and association, democracy, the rule of law – are simply accidents of culture or vital social principles. It seems to me that the kind of liberal tradition of which I feel a part recognises not just the rights and freedoms of the individual, but also the responsibilities and duties owed to the society that secures those rights and protects those freedoms. And perhaps the prime responsibility is to recognise the enemies of what Karl Popper termed the open society, which at the very minimum entails the refusal to pretend that the censors and gangsters and extortionists that seek to restrict freedom and enforce religious, racial or class divisions are in some way progressive forces. No holy book guarantees the amazing wealth of opportunities that Western society has developed. They are the result of centuries of thought and struggle. To disown or downplay these achievements out of a sense of cultural guilt is an insult not only to all those who fought to establish an open society but also to countless millions who dream of one day being members of it. It's essential to maintain a sceptical vigilance of those in whom we entrust our governance, and British society, for one, is nowhere near as open as it could or should be. But to think in the post-9/11 era that the main threat to democracy comes from democratic government is an indulgence only fantasists and dissemblers and the incurably naive can afford. The rest of us must contend with reality and its endarkening fallout.

Acknowledgements

I must here acknowledge the unacknowledged, all those writers, journalists, bloggers, letter correspondents and friends whose ideas have shaped this book in countless subtle and not-so-subtle ways. I'd like to express my gratitude to *Observer* editor Roger Alton and his deputy, John Mulholland, for their encouragement and understanding. Ian Katz and Georgina Henry at the *Guardian* for giving me the column space to think out loud. Dan Franklin, Rachel Cugnoni, Alex Bowler and Katherine Fry at Random House. Georgia Garrett, David Matthews, Maad Fayad and the al-Khoei Foundation. And most of all I want to thank Louise Chunn for her patience, wise words and support.